"Belleville reveals the waterway's exotic voluptuousness . . . in writing that is both silvery and refreshingly unrehearsed . . . two qualities much in keeping with the milieu. Belleville creates in the reader a protective affection for the St. Johns, all any river can ask of its lover."

—*Kirkus*

"[Belleville] establishes his kinship with William Bartram . . . and other artists who have felt the tug of [the river's] currents."

—*Audubon*

"Eloquently captures one man's quest to explore both the known and unknown about a mesmerizing body of water."

—*Southern Living*

"A wise and inspired book . . . This is an important and beautifully written work that deserves to be widely read as a lesson in learning to know and love the damaged places that surround us."

—*Alison Hawthorne Deming*

"Filmmaker Bill Belleville has written a fine account of the St. Johns. . . . a definitive book."

—*Miami Herald*

"[Belleville] kayaks and boats the St. Johns, hikes its forests, dives its springs. He talks to scientists, fishermen, historians, and residents. And he depicts, with finely tuned prose, the many threats [the river] faces from haphazard development and destructive pollution."

—*The Tampa Tribune*

River of Lakes

A Journey on Florida's St. Johns River

BILL BELLEVILLE

The University of Georgia Press

Athens and London

Paperback edition published in 2001
by the University of Georgia Press
Athens, Georgia 30602
© 2000 by Bill Belleville
All rights reserved
Designed by Erin Kirk New
Set in 11.5 on 14 Fournier with Cochin display

Printed digitally

The Library of Congress has cataloged the cloth edition
of this book as follows:
Library of Congress Cataloging-in-Publication Data
Belleville, Bill, [date]
River of lakes : a journey on Florida's St. Johns River /
Bill Belleville.
xxxi, 220 p. : 1 map ; 24 cm.
Includes bibliographical references (p. [203]–210) and index.
ISBN 0-8203-2156-7 (alk. paper)
1. Saint Johns River (Fla.)—History. 2. Saint Johns River
(Fla.)—Description and travel. 3. Saint Johns River Valley
(Fla.)—History. 4. Saint Johns River Valley (Fla.)—
Description and travel. I. Title.
F317.S2 B45 2000
975.9'1—dc21   99-33373

Paperback ISBN-13: 978-0-8203-2344-2
        ISBN-10: 0-8203-2344-6

British Library Cataloging-in-Publication Data available

Map on page xiv by Karen Harrod Miller.

To my Dad,

who taught me not to be afraid of the woods

and knew the names of all the trees.

Contents

Contents

Preface

Journalists, as Bill Moyers once noted, enjoy a license to be educated in public. And the research for this book has been nothing if not a public education, a joining of many pieces—some known, some not very much so—into a larger whole.

This is especially true with a resource that hasn't been approached inside a single book cover in more than half a century. The world has changed since then, with the peninsula of Florida transmuting as suddenly and as thoroughly as any environment in our country.

There is chronology to this book, as there is to the river itself. The narrative begins at, well, the beginning. From here, it flows with the current of the St. Johns, from south to north, each chapter taking it a little farther downstream to its confluence with the ocean, to its consummation.

To flow north is highly unusual for any large river in this continent, and my constant referral to "downstream" as north and "upstream" as south will perhaps be unfamiliar at first.

You'll have to blame the river for this—or more historically, blame the ancient seas. As Walter Schmidt put it in *The Geology of Florida* (edited by Anthony F. Randazzo and Douglas S. Jones), "Florida's landforms show the dominant effect of marine forces. . . . Ancient seas have left behind extensive flat plains that were their shallow floors, and scarps where old coastlines were cut into the uplands." The St. Johns has filled one of these almost flat, barely northward-flowing plains with its waters.

Like the river and its tributaries, the narrative digresses here and there, wandering into figurative sloughs and bayous, springs and creeks—places of discovery. Sometimes, it lingers on critters I've found fascinating; other times, it reveals a bit about other people who have developed an affection for this unique riverine environment.

You won't find the river matched, word for water acre, along its route. If it were, the massive "main stem" of the Lower St. Johns would consume 90 percent of the narrative, for that is about how much water surface is represented by that broader stretch of river during its final eighty-mile run from Palatka to the ocean.

Instead, I've devoted more energy to the river that comes before, in the belief that the river upstream defines in many ways what goes down. Besides, most of us simply find a narrow, twisting waterway more appealing than a broad thoroughfare.

By the end—or perhaps somewhere in the middle—you might even feel the urge to put the book down and go out on the river to see it for yourself. I hope so—because I believe we don't protect what we don't value. And one of the surest ways to value any place is to connect with it, even if only a little bit.

I have made this a bit easier for you to do in the list of public access points in the appendix, grouped chronologically as to how each point appears along the river or in its valley.

As for private access points—the marinas and private ramps and boat-yards—they can be highly transient, as shifting as the river itself. They open or close, expand or change names. Perhaps the dynamic of the river breeds in this whimsy; maybe it's a function of living in a rootless place like Florida.

Public land usually remains public. And, thankfully, more land is becoming public all the time as folks come to understand the finite value of such resources. But this also means new parks and preserves take shape in places where, the year before, there were none.

If this book whets your appetite for more specialized information about the river, or if you need to express yourself about its well-being to those agencies charged with its care, you will find another list in the appendix that will help you accomplish both.

As for your own expression, it is important to know that public agencies seldom have enough ammunition to do the job they need to do to protect the river—it is rare for them to have adequate money or clout. In addition, staff members are being hammered routinely by those who would dilute laws and rules regulating the health of the St. Johns and its tributaries, usually in the name of short-term and selfish gains. Your voice counts as part of a building consensus that brings conservation to reality.

Today, the St. Johns and its wildlife teeter on the thin line of survival, balanced dangerously on the curve of biological sustainability, sometimes even dipping below. Chipping away at its many small parts sooner or later reduces the ability of the whole river system to regenerate itself. Such a loss would be not only a massive economic blow but one that would also drain the natural aesthetic, eroding the fragile well of its soul.

In this reality, protecting the St. Johns is a never-ending process that requires eternal vigilance from individual citizens, the media, civic groups, and religious congregations. Wanting to do right by the river is a beginning, but expressing that concern to top administrators and elected officials goes a long way toward making it happen.

Yet on occasion expression can get sucked into that great political stew of politics, a thrice-removed, emotionally driven theater in which logic is only a bit player. When, in 1998, the St. Johns joined a select national list of other waterways to become a prestigious "American Heritage River"——besting 126 applicants in the process——the reaction was not unanimous. Although the designation promised to help the river with badly needed cleanups, environmentally sound economic development, and historic preservation, not everyone was pleased about its new status. Conspiracy zealots went to work, figuring a federal sanction would mean everything from more government interference to UN troops bivouacked on its shores. Controversy, even the kind that courts haywire opinion, helps. When the dust settled, the publicity at least brought attention to the needs of the river, and officials began to respond.

After all, a river is a rare thing all by itself, a conveyor of water and history and myth. Of the water on earth, 97 percent is in the oceans; most of the rest is locked in icecaps and glaciers. Less than 1 percent is left as surface water. Yet it takes work to release a single drop of water from its commercial boundaries, to make it more than just a backdrop for our clever human contrivances.

If we are all students in this great shared learning process of life, then perhaps we can see the river as a great lesson in ecology, as a metaphor for learning how the integration of each natural part affects the whole.

I believe it is in *seeing* that true affection, of the kind that leads to an ethic, really begins. And you'll find that to be a theme in all that follows here. If I have helped the reader see a river that has been notoriously "unseen" in modern times, then I'll have done my job.

Acknowledgments

My deepest gratitude to poet and essayist Alison Hawthorne Deming for her belief in this work, as well as to Barbara Ras of the University of Georgia Press—they were among the very first to "get it." And certainly Grace Buonocore's intelligent and thoughtful copyediting has helped make this a more readable book.

At the St. Johns River Water Management District—in addition to those who appear in the book—I owe a special gratitude to Patricia Harden, formerly of the Board of Governors, for her support of the book, at the beginning and end. Also thanks for professional assistance to scientists Kimberli J. Ponzio, Palmer D. Kinser Jr., Doug Munch, and David Toth, outreach coordinator Jeff Cole, and information specialist Beth Hickenlooper.

Also very helpful were Fred Harden, a true Bartram disciple, of the Friends of the Wekiva River, Dan Ragan of the Florida Times-Union's Web site (www.jacksonville.com), Bob Giguere of WMFE-TV, Herb Hiller and Mary Lee Adler of Drayton Island, Judy Armstrong of Holly Bluff Marina, Dr. Robin Denson of Gulf Archaeology Research Institute, Gray Bass of the state's Game and Fish Commission, Dr. Jim Miller of the Florida Department of State, Jerry Clutts and Dr. Ray Willis of the U.S. Forest Service, Alicia Clarke of the Sanford Museum, David Brown of Florida's Backcountry River Adventures, Jody Rosier of the Florida Defenders of the Environment, longtime friends Russ and Katie Moncrief, and kayak buddy Dr. Steve Phelan of Rollins College, who, besides giving an extremely thoughtful reading to the manuscript, provided spiritual counsel, even when he may not have known he was doing so.

Thanks, too, for the conscientious work of Patrick Harvey of Rollins College's Environmental Studies program in Winter Park, Florida, in researching and assembling the list of public access points, as well as assisting in fact checking of the narrative.

Finally, I can't leave the river without expressing my appreciation to Eugenia Stefan for the support and encouragement she provided during the research.

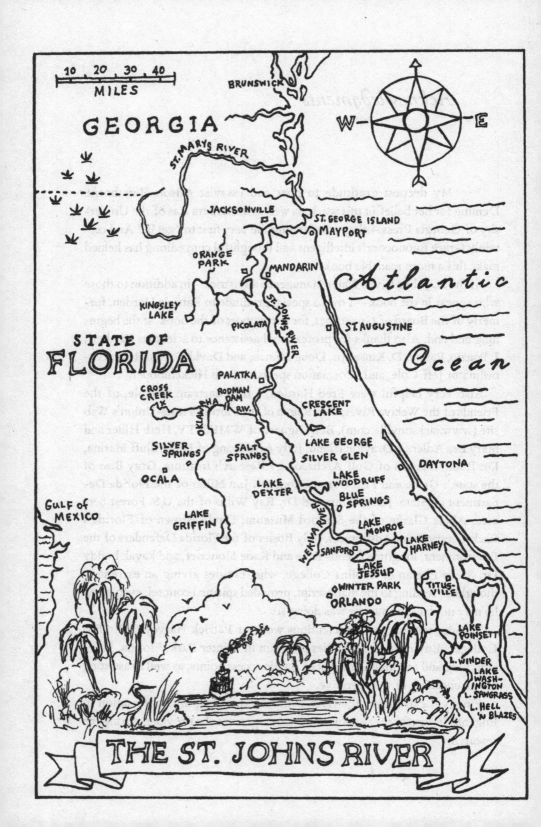

THE ST. JOHNS RIVER

Introduction

〜〜〜〜〜〜〜〜〜〜〜〜〜〜〜〜〜〜〜〜〜〜〜〜〜〜〜〜〜〜〜〜〜〜〜〜〜〜

> Unlike the mountains and sea-shore of the North, the scenery of the Tropics is
> greatest in its little things.—A traveler who journeyed up the St. Johns by
> steamship in 1870

*J*ust moments after full dark, when the last shards of twilight slip away into the night, the junglelike woods outside my tent abruptly turn on, as if someone has thrown a switch. There are raspy screeches and deep, throaty grunts and the unsettling crack of branches being snapped in the underbrush. From the river nearby, something very large splashes and then exhales loudly. As I stretch out to rest, the hard-packed shell mound under me pushes through the thin tent fabric, outlining the knobby relief of thousands of freshwater snails gathered here by aboriginal campers centuries ago.

I am not in a tropical rainforest in Latin America but on the banks of a river that parallels the eastern coast of Florida, from Vero Beach to Jacksonville: the St. Johns. Tonight, I have made my camp on Idlewilde Point, a rich, lush oxbow in the middle river basin rimmed with towering cypress and sabal palms, bermed by the high, chalky earth of Indian shell middens.

Historically, other chroniclers of Florida's longest river have come here before me over the last several centuries—from the early French artist Jacques Le Moyne de Morgues and naturalist William Bartram to composer Frederick Delius and novelist Marjorie Kinnan Rawlings. All of them found something that touched them deeply. In turn, they helped create a legacy of art and artistic science, themed by the river and the people it nourished.

At times, their discoveries and creations could be astounding, affecting those who lived far beyond the boundaries of the St. Johns. For instance, Bartram found that northern songbirds didn't spend the winter under the ice of lakes or fly to the moon, as commonly supposed in the mid-1700s. Instead, he reported, cardinals and robins like those he had seen back home in Philadelphia migrated south, down along the great winding, exotic valhalla of the "sublime" St. Johns River valley.

For American and European readers who followed Bartram's *Travels* up the wild Florida river from the civilized comfort of their parlors, this junglelike St. Johns may well have been on the moon. Although several degrees north of the Tropic of Cancer, this was, indeed, the tropics, with an exotically voluptuous promise locked inside its green walls. Wedged in between these more aesthetic travelers have been a checkered lot of conquistadors, soldiers, renegades, and—this being Florida—unabashed promoters of tourism and development.

Steamships, which first hauled cargo up and down the river for early settlers and rugged frontiersmen in the 1830s, became larger and fancier, accommodating visitors lured by blue sky dreams here in the land of flowers. These archetypical snowbirds descended on the swampy peninsula in a mad quest for health, wealth, and adventure, riding the "highway" of the St. Johns each winter into the heart of known Florida, like today's snowbirds ride Interstate 95 and the Florida Turnpike. Between 1830 and 1920, there were some three hundred paddlewheelers trailing their distinctive plumes of black, pine-fed smoke up and down its shores.

In this way, the St. Johns also became Florida's first tourist attraction, with luxury hotels, boardinghouses, and busy "landings" dotting the riverbanks from Mayport at the river's mouth all the way down to Lake Poinsett, more than 225 miles south. As for the rest of Florida, it was simply too wet or too remote to catch on: a census in 1880 revealed that only 257 people lived in Dade County, including Miami, while 4,535 swarmed over St. Johns, a county bordering the lower river.

For those who would promote such travel, it seemed almost impossible to describe the St. Johns without using the word *salubrious*. Promotional pamphlets and guides to the river from the late nineteenth century told of a surreal waterway that was, apparently, not only free of bugs and frost but a sort of balmy Shangri-la—a geographic version of the Eagles' "Hotel California" where you can check out but you can never leave.

There "are men and women, healthy and vigorous, who in years gone by, came to Florida as a last resource from death," observed the writer of *A Hand Book of Important and Reliable Information for the Use of the Tourist, Settler and Investor* in 1885. "They dare not return to their old homes where the enemy still lies in wait for them." As for reality, it was given a sort of backhanded acknowledgment. "There is malaria in Florida," noted the same writer, "but not to the extent commonly supposed."

Predating this deluge of Europeans by several millennia were the original natives of the river valley. When the climate of Florida became moister and the flow of the St. Johns surer after the end of the last Ice Age, pre-Columbians began to settle along its shores. The certainty of this river and its bounty helped these people become less nomadic, more given to geographic commitments. They had time to invent pottery and myth, time to interpret the nature that sustained them. The culture that arose was as complex and organized as that of any North American tribe, with ceremonial centers, pyramidal temple mounds, plazas, and playing fields for a sort of ball game—a contest simmering with religion and allegory.

Of the dozen or so tribes that flourished here at the time the Spanish "discovered" La Florida, those known as the Timucua lived along the shores of the St. Johns, worshiping the sun and the stars, imbuing the eagle and rattlesnake with mystical powers, and using wild herbs to fire the magic that created a successful hunt, a victory in battle, an everlasting love.

It was Le Moyne who first captured these Indians at work and play in the valley of the late sixteenth century, rendering indelible likeness of them in forty-one finely detailed drawings. Theodore de Bry's engravings of Le Moyne's art were published in England in 1591, giving the world its first glimpse of the people of the St. Johns.

Although they were only here a short time, the French related to the Timucua in an intimate way, telling us more about them in three years than the Spanish could in two centuries.

Before the Timucua, there was a succession of even earlier peoples, stretching all the way back to the Paleo-Indians who briefly shared the river valley with huge Pleistocene megafauna like the mastodon, bison, sabertoothed cat, and the glyptodont, an armadillo-like animal the size of a Barcolounger.

After the Timucua were enslaved, diseased, and driven away by the Spanish, Creeks from Georgia and Alabama migrated down, often living atop the same middens and village sites the Timucua and others had created. Adapting to their new riverine environment, often accepting escaped slaves into their villages, the Creeks became known to the Spanish as *cimarrones*, "wild ones" or "runaways." In the Muskogean language of the Creek, cimarrón became *Seminole*—a description not of themselves but of how the Europeans saw them.

The river fed them all, man and beast, bringing them to life on the banks of its channels, lakes, and springs and then—just as quickly—turning them into detritus upon which the ever-changing, water-rich system would continue to grow and reform itself.

From the Seminoles came a version of a word first used to describe the St. Johns, *Welaka*—a corruption of *Ylacco*. It was said to mean "river of lakes" or "big water." *Ylacco* is surely a graphic description of a system that seems to be a series of broad inland bays linked together by a channel. There is another, lesser-known interpretation of *Ylacco*. For me, it fits just as well, for it wanders into poetry: It hath its own way, is alone contrary to every other.

The clues earliest men and women left behind from their occupation of this river tell us not just about life in another time but about how any environment shapes the social evolution of a society. And it leaves us with questions about what happens when we become clever and industrious enough in turn to shape the environment that will ultimately reshape us.

The history of this river was a heady one, to be sure. It was not only the first trail down into Florida but, in fact, the first great river in North America to be explored by Europeans.

When I prepared to examine the St. Johns for myself, I was more than aware of the distance between today's expedient Florida realities and the slower, less frenetic times that set the backdrop for earlier visitors here. Since the turn of the century, the river has undergone marked changes, most having to do with humans' conceit that they know how to run things better than nature.

Could I still find an authentic experience here, in a go-fast state that seems either in a swoon with "progress" and contrived, theme-worldish fun or randomly sullied by crime and violence? When I told two friends of my extensive plans to visit the St. Johns and its swamps, one wondered whether there was anything truly wild left to see; the other suggested I carry a gun.

The advice was well meaning, if uninformed. But I understood: pinning down any reality in a transient, pro-growth state like Florida nowadays is a bit like nailing Jell-O to the wall. What was true last year, even last week, may not be true today or tomorrow. Change can sometimes be heartbreaking: I have a very good 1966 field guide, *Birds of North America*, in which the local endemic known as the dusky seaside sparrow—found in the salt marshes just east of the St. Johns—was listed as "uncommon," a step before rare and surely far from extinct, which it now is.

Into this uncertain equation comes the factor of perception. The riverine environments of the St. Johns have never been easy to figure. For one thing, by the standards of other North American rivers, it is a virtual newborn, having configured itself into its present condition barely more than five thousand years ago.

For another, the St. Johns is a slow-moving, tannic-stained blackwater river that meanders through a floodplain, leaving in its wake a shore that is more often flat and swamplike than high and banked. Because they are still and given to nuances that leak into the consciousness, swamps confuse many people into thinking these complex resources are much less than they are.

Perhaps the most famously confused was artist-scientist-woodsman John James Audubon, who came here in 1831–32, precisely because of the wonders Bartram had described forty years before. Although he had dreamed of exploring the St. Johns since he was a child, Audubon picked up a quill and wrote to his wife soon after his arrival: "I am now truly speaking in a wild and desolate part of the world—no one in the eastern United States has any true idea of this peninsula. My account of what I have or shall see of the Floridas will be far, very far from corroborating the flowery sayings of Mr. Bartram, the botanist."

Harriet Beecher Stowe, better known for *Uncle Tom's Cabin* than for her 1873 nonfiction paean to the St. Johns, *Palmetto Leaves*, was more sympathetic. In that later work, she noted, "Fully half the tourists and travellers to Florida come back intensely disappointed," because visitors arrive on the river "with their heads full of certain romantic ideas . . . [expecting] flowers and arabesques and brilliant coloring."

If travelers are not put off by the lack of melodramatic relief in the flat terrain, said Stowe, then they're confused by the absence of distinct seasons, in a place where "nature is an easy, demoralized, indulgent old grandmother who has no particular time for anything and does everything when she happens to feel like it."

Oddly, a contemporary state-funded tourism slogan popular a few years ago decided "The Rules Are Different Here." Although I'd like to think this meant the uncertain and enchanting natural rules Stowe described, it undoubtedly had to do more with the popular concept of the place—an arabesqued and umbrella-drink–studded playpen—rather than one full of dark swampland and natural discovery.

To their credit, a few savvy outfitters up and down the river today have found that Stowe's blackwatered mystique can be sold. There are now a handful of "eco tours" on the St. Johns offering visitors a chance to bird or photograph or simply exalt in this unique environment, to help displace the audioanimatronic Florida with the real.

Yet, as always on the river, some folks just don't know when to stop when it comes to putting a spin on natural history: I think of the ambitious Realtor who sold lots near a little creek off the Wekiva, a major tributary of the St. Johns. Here, more than 160 river miles from the sea, buyers were solicited not for the chance to listen for kingfishers in the cypress boughs and watch otters play in the clear, spring-fed water but to have real estate with "ocean access."

Adding to the confusion is the reality that the river is different things at different places, that local "experts" on one leg of the river may think they have it all figured out when, in fact, all they have figured out is their place on it.

Rivers also seem to birth exaggeration in the best of us—especially when it comes to sizes of things, and particularly when those things are cold blooded. As the great Florida naturalist Archie Carr facetiously explained in the introduction to his book about reptiles, amphibians, and fishes of Florida, "There is a great deal of irresponsible talk about the sizes attained by some of our cold-blooded animals, particularly snakes and fish." In fact, "the whole subject of fish sizes is so delicate and dangerous that talking about it would probably only lose . . . readers."

Still, it is hard to resist: How can I forget the good old boy on a tributary who bragged to me about his catch of a "26¼ pound" black mullet—a fish that usually gets no larger than around 3 pounds? Or the modest conservationist who insisted he routinely encountered an 18-foot gator on a river-fed lake—about a yard beyond what any known alligator has so far achieved in the world.

Hydrologically, the waters that feed the St. Johns are grouped into three basins—upper, middle, and lower—that chart the river's progress from feral wetland creek to broad lake to deep tidal estuary. Because it flows north-ward, the upper river—as in "upstream"—is south and the lower river is north. There are officially fifty-one artesian springs charted in this valley, many with their own narrow creeks or spring runs, some with limestone por-tals leading to the underwater rivers that feed them.

Within this reality, a maze of serpentine twists and isolated oxbows still remains, many with inviting tributaries and bayous, making it impossible to experience the entire St. Johns fully in a short time.

In fact, it would take me months to cover its entire territory, an act accom-plished in bits and pieces, taking place aboard kayaks, canoes, research ves-sels, houseboats, airboats, and small airplanes and even while wearing a wetsuit and a set of scuba tanks.

In making this journey, I wasn't looking for speed but for more of a com-mune. Biologist Edward O. Wilson has written of such intimacies, explain-ing them as the primal affinity we humans have for a subconscious connec-tion between ourselves and the rest of the natural world. He calls this quest *biophilia*, a link to the great expanse of time before industrialization, when humans lived directly on the land and from it. For this connection to soothe our soul, some form of wilderness must be left, says Wilson, a place for people to travel "in search of new life and wonder."

Thus I was searching for a way not just to traverse the river but to know it, to feel a hint of what it was that had evoked such passion in others over the centuries.

Ultimately, I suppose, I was hoping to hear a few notes of Delius's *Florida Suite* in the breezes that rise from its waters, to understand why Bartram so loved its plants and animals that he drew them as almost human, to find that place—or one like it—where Rawlings camped on the shore of the upper river one night and never fully let it go.

"If I could have, to hold forever, one brief place and time of beauty," Rawlings later wrote, "I think I might choose the night on that high lonely bank above the St. Johns River."

Along with 3.5 million others, I live in the St. Johns River "valley" in east central Florida. For a person to reside in this sprawling 8,840-square-mile basin is not a particularly rare or special event. To realize fully that you do surely is.

Like much of the rest of natural Florida, this is a valley unique unto itself: there are no towering hillcrests, no mountainous slopes, no high-profile ravine walls. Instead, it is an enormous sprawling sand and limestone basin gradually drained by the nearly imperceptible slope of our young terrain, a landscape that has repeatedly been carved and molded from the sea in recent geological time. It is a sculpting that continues today, with the dynamics of currents, tides, weather, ship traffic, and dredging all leaving slight but sure thumbprints on the malleable channel that marks the river's course.

From its headwaters to its confluence with the ocean, the river in this valley falls only 27 feet—barely an inch a mile. If I lived atop more hardfast land and rock back on the mainland, this distinction of inches would be virtually lost to all but a few concerned with the measuring of topography by degrees.

But in Florida, where an average of five feet of precipitation falls on this region yearly, an inch means something: here, the slightest depression in the terrain becomes a slough. Natural furrows are transformed into creeks. Broad, pancake-flat savannas brim with rain, birthing entire headwaters.

Because this is all done under cover of magnificent subtlety—inside a fretwork of wetland plants, spread over a massive basin, miles from dry land—this process can seem tedious, even cryptic. For those used to having the world neatly delivered to them in this turbo-charged age of immediate gratification, figuring out a river as complex as the St. Johns is a monumental task. For believers, it can be done, but it just takes time.

Yet the entire process of discovery can be entirely missed unless one focuses on the act of looking—not just where to look but how. "Nature and books," as Emerson once observed, "belong to the eyes that can see them." To see fully a river like the St. Johns, then, is an act accomplished by patience, a matter of degrees. For me, this act of seeing the river begins in my own backyard.

The weathered "cracker" house I call home was built on a chunk of drained wetland almost a full mile from where the St. Johns dilates itself into Lake Monroe, near Sanford. The resourceful farmer who once raised livestock and row crops here inside a perimeter of bamboo and sour root citrus trees—his tinkering with twig grafts never fully complete—is gone now. So are most like him, an entire community that once farmed celery and tomatoes and squash in the black, muck-rich soil where the wetlands used to be.

The hope that drew them all here—as well as the methodology that kept them—are still imprinted on the land. And so it is with my own land, down here at the end of a dirt road, next to the freeze-burned citrus grove, overgrown now with sabal palm and live oak and a thicket of blackberry vine, still guarded by the shrill cry of red-tailed hawks.

The boundaries of my yard, like those of my neighbors, are bracketed with ditches. Layered with grasses and ferns, they seem almost natural—except, of course, for their sheer linearity. They run east and west and then north to the river, precise and angular routes that efficiently expunge the wet from the wetlands. In turn, they offer expediency and rich, tillable soil in a Faustian trade that—even a half century ago—probably seemed like a great deal.

Since most of Florida's population is new, we see only the grooves left behind in the earth. There is scant cultural memory of what was here before. Even on my little dirt road, which seems lifted out of a corner of Cross Creek, none of my contemporary neighbors can recall a landscape without ditches.

It takes an aged, faded survey map of the property to show a time when there were none. On that seventy-five-year-old map, there is only a light line meandering through what is now my back yard, intent on making its way to the St. Johns in the full spirit of whimsy God grants to tiny creeks.

This little stream with no name has only vanished in part. Its flow still lives, revitalized during the wet season, filling the narrow ditches with two and three feet of water and gambusia, fed by a larger earthen gutter on the far side of the dead grove. All of it is geometrical, ordered, like lines drawn by a diligent youngster on a giant Etch-a-Sketch. This is water management in its most simplistic form, a technique that has drained at least half the wetlands from our peninsula—including the basin of the St. Johns.

But there are more secrets here in the valley. In my front yard, I look closely at the edges of the clay road to see how its foundation is composed. Underpinning a road like this in a region as wet as Florida is not easy. Boulders and smaller igneous rocks that you might find in more ancient terrains are virtually absent. How could the road builders in the 1920s and 1930s build solid, dependable pavements?

The resource they often used was not geological but cultural. I look closely at the hardpan and see that it is composed of millions of tiny, sun-bleached freshwater shells, gastropods and bivalves, that were once part of a midden heap—maybe even a burial or ceremonial mound—created by pre-historic Native Americans in the valley over thousands of years, an edifice rich in the hardness of calcium. For road builders with no where else to look, folks anxious on "reclaiming" this moist terrain, the mounds spelled cheap and abundant fill.

As a result, the dirt road to my house is paved with the remnants of just such a mound, virtual pages of long-forgotten aboriginal history scattered from mailbox to mailbox, flattened more thoroughly with every crunch of our modern tires. On other such older roads throughout the basin, children sort through the fill rubble for arrow points and pieces of pottery. And so my own little rustic tract of Floridiana graphically tells the larger story of how humans have generally regarded the St. Johns and its cultural history, here in the deepest heart of the river valley.

The fact that a healthy river remains at all, that it is still magnificently wild in many parts, and that its banks are still dotted with ancient Indian mounds is a testament not to humans' restraint but to just how pervasive and pow-erful this resource actually is.

If memory is the simplest form of prayer, as the poet Marge Percy once wrote, then we are perhaps losing our collective memory about the river, forsaking our right to exalt with this self-induced amnesia of its historic ecol-ogy. Examining the traces of my yard—indeed, any land—in the St. Johns River valley will set loose this history, providing clues of where the river has been.

The most vital questions then become: Where is it today? Where is it go-ing? And, for the kid in us all: How do I hop aboard to see?

The St. Johns may seem to be one of the most accessible rivers in Florida. Although its marshy headwaters extend farther southward, the St. Johns has a channel that stretches, in some fashion, from just below Lake Hell 'n Blazes, 275 miles upstream. Some twenty bridges and three ferries span it, roads run near it, one large city and two towns are built next to it, and near its mouth office buildings and industry sprawl over its banks.

Beyond its three major tributaries—the Ocklawaha, Wekiva, and Econlockhatchee—there are also dozens of smaller creeks and spring runs that wind through its floodplain, many with their own bridges, even neighborhoods.

This illusion of accessibility is both its joy and its dilemma: it fools us into thinking we know it—that the river is static, unchanging, permanent, like a familiar intersection we routinely pass on the way to work or school.

"The St. Johns is one of the premium ecological resources in the Southeast," Ed Lowe, a scientist with the St. Johns River Water Management District, told me as I was preparing to begin my journey. "But I don't think there's a recognition among locals of the treasure that it is. It's sort of like the 'unseen river.'"

In thinking this way, we not only short-change the river but fool ourselves, limiting our chance for experiences on it by narrowing our own perceptions about it. In short, we take it for granted. And so it is for science as well. Although Bartram sent back early reports about new plants and animals he discovered on the river in the late eighteenth century, the examination of the St. Johns in the interim has been spotty and often unintegrated.

Some of this has to do with economics, which too often decides for us what is important. The St. Johns lost its modern clout in this arena when the steamships first began to give way to railroads at the turn of the century, inaugurating the process of funneling visitors and commerce off to someplace else. A statewide highway system completed that transformation in the 1930s, making the once popular practice of doing business on the highway of the St. Johns an old-fashioned notion. No longer the panacea for every ill of northern invalids, or an El Dorado for land and citrus investors, the river was left to itself again.

"In time, it was only the exceptional tourist who returned to the well-nigh deserted St. Johns," observed the authors of St. Johns: A Parade of Diversity in 1943. "Finally, all steamboat and hotel life reached an unarguable close . . . with the last trip to Sanford of the lone remaining steamers."

In addition, Florida has lagged behind other continental states in developing its interior because of its wetness. At least 80 percent of the population sprawls along the coast today, leaving an inland riverine wilderness like the St. Johns a chance to breathe. A 1995 assessment of Florida's natural lands concluded that "some of the state's most significant wildlife habitat is found in this region, particularly in the freshwater marshes, forested wetlands, mesic [moderately moist] pinelands and dry prairies."

Although there is little true "virgin" territory left here, there are still chunks of riverbanks and tributaries and marshes that appear as unscarred as they did during the time of first European contact, with third-, fourth-, and fifth-growth trees filling the landscape convincingly. Surely, there are still plenty of secrets left to be told.

Modern scientists, for their part, are now scrambling to do everything they can just to "manage" the river in a progressive, eco-sensitive way, to keep its health ahead of the population boom—and accompanying downward curve—that stamps the environment with the heavy footstep of humans.

The story of how they have done so in the upper river basin is one of the great successes in "resource management" of Florida, perhaps far more realized than the campaign to save the Everglades. The idea is simple: if the upstream source is not clean, then the downstream river stands no chance at all.

Surely, recurring pollution problems remain from urbanization inside the sprawl of Jacksonville, a disparagement through which the river and its animals must travel. And, without a stronger local commitment to fix it, water quality there will continue to approach levels that are alarmingly grim.

Were it not for the aggressive purchase of public land adjacent to the upper St. Johns and the passing of laws to restrict filling of valuable wetlands elsewhere, the river would be far less than it is today. Other plans are under way to perform similar work on the Ocklawaha, restoration that will revive aesthetics as well as ecology, enticing wildlife back to where it used to live.

Humans are still in dominion over the St. Johns, certainly. But their science of choice today is now more likely to be biology than engineering.

In the rare lulls between efforts to restore and preserve the river come chances to do actual inventories of its natural and human histories. Each one of these studies reveals surprises, weaving a richer and more complete tapestry of the complex river system that is the St. Johns. In my lifetime, new plant and animal species have been identified here, new freshwater springs found, new information about long-lost cultures revealed.

Naturalists who travel all the way to Latin America looking for hidden taxonomic closets to poke about in might do well to spend some time here in the valley. As one wildlife biologist told me, "We've got things living here in the river that we're not completely sure what they are."

Biology that is provocative—even balanced and sound—may not translate directly into values that are shared by everyone. But when one realizes that fishing and hunting, as well as bird watching and nature observation and photography, all depend on the availability of good land and water to sustain them, such science takes on new meaning.

A 1958 state wildlife study of waterfowl distribution in the valley analyzed how an exploding population base could easily Cuisinart the land people use for natural "recreation." Using emerging patterns, it made a prediction— one that has become alarmingly true: "Hunting and fishing in Florida has, in the past, been such an available commodity and utilized by such a relatively limited population that it is often taken for granted. Twenty to 30 years hence, when the population of Florida has tripled, the premium may well be on lands affording these recreational activities."

Economics are seldom static; like the river, they change course over time. But dollar figures are now used to justify ecology, values that folks who don't give a twit about a blue-winged teal or a warmouth can understand. There is more than parity here: with a relatively small investment, the river gives back many times.

In fact, a state study that puts a dollar figure on the more complete "socio-economic value" of the river—from real estate to boat rentals—took a hard look just at the lower St. Johns, from the Ocklawaha north to the river's mouth. If this portion of the river disappeared tomorrow, the two million folks who live in this lower valley would be poorer to the tune of $2.5 billion. It is a value that is many times what has been spent to make the river healthier, a good investment return by any account.

If a river can be said to have distinction, the St. Johns surely has a great deal of that. At 310 miles, it is the longest river wholly within Florida. It is also one of the few main rivers on our continent to flow from south to north.

Early promoters of the St. Johns in the 1800s capitalized on this, calling it the "Nile of America." To flow this way is a neat trick in North America, where most rivers run down out of mountains and hills, headed south, east and west, for the sea.

But this is not its most truly distinguishing characteristic.

Like the emotional desperadoes who came—who still come—to Florida seeking a geographic cure for their past, this river has a complicated persona. There are enough twitches and quirks left from its distant marine inundation to give it a character special unto itself. Figuring where these prehistoric tics will surface and why is part of the grand and wonderful puzzle of the river.

"Faunally speaking, the St. Johns river is an extraordinary stream," wrote naturalist Archie Carr after many visits to its waters, "like no other in America." It is made so because of the rare mix of fresh and salt water far upstream.

This creates a Whitman's Sampler of diversity, fed by an infusion of spring-borne salts, the leakage of prehistoric sea water up into the riverbed, and incoming tides that may meet and overwhelm the river's sluggish current as far south as Lake Monroe 161 miles away.

This ecological drama is played out against a climate that ranges from subtropical in the river's southern basin to warm temperate in its northern one. Some climatologists even describe the valley as "distinctly maritime," with temperature extremes moderated by the offshore Gulf Stream.

The sheer variety of plants and animals—which skyrocket when an environment is wet and warm like this one—is further hot-wired by the odd salt-fresh mix. The river itself is home to some 183 species of fish, many of which are saltwater. Some of these marine critters maintain a link to the ocean through spawning or migration. But others now spend their entire lives in the St. Johns.

For example, in Lake Washington near the river's headwaters, there is a resident population of southern stingrays. They coexist next to scads of freshwater grass shrimp (*Paleomenetes* spp), lilliputian and ghostlike versions of their far more massive marine brethren back in the sea. It is as if evolution has turned in on itself, making up its own rules as it goes along.

If you take this singular, diverse riverine environment and populate it with endangered wildlife—like wood storks and bald eagles and manatees—then chunk in some endemic plants and animals found nowhere else on earth, you have one long, winding natural corridor where most anything is possible.

Adjacent to and even under its waters, there are powerful artesian vents, and in its woods, black bears, bobcats, and, in places, wild—albeit introduced—rhesus monkeys. Within this system, we find at once one of Florida's most pristine lakes, in Blue Cypress, and one of its most polluted, in Lake Apopka. The rules, surely, are different here.

This *Welaka* of a river is a blackwater system of tributary creeks and lakes, gigantic aquatic boulevards that both store and slow the movement of the water. Although it's longer than any other major river in the state, its broad character and scant gradient diffuse its flow.

When it finally confluxes with the Atlantic at Mayport, its discharge ranks a distant fifth behind the Apalachicola, Suwannee, Choctawhatchee, and Escambia—all rivers that weren't coveted enough by early Europeans even to be renamed. If naming implies covetousness, then this river has had its share of both.

Early Spanish, who mapped the east coast of Florida in the early 1500s, noticed the strange eddies of water at the river mouth and called this Rio de Corrientes—River of Currents.

But it was French Huguenots led by Jean Ribault who first landed here on May 1, 1562, naming the river *Mai*, for the month of spring when they arrived. Before sailing on, they erected at the river's mouth a stone column with the crest of France. The friendly Timucua and their statuesque and brave chief, Saturiwa, welcomed the newcomers, and—thinking the French were honoring a phallic god of fertility—decorated the monolith with garlands of wild magnolia blossoms.

When some three hundred French soldiers returned in 1564, they built Fort Caroline, a triangular fortress of earth and wood, five miles from the mouth. It was a half century before Jamestown was founded.

On a warm summer day in the following year, an English slave ship stopped to take on fresh water upriver and found the colony of soldiers, which, despite the abundance of fish and game in the surrounding woods, was not doing so well. Englishman John Sparke, who recorded the visit, seemed dumfounded that the French were not able to sustain themselves from a natural bounty "with commodities . . . more than are yet known to any man."

After reporting a rich inventory of flora and fauna, Sparke casually mentioned he also saw a strange animal at the edge of the river Mai, quenching its thirst. It was, said Sparke, "a beast with one horn, which, coming to the river to drink, putteth the same into the water before he drinketh." By Sparke's description, it was a unicorn.

The Spanish, ever diligent, reclaimed their territory soon afterward, brutally slaughtering the French colonists and changing the name of the fort— and the river—to San Mateo, to honor the gentle Catholic saint whose feast day closely followed that capture.

By the early 1600s, the Spanish built a new mission of wood and palm fronds near the *puerto*, the port or mouth, christening it with the name of a Christian apostle as San Juan del Puerto. Soon, San Juan became known as the river itself, a title by which it has long been mapped and, since the first British occupation in 1763, anglicized.

The St. Johns, then, becomes a river of infinite potential, a place to indulge myths, to evoke shards of timeless magic, to search for the natural realities that are sublime instead of merely virtual and safe. After all, this is a river where dreams have been chased through the early morning mist for centuries on the peninsula, from inside the heart-pine log dugouts of the earliest Paleo-Indians to the sleek polymer hulls of the most modern canoeist and boater. It is a place where strange, single-horned beasts, before being relegated to legend, once came to drink.

If we are lucky, we may yet find enough wildness left here to take the shrillness of civilization out of us, to discover a place, as Sherwood Anderson once wrote, where we can still "learn the trick of the quiet."

To accomplish this in modern Florida, a state to which a thousand people move each day and where developers ceaselessly extrude new tract neighborhoods from natural land, is not a small thing.

In my own sojourn on the river, I have relied not just on those contemporaries who know and care about the St. Johns but also on others who have experienced it through the centuries. In this way, I have invited the entire lot of them aboard my allegorical raft as I travel its distance, from its headwaters to its confluence with the ocean. In a transient state that yearns for connectivity, you might think of us as a single tribal community, without the constraints of time.

It is, as you might imagine, a highly variant and sometimes contrary community. But we are all bound by the thread of the river itself, a linkage that rises and falls through the consciousness of history, reborn again in each cry of the limpkin at dawn, each new spring bloom of the cypress and sedge, each pale reflection of the full moon light on the black, tannic water.

As a reader, you can remain stationary on the riverbanks—like the audience in John Barth's *Floating Opera*—and wait for this grand play to reveal itself from the stories that drift by.

Or, you can come along for the ride.

It'll work either way.

River of Lakes

> The St. Johns takes its rise in a small lake . . . [and beyond the lake] extends
>
> a marsh as far as the eye can reach . . . with as level and uninterrupted a
>
> horizon as the sea itself. . . . It is constantly underwater and may be considered
>
> as one great spring from which water is slowly but continually oozing out
>
> —Naturalist John Eatton Le Conte, who explored the river for the U.S.
>
> government in 1822

Whales once breached here, somewhere above where I am now standing, thigh-deep in sawgrass at the river's headwaters. They did so worldwide, of course, back when they were something other than whales and land was little more than the remnants of angry, fuming volcanic pinnacles. But age is the great divider, and geological time—or the lack of it—was, and still is, what has made Florida and its waterways unique.

A quarter billion years ago, when the Shenandoah Valley was becoming the mountainous gully that would carry the river of the same name, Florida was where marine animals still came to dream. It was the sea, blue and endless, and it swept freely over sand and coral, unrestrained.

It did so at least until twenty million years ago, when the sandbars and cays that represented the nascent peninsula first emerged from the sea, west of my spot here in the grass, water, and peat. The oldest and highest of these sand spits would evolve into the Central Ridge along the spine of the peninsula, providing a point of reference against which subsequent shorelines would later define themselves. And define they did, re-forming at least eight different prehistoric coasts during assorted ice ages, sending the sea level up and down by as much as four hundred feet. The oceans ebbed into ice at the massive polar caps and then—during interglacial warming—flooded back out again, repeatedly soaking the shore that would rim modern Florida like the froth of the surf over coquina shells.

During the last series of these re-formations, when the appendage that would be Florida was as truncated as it appears on old Spanish maps, the terrain that would hold the St. Johns River valley finally arose. This valley was born as a deep saltwater lagoon, bordered by a perforated line of sea islands and bars to the east and by the ancient ridge to the west. The time was one hundred thousand years ago, and sea level was forty-two feet higher than it is today.

In this way, then, the basin that would one day cradle the St. Johns was not molded by the torturous chasm of shifting plate rocks or scooped out by tedious erosion through a steep ravine. Rather, it cascaded down from the sea in a timeless trickle of shell and sand and bone of animals and calciferous plants, marine life that once swam, crawled, and took root here. The walls of this valley were constructed of ancient dunes and terraces, shaped into north–south contours by the energy of the wind and the spindrift of the prevailing currents offshore.

But the ocean that shaped the early basin of the river was not through yet. When the sea level dropped one last time and the coast and dune line migrated even closer toward the Atlantic, the function of the marine lagoon moved with it, setting up shop inside the parallel basin of what would become the Indian River. Left behind, bereft of its estuarine nature, the just-slightly-older inland valley did what many of Florida's brand new residents continue to do today—it re-created itself.

It did so with the abundance of rain in the southern subtropic realm of this peninsula, an act that relies on the wealth of foliage and water to keep the cycle in good working order. The warm sun sucks moisture up into the cumulus, and the sky sends it back down again onto the great sprawling basin as drizzles and showers and great heaving bursts of thunderstorms. And somewhere here, somewhere around me, west of Vero Beach and Fort Pierce, the alchemy of a river is fused from the oversaturation of water into the land, birthing a tenuous flow that slowly—if not always surely—heads north for the sea.

In the greatest of ironies, of the kind only a flat place like Florida can acknowledge, another giant river system parallels the St. Johns on this same latitude, not so far away. But instead of flowing north, it is busy moving south. It is inland from here, barely twenty miles away on the other side of the relic marine terrace of the seminal river valley. It is the Kissimmee, and the scant rise of geology moves it through its own basin, south to Okee-chobee, for it is the origin of the grassy river of the Everglades.

Anyone can, if so motivated, travel to ground zero of these headwaters. Yet it's a place in which few ever step foot. That's because it's a shallow marsh, remote and isolated. Although anglers and hunters pass nearby on narrow airboat trails today, most are headed for either deeper waters to fish or higher ground to hunt.

To come here helps me better understand why the wet, low interior of Florida was the last part of the state to be settled. When cities and towns far beyond the western "frontier" of the country were thriving at the turn of the century, the river's wetlands were still immeasurable, uncharted. As recently as 1943, the authors of *St. Johns: A Parade of Diversities* reported that the headwaters of the St. Johns "as yet await a cartographer, for none knows how many miles [there are] among the ambiguous and lonely, wild huge bogs about the river's source waters."

I have traveled here with Dr. Ed Lowe, chief scientist for the agency charged with somehow "managing" the water quality and flow of every vein of the St. Johns. Lowe, trained as a biologist, wants to show me not just where this river is born but how the condition of a headwater can influence a river's disposition miles away. This should be an observation of great pain for any biologist because, like the great Everglades of Florida, the headwaters of the St. Johns have been under siege until recently by drag lines and dredges, all in the name of "land reclamation" and flood control. Unlike the Glades, though, the river has not become the cause célèbre that fires imaginations far beyond its boundaries. Defenders, like Lowe, are rare.

Lowe, earnest and resolute, also embodies a quality that sets him decidedly apart from many public agency scientists—or private environmental consultants—who often stuff their conscience here in Florida: he seems to really *care* about what happens to the resource he is charged with managing. Quietly, unashamedly, he often speaks of the need to have an "ethic" for the land, a belief system that can be far more powerful than paper-intensive environmental rules.

However, he is not naive. For decades, people have settled anywhere land promoters have convinced them to in Florida, often circumventing "growth management plans" via politically granted exemptions to do so. Even now, with progressive strategies written into law, the state is hemorrhaging its natural lands to development at the rate of twenty acres per hour. Bubbaism, whereby personal connections sneak around the most well meaning of laws, still widely prevails, not just in the nineteen counties of the St. Johns River basin but throughout Florida.

What is left is often fragmented, like a'fine plate of china broken into many pieces. It is Lowe's job to help glue it all back together again, a vast chore. "We have such a wealth of water in this state," says Lowe, partly in awe, partly in lamentation. "There are plenty places for everyone who wants to live here. But, why does everyone have to live *everywhere*?"

Not only do they want to live everywhere, but they apparently want to farm everywhere, as well. In its earliest days, the agency for which Lowe now works was not a "water management" district at all but one of "flood control." The U.S. Army Corps of Engineers, which performed the actual structural work on the terrain for the district, was unleashed on Florida's wetlands, helping to build dikes and dig arrow-straight canals to keep seasonally dry wetlands from being flooded, as nature intended.

Farmers and cattlemen worked hard to do their share, piling up berms of dirt to make levees and backhoeing ditches for canals on their land. In the simplistic, linear reality of the first three-quarters of the century, dry was always good, and wet was always bad.

As the historic marshland around the headwaters shrank from thirty miles to barely one mile in width between 1900 and 1972, the quality of the river downstream suffered tragically. Without the kidneylike cleansing function of the wetlands to filter impurities, the entire river simply started badly, loaded with sediment and agricultural chemicals. By the early 1970s, most of the forty-six tributaries that had once seeped over adjacent marshes and wooded swamps were surging ditchlike into the upper river channel from the western ridge.

Since the early 1980s, the water managers in the St. Johns Basin have decided to try to balance ecology with farming needs—such as the use of natural reservoirs to filter pollutants, store water, and provide habitat for wildlife. These are precisely the type of benefits a deep natural marsh, if left intact, would have generously given of itself.

To reverse the damage done earlier in the century, farmland had to be bought and then reflooded, maintaining some levees to segregate the newer artificial "water management areas" adjacent to the groves and row crops from the more natural "marsh conservation" zones that actually hold the headwaters. Biologically, the hill-like levees separate the evil twin from the good one. The cost of buying and fixing land here between the early 1980s and the late 1990s is around two hundred million dollars—a fraction of the worth of the entire river.

The result is a drainage basin that is a hybrid of nature and human efforts. "We are at heart, manipulators, gardeners, controllers," admits Lowe. "Now, we're trying to ask the question: What's the least we can do?" In this way, the quest for sound ecology now controls the engineering, and not the other way around, as it once did.

Lowe tells me that some 235 square miles of land has been reclaimed in the upper river, more than tripling the size of the functional drainage basin from what it was in 1972. Government canals that once functioned as gutters to empty the marsh water into the adjacent Indian River lagoon on the other side of the terrace are being plugged. By 1976 they had reduced the outflow by 70 percent of what it once was. Today, the only fresh water that goes into the Indian River from these canals does so only to abate flooding after a severe storm—an event that occurs once every twenty-five years. The result is not just a more actualized marsh but a healthier coastal estuary not nearly as diluted by fresh water as it once was.

The contemporary Army Corps is helping to make this happen, undoing work their predecessors did years ago. If this is one of the largest wetland restoration projects of its kind in the world, it may be—like the St. Johns itself—also one of the most unsung.

Lowe and I are journeying to the most undisturbed of these headwaters via airboat, a sledlike vehicle torqued by an aircraft engine and giant wooden prop, designed to push us across the top of the water-sogged earth and weeds. When pilot Ken Snyder, sitting behind and above us in a leather flight jacket, revs up the engine, the noise is so ear-splitting that we have to put on muffling headsets to blunt it. To steer left or right, Snyder uses a sticklike lever to manipulate narrow, vertical wings on each side of the prop, not unlike navigating an aircraft. When this hybrid vehicle is cranked up at top end, it soars, more like a hydroplane than a boat, pressing the wind against my face and letting loose torrents of adrenaline as effectively as a good carnival ride.

The downside to soaring is that there are no brakes. To stop, both flaps and throttle are disengaged, and the sled gradually coasts to a halt, tall grasses finally giving way just a couple of feet from my face. I wonder out loud why the boat has no "reverse." Lowe informs me that if the powerful prop were to spin in the other direction, it would simply blow us off the front of the sled.

When we approach fifteen-foot-high levees between the marshes, pilot Snyder pulls back hard on the throttle and we slide up at a forty-five-degree angle and over the human-made hills, our hull scraping and grading on the bare, packed earth, the engine roaring like a small plane on takeoff. It is a testament to the nature of this great vast tract of unroaded Florida in the river basin that an agency like Lowe's—the St. Johns River Water Management District (SJRWMD)—would have as part of its official vehicle fleet several high-powered airboats designed to travel at a fast clip across very wet mud.

And travel it does, finally taking us four or five miles from where we put in at a nearly deserted boat ramp at the edge of the Blue Cypress Water Management Area. After leaving the ramp, the airboat had first skirted over the six-thousand-acre water management area (WMA), a tract that in 1989 was a cattle ranch known as "Lake Miami Farms." Reflooded by the scientists, the WMA today is a deep, cattail- and coot-studded natural impoundment where runoff from the adjacent citrus groves can be drained and cleansed of chemicals and silt without environmental damage to the wilder "marsh conservation areas" on the far side of the levees.

The farmers not only get to pump water for irrigation out of the WMAs, but their groves also benefit from the natural warming effect the rewetted public lands provide. When a killer freeze blew in across the state in 1989 with temperatures as low as the teens, the results could have browned out the nearby crops as thoroughly as a brushfire. But as the chilled air mass moved over the new wetlands, it warmed by several degrees, enough to save some seventy thousand acres of citrus to the east. The farmers, who initially resisted the purchase of their land for the restoration, began to realize there might be some wisdom in the forces of nature after all.

But turning winter marsh into a giant space heater is only one of reclamation's many gifts. Another is found in the rectangular 4-square-mile "Stick Marsh" and the adjacent 6.25-square-mile "Farm 13" reservoir, both of which have converted farmland into the state's hottest fishing holes for large-mouth bass. Topography has been redefined again, with the thick-bodied, hard-hitting bass roaming atop the former pastures in six to eight feet of water, swimming between the ghosts of cows and cattle egrets.

All of this brings up the question of who, ultimately, can presume to own the title to any land—humans, cows, fish? Author Marjorie Kinnan Rawlings pondered that same dilemma when she considered the little plot of land she lived on in northern Florida: "Who owns Cross Creek?" "We are tenants and not possessors, lovers and not masters," she answered. "[It] belongs to the wind, the sand, the rain, to the sun and the seasons, to the cosmic secrecy of seed, and beyond all, to time."

Aborigine cultures, like those who lived in the river basin of Welaka, saw the occupation of the earth similarly, not as dominion but as stewardship, one for which they developed a deep and mystical appreciation.

Yet to occupy land soaked with water is far trickier. It is a responsibility that continually seeps, leaks, and flows downstream, ecologically if not spiritually.

Snyder, with a twist and pull of the stick, puts us into a coasting stop near a low-lying tree island and cuts the motor. Seminoles who treasured the higher ground the islands offered called them *hummocks*—from a word meaning "home." Like other Indian words that have slipped into our vocabulary under disguise, hummock has now become *hammock*.

Lowe and I each put on rubber, chest-high waders and slip down off the flat deck of the airboat into the grass, which towers above and around us like an African savanna. It is somehow hard to believe I am standing inside the genesis of a river, one that near its mouth will be strong and deep enough to hold eighty-five-thousand-ton aircraft carriers.

It is a bright Florida fall day, with a deep blue sky bridged by a bank of puffy cumulus, the same kind of broad, water-rich sky that nurtures the Glades. From out of one of the clouds, a pterodactyl of a winged figure emerges. As it flies over, I see it is an Audubon's crested caracara—*Caracara cheriway*—an elegant-looking tropical scavenger, with a white throat and large crested black head setting it apart from the more common vultures. *Cara* is Greek for "top of head," and it is so distinguished in this way that its genus repeats the word twice.

In the art they left behind, the Aztecs of what is now Mexico depicted a caracara eating a serpent. Considering the sanctity they afforded snakes, that was mighty praise indeed.

In water to my waist, I bend to feel the blades of the sedge called sawgrass, letting the sharp, serrated edges brush over my fingers. Golden now from the end of its growing season, the tops of the sedge will soon brown out and die, settling down into the muck.

Although associated only with the Everglades in popular lore, sawgrass is found scattered along the entire corridor of the river. At Lake Poinsett, it actually grows in vast pastures; in other places, it thrives in patches, all the way up into the tidal lower basin around Jacksonville.

I look closely between the sawgrass plants and see that this is far more than a monoculture: scattered about are the flowers of the string lily, the grassy maidencane, the buttercuplike white bloom of the duck potato. From the water's surface, I pick up a strand of bladderwort, an aquatic plant that captures tiny zooplankton inside its little swollen bladderlike leaves and then— perhaps in payback for every nibble an animal has ever taken from a plant— digests them.

By spring, this wetland pasture will be alive again with the bacchanal of renewal, greening the plants here as far as one can see. But that's not all that will come back to life: in the warm days of March and April, the marsh will be consumed with the chorus of frogs—green tree and cricket and pig—all reaffirming their rights at once in a series of croaks, squeaks, and grunts to these "ambiguous and lonely, wild, huge bogs."

But today, it's quiet around us, the unearthly silence in which the air actually seems to hum to make up for what's not here. Part of what's not here is the chirp of the Carolina parakeet, the sharp call of the ivory-billed woodpecker, two now extinct birds that made their last stand here in the protection of these lonely bogs. Perhaps their spirits are still here, fluttering somewhere inside the hum.

Lowe sticks a sharp metal pole tipped with a pipelike probe into the soft bottom to capture a plug of the peat below. His arms go down below the surface of the water as the six-foot-long pole sinks into the murk. When he pulls it back up, the pipe is stuffed with peat, the same rich organic matter that makes the drained marsh so attractive to farmers.

Deep below, says Lowe, is fifteen to twenty feet of this peat, the centuries-old accumulation of sedge long gone, dating from the earliest days when freshwater plants first colonized this basin.

We trudge through the water to the edge of the tree island, a just slightly higher plateau crowded with stunted shrubs like the primrose willow, the St.

Johns wort, the wax myrtle. I see the little purple fluff of a wildflower—a climbing astor—that seems scattered like an afterthought in the darker foliage.

This is a bonsai of a hammock, one far older than its height would have us believe, sized down through time like the dwarf bald cypress found inside the savannas of the Glades. It may well have been here when Florida was first colonized, creating itself from the marsh simply because it could. "We haven't done enough science to know really how old trees like this even are," says Lowe.

Water here moves so slowly as to be immeasurable. Mineral nutrients that might nourish growth in the subtropical climate come not from an enriched upland flow but from the rain, pure and nutrient-poor, like the distillant-quality waters that fall on the Amazon. There is oxygen at the top but little at the bottom.

If this tree island is low, it is also too dense for us to make our way more than a few feet inside. Lowe and I slosh back to the airboat and flop back over the side like netted tuna. Snyder fires the craft back up, and we head off to a hammock in the distance with a higher profile, one that promises enough open ground to enable us at least to walk inside.

As we go, flocks of white ibis rise from the marsh in great sheetlike waves. Here and there, I see the distinctive black "iron" head of the wood stork poking out at the edge of the grass, watch the gallinules madly paddling for cover like wind-up ducks.

I also see a rare bird made remarkable by the fact it still exists here at all, a raptor known as the Everglades snail kite (*Rostrhamus sociabilis plumbeus*). Crisply etched into the sky like a finely folded work of Japanese origami, the kite is scored by a distinctive white stripe across its tail.

With fewer than five hundred snail kites left in the world, the hawklike bird teeters in the moment, just a few threads above the threshold through which the Carolina parakeet and the ivory-billed woodpecker have already flown. Reports of kites from the 1930s told of them once being abundant from the Florida panhandle to the southern Everglades. But as they declined to only a few dozen birds in the 1960s, biologists figured the widespread destruction of wetlands would finally do them in.

Virtually flushed from the Glades by the skewed, dysfunctional nature of the artificial water cycle there, the kite is as dependent on the delicate seasonal balance of water as any animal can be. That's because it's bound not by territory but by habitat. "It's nomadic," explains Lowe, "so it follows the habitat it needs over the southern range of the state."

The habitat it needs must have some vegetation but not too much, and it should be full of water that is both clear and clean. Perhaps most important, the water level must be stable enough so it doesn't suddenly swamp the low-lying nests of the kites or short-circuit the cycle of what the bird hunts—the fat apple snail.

Although I see several empty shells, I spot no live apple snails at all around us. But the snail kites do, and that's what counts, for they must dive and grab the mollusks with their talons. I do observe several birds, perched on low scrubs just above the water, pulling the snails from their shells with their curved beaks. Before the day is over, I will count almost two dozen snail kites, more than I have ever seen in my entire life.

Later, I will encounter the giant apple snail (*Pomacea paludosa*) thriving throughout most of the length of the St. Johns, for, after all, it is the largest freshwater snail in North America and is not so hard to spot if you are in the business of searching for snails.

After a while, I will look forward to watching carefully for its pinkish, opalescent eggs, laid in rows on leaves and stems just above the water's surface. It is this egg—the beginning of us all—that must survive if the kite is to endure: a sudden rise or fall in water level will either strand and dry the eggs or, more likely, drown them. With no eggs, there will be no snails, and the birds who live on them will fly away, perhaps, one final time.

As the upper river restoration has rewetted at least a chunk of the bird's historic habitat, the raptors have increased today to a population of four hundred to five hundred—one-fourth of which are found around us in the headwaters here, a bottom-line affirmation in which nature itself forges the grade by returning ecological links to the land.

If the revitalization of natural water levels has driven restoration, so has fire. Generally portrayed as a natural disaster good only for its terror potential in B-movies and Bambi cartoons, fire helps periodically clear away the dense cover of one dominant species or another. In this way, it continually allows the valuable wet grasses to reemerge, instead of climaxing into shrubs and, eventually, forests.

"Fire is important for the biological diversity of the marsh," explains Lowe. Besides stabilizing the grasses, fire releases nutrients—both from the ashes of what is burned and from the oxidization of the foliage. "It helps shift the balance between all these species that are competing furiously between each other here for space and light," says Lowe.

Once solely introduced by lightning here in the valley, fire is now coaxed to life by humans to do the sort of things it does so well. Used in "controlled burns," fire then becomes part of the process of "helping nature heal herself." In doing so, it also helps keep water-sucking exotic trees like the Malelecua—a scourge of the Glades—out of the headwaters.

Our second hammock finally approaches from the bow of the airboat. Snyder again kills the engine, and this time we all slide off the deck onto soggy ground that only covers our shoes. We walk single file up into the drier territory of this island—a hill by scant degrees—where bay magnolias tower up into an impressive canopy they share with bald cypress. From a ground cover of royal ferns and fallen cypress needles, greenish moss-covered knees randomly poke out, venerable and gnarled, troll-like monoliths. A cat brier vine with its banana-shaped leaves winds high into the foliage, next to an old water oak with bark that seems naturally corrugated.

The wind wafts through the foliage canopy, releasing a scent both fresh and rarefied, the smell of land seldom visited, one that it has kept to itself for a long time now. If I were a Native American, returning across the lonely sedge in my dugout, this would surely be a fine home.

Pausing, Lowe takes stock of the largest cypress: About one hundred feet tall by four feet around—a youngster compared with the thousand-year-old trees clear-cut from the basin for lumber in the earlier part of the century by loggers.

"This one will never be logged," says Lowe. "At least we know that."

All things considered, Lowe is optimistic about the prospects created by the enlightened public policy that manages the river basin. There is simply more land than ever protected by public ownership, more ecological restoration of damaged terrain, stronger laws on the books to support conservation.

"In the next fifty years, I think we're going to see a blossoming of fish and wildlife in Florida," says Lowe. "At least until the population finally overwhelms what we've been able to do. . . . Then it'll be up to another generation to solve it."

Ecology is all about connections—not piecemeal slabs of habitat left standing as zoolike islands to assuage our curiosity or guilt but true, natural connections. When I read about early travelers riding up the St. Johns on steamboats only a hundred years ago, it still astounds me to hear them describe their journey into the "everglades."

But that, in fact, is what these headwaters once were. The sawgrass marsh that surrounds me today used to sweep southwest to Lake Okeechobee, and from there, across most of southern Florida. The Seminoles, who migrated down into the peninsula in the late 1700s as Creeks, believed the St. Johns originated in what they called Lake Mayaco—Okeechobee—and perhaps it once did.

The Seminoles, like the pre-Columbian Indians who lived here before them, could travel the entire length of this ecologically linked peninsula by dugout, from the Ten Thousand Islands up through Shark River Slough into Lake Okeechobee and out across Florida's horizontal ridge that divided the newer, lower terrain of south from central Florida. Wetlands were dominant then, water was higher, and physiographic zones like this could be seasonally navigated by running creeks and deep marshes, up over the Allapattah Flats to Blue Cypress and through the channels of the St. Johns, all the way to northern Florida.

Artifacts found today in burial and midden mounds hundreds of miles from where they were first carved, hammered, and molded remind us of how profoundly vital such waterborne routes had once been. The Everglades didn't begin and end at the boundary to a national park in the southwest corner of the state then but truly seemed to be eternal and wet and everlasting. In this reality, the headwaters of the St. Johns sometimes overflowed south and sometimes north into the river basin, depending on the rain and the winds.

The Mickosugees, the culturally entrenched tribe of Seminoles who still live on reservations at the edge of the Glades, harbor a creation myth that is a haunting intimation of Florida's aquatic genesis. In it, their ancestors dropped from the sky like rain into Lake Okeechobee and from there swam ashore. If they did, they would have shadowed the molecules of water that birthed all the great wet marsh and swamp overflow that was once central and south Florida.

Okeechobee, in fact, is barely thirty miles from here, and streams like Taylor Creek lead into it and out of its northern rim toward the sawgrass. Southwest of Blue Cypress, stream relics, like Fort Drum Creek, wander through the marsh like dotted lines begging for connection. Together, they provide traces of a prehistoric trail, of a natural link between here and Okeechobee.

But they are only shadows of their former selves: the big bowl of a lake was fully diked after a devastating hurricane in 1928, and the only waters that flow into or out of Okeechobee today do so on behalf of canals and locks that breech the encircling Hoover Dike.

And so, the St. Johns is on its own now, rising alone from a marshland to create an excruciatingly gradual sheet flow, a second "river of grass" that moves north inside the old marine lagoon, instead of southwest like the Glades.

How long truly is this river? By water management standards, it is 310 miles, with its headwaters beginning somewhere around the southwest border of Indian River County. But its biological genesis may even be a few miles south of there, deeper in St. Lucie and Okeechobee Counties. An old United States Geological Survey chart that mapped the river long before the district's restoration project was in place charts the St. Johns as 318 miles.

Blue Cypress Lake is just north of here, and it is a magnificent body of tannin water rimmed with cypress, as clean and deep as any lake in Florida can be. Unlike other lakes in the middle river system that sometimes turn green with algae blooms from human activities, Blue lives up to its name, reflecting the trunks and canopies of cypress on a mirrorlike surface that is nothing if not cerulean. It is a far more poetic name for a lake that, just a few decades ago, was called Lake Wilmington.

Thoreau never saw this river system, but he surely read Bartram's description of it. And, as well as anyone, he understood the beguiling powers of water. When our airboat finally reaches the edge of Blue Cypress and coasts to a halt, we ascend again into the magnificence of absolute silence, broken only by the cries of the ospreys, and I think of Thoreau's evocation of such places. "A lake is the landscape's most beautiful and expressive feature," he once wrote. "It is earth's eye; looking into which the beholder measures the depths of his own nature."

Because it is almost entirely encircled with wetlands, Blue Cypress is fed with the drainage of these moist systems. Like wetlands everywhere, they cleanse the waters of any earthen depression lucky enough to be surrounded by them, functioning as eyedrops for this natural eye.

To have many different species in any one place is a phenomenon to be-hold, nature's version of a well-faceted personality—or the real-life appli-cation of Noah's Ark, a single place where a multitude of critters coexist, some on deck, others below in steerage.

Lowe tells me that a biologist who studies little insects that live down in the mud once found a higher biodiversity of them at the bottom of Blue Cypress than in any other lake in Florida. This is not just good news for the mud-loving arthropods of steerage but a vital sign that the rest of the food chain may be just as healthy.

Most lakes in Florida, including the thirty-five hundred in the St. Johns Basin, were once as clean and clear as Blue Cypress—and not so terribly long ago. A 1941 aerial photo of Lake Apopka, which is today a sad, forlorn body of plankton-clogged water that feeds the Ocklawaha tributary in the middle river, shows a water body so clear that you can see bottom vegetation five and ten feet under the surface.

North of Blue Cypress, there is a vast, spongelike wetland that sneaks water quietly across the Brevard County line, up to and around Lake Hell 'n Blazes, which some more puritanical cartographers have named Hellen Blazes.

Although road maps show nothing between Blue Cypress and Hell 'n Blazes but the great blue marsh of the river, there is actually quite a com-plex corridor here that is half natural, half "structural"—as the engineers like to call their handiwork of dikes and levees.

Lake Hell 'n Blazes is where the natural channel for the St. Johns River historically has emerged. From here, on a good map, you can trace the river with your finger for 275 miles, all the way up to Mayport and the river's mighty confluence with the Atlantic.

But, as I will soon find, a line traced on a map does not always follow one traced into the earth.

2   *Lake Hell 'n Blazes to Puzzle Lake*

> Florida is so watery and vine-tied that pathless wanderings are not easily
> possible in any direction. . . . Oftentimes, I was tangled in a labyrinth of armed
> vines like a fly in a spider web—John Muir, reporting his walk across the
> St. Johns Basin from the Atlantic in 1867

*I*f Jackson Pollack were God, this is how he likely would have painted the upper St. Johns, a terrestrial canvas covered with tannic splatters and veins, elliptical cobwebs one step away from being random. Instead of following the sheet flow of this grassy river northward from the headwaters into the place where the map tells me the river should begin, we soar back to our put-in ramp at Blue Cypress Marsh, the speed of the airboat pressing the wind into my face.

If the Florida winter has browned out the marsh, it has also kept a check on the multitude of flying insects that might otherwise be smashing themselves into our heads as we go, as if we were organic windshields. This splatter factor can take curious forms, a way of identifying arthropods by the way they crash like teensy meteorites into human foreheads and cheeks. "It makes you appreciate how durable the exoskeleton of a dragonfly really is," says Snyder, the memory from summer still fresh in his mind.

From our ramp, we trailer the craft up to just south of Hell 'n Blazes on a country highway, passing the little village of Fellsmere as we do. Fellsmere is the cultural underside of the grand scheme to drain the river's wetlands, one that depended on the promise by early developers that "reclaimed" bottomlands would, indeed, stay reclaimed. The local company-owned newspaper, the *Fellsmere Farmer*, was shameless in its promotion of "Fabulous Fellsmere," bragging in 1912 that this was "the first and most efficient drainage project of a permanent nature ever completed in the state." The interior, at last, would be open to development, establishing a prosperous city that would dwarf all else in Florida.

A massive dike and canal system, the Fellsmere Grade, was constructed horizontally across the middle of this system. This canal didn't just interrupt the northerly sheet flow of the river—it actually channelized millions of gallons of fresh water into the nearby Indian River lagoon. As for natural repercussions of draining the headwaters and diluting the saltwater lagoon, there were none: "The dredge work," reported the *Farmer*, "is but an engineering problem with little consequence."

Marshland bought a few years before for $1.25 an acre was resold for $100 an acre. Anxious, starry-eyed home owners began to settle here, some of whom grew sea cotton, corn, citrus, and sugarcane on adjacent fields. But when a storm dumped sixteen inches of water on the town in 1916, dikes ruptured, and Fabulous Fellsmere became marsh once more.

After the flood, even the Orwellian newspeak of the company paper couldn't make the development's image right again. Homesteaders fled in droves, bankrupting the Fellsmere Land Company and leaving behind a boomtown village that to this day remains incomplete, like an HO gauge train set with most of the pieces of the little town missing. More reliable "structure" would later conspire to keep Fellsmere drained for farmers, but the scare of a flood lingered for home owners. Fellsmere was not a salubrious place to be.

There is more wonderful irony in all this: Fellsmere today radiates a retro, slow-lane village charm that is the flip side of the congested, edgy place it could have become if it had indeed been dry and efficient and Fabulous.

North of Fellsmere, we wait our turn in a line of other trailered airboats commandeered by deer hunters—accessorized in camos and guns and machismo—before Snyder can put us back in the water. Here, the vague but discernible channel of the St. Johns first begins.

Safely afloat, we zoom north through Three Forks Run to the edge of Hell 'n Blazes, a remote place where I can imagine some lost soul—quite literally—wondering where in hell 'n blazes he had ended up. Some might think this of the entire upper basin. To me, this region of the river seems more unformed, more biologically raw than what follows. It is the primitive, fire-spitting volcano to the worn, aged mountains that are further downstream in time. But raw doesn't mean it isn't static enough to be measured: in purely linear terms, the upper valley is 83 miles long and 22 miles wide, bordered by the Atlantic Coastal Ridge to the east and the older Central Ridge to the west.

If it were not for the natural berm created by the prehistoric oceanic terrace, the waters in this newly created river would inauspiciously leak more or less eastward toward the sea after not too many miles. It would be a nickel rocket of a river, full of unrealized promise.

As for Lake Hell 'n Blazes, it is protected by a broad, marshy shoreline, a buffer that ought to guarantee all is biologically well here where the natural channel once began. But as we approach the lake, I see it is as green as a golf course fairway. Our airboat drifts to a stop, and the scent of newly cut grass fills the air. It is coming from the lake itself.

Lowe pushes a PVC pole overboard to test the depth, down to five feet. It comes up covered with hydrilla, an underwater plant first brought into the state in the early 1950s from Sri Lanka to be sold to aquarium owners. "This is bad stuff," says Lowe, shaking his head, stuff that wasn't in the river system when he began his work here in 1981. Hydrilla, which is also the name of its genus, sounds suspiciously like some B-movie Oriental monster that glooms the world alongside Godzilla—the *Attack of Hydrilla!*—and that image isn't too far-fetched.

Under control inside a low-lit fish tank, the single-stemmed water weed with whorls of soft green leaves looks fragile enough to seem delicate. But on its own, under the warm Florida sun, it fulfills its potential as its scientific namesake, *hydra*—a fabulous, many-headed serpent. In this way, hydrilla becomes a Godzilla of a plant, growing up to thirty-five feet in length—an inch or more a day. Introduced here by hobbyists dumping their tanks after one Fellsmerian tragedy or another, hydrilla has become the subsurface counterpart of the floating hyacinth, another non-native exotic that in a relatively short period has threatened to crowd out all that came before it on the river.

It is this hydrilla I smell today, and it chokes the entire water column from top to bottom, a true prop-grabbing monoculture that makes it difficult for all but a surface-skimming vehicle like we have to navigate. Spraying herbicides kills the invasive weed, says Lowe. But it also destroys native plants, poisoning God knows what kind of related natural fauna in the process.

Foreign exotics like this have entered this river system without the dangers they might face from predators savvy to their tricks back home. To try to correct this imbalance, two flies that specialize in eating the plant have been released in the basin, along with a weevil that likes to munch on its tuberlike roots. But controlling the weed seems a Sisiphian task, and the introduction of any new exotic to the vast, inviting aquarium of the St. Johns Basin for natural predation has its drawbacks: a hybrid Asian grass carp was brought in a few years ago specifically to eat the hydrilla. But the cute, manageable little carps ballooned up to thirty and forty pounds—at which point they decided to eat every other native plant they could in the lakes in which they were released.

Environmental officials threw up their hands and decided to launch the sort of decisive action legislators often resort to when something is already far beyond control: they outlawed it. As a result, possession of *Hydrilla verticillata* is now a second-degree misdemeanor, punishable by a five-hundred-dollar fine and/or sixty days in jail. The rules, surely, are different here.

From Hell 'n Blazes, we roar north to Lake Sawgrass, passing the narrow, tree-lined Jane Green Creek to the west, where we make a brief detour. More slowly now, we travel up the winding stream, past low shores of bald cypress. I notice that almost all the trees are scored with water marks almost four feet above where the creek level is now, creating a whiter, unmarked trunk over the uniformly darker one that was stained with tannic water during the warmer wet months. It reminds me of how critical rainfall is to the river's level, not just here but far downstream. When nature scores trees in a hardwood swamp like this, it lets us know the forested wetland is still intact, that it rises and falls with seasonal overflow, just as it was made to do.

Up inside the canopy, I see thousands of bromeliads studding the branches like holiday decorations—some no bigger than a silver dollar, others as large as a pineapple plant. Each is a micro explosion of fauna bred by moisture and rain, spiky clusters of tapering green fronds bound at their base like wetland corsages.

Along with orchids and Spanish moss, bromeliads are part of the family of air plants known as epiphytes. They are germinated by Florida's moistness, and many of them are firing out reddish spears, tight scarlet buds bursting unexpectedly at the ends. There are seventeen different kinds of bromeliads found along the Florida peninsula, and almost all thrive in places like this, around rivers and swamps and marshes. Snyder reminds me that one of the advantages of being on the river in winter is that the thick cypress foliage of the warmer months that hides the bromeliads has now thinned to reveal them.

Our winding creek trails off into the cypress, clear and enchanting, like others I will find later along the river, offering the very complete illusion that humans have never stepped foot here. It is late, nearing twilight now, and as we travel up through Lake Sawgrass, we spook hundreds of long-legged wading birds—white ibises, herons, wood storks—and a gaggle of cormorants, their crooked beaks easily distinguishing them from the look-alike anhingas with sharper bills. Four roseate spoonbills fly above us, their cartoonishly pink wings backlit and made even more surreal by the crimson sky. Gators swirl in enormous vortexes to get out of our way, and gallinules flap madly just inches above the water, neither fully flying nor swimming.

There are wading birds everywhere, rising from the high savannalike grasses in great white clouds, like they once did in the Glades. Snyder wonders out loud how in the world they can stay so white, after spending most of their day amid the consuming blackness of mud, and we laugh at the anthropomorphic notion of it all.

Lake Washington, often incorrectly cited as the "headwaters" of the St. Johns, lies just north of Lake Sawgrass, connected by a weed-choked channel that sneaks under U.S. 192. I am on my own for this piece of the river, and I head out to Lake Washington in my jeep, driving due west from Interstate 95 on a road that turns from asphalt to dirt but remains straight and true all the way to the rim of the lake.

Like most roads built through river wetlands, this one is paralleled by a canal, a farm ditch from which fill dirt for the higher roadbed is constructed. Fish fan out from lakes into canals like this, sometimes constructing circular sandy beds at the shallow edges of them in the early spring, little ichthyological homesteads where new broods of bass and bluegill are brought to life.

The wading birds know this and station themselves at the edges of these canals, like several great blue herons are doing today. So, too, do humans, and several families are parked next to this canal, perched atop little stools and overturned plastic buckets, under colorful umbrellas, cane poles with short lines of mono attached to bobbers, hooks with worms wiggling enticingly somewhere below the surface.

The state of Florida, in one of its more beneficent acts, waives the need for licenses for those residents who fish with cane poles in their home counties—figuring that many who do so often benefit more from the sustenance of what they catch than from the sport of it all. Bamboo cane pole fishing, while not special to the St. Johns, is a distinctly southern tradition, one that requires a certain unhurried, low-tech patience to master fully, an attitude best suited to slow-moving blackwater rivers and all their watery veins. It is Opie in a straw hat with a can of worms, long-gone Florida rocker Duane Allman squatting on the bank with a cane pole next to him on a nearly forgotten album cover.

I drive as far as I can, up to where the dirt road turns into a deep quagmire of the sort favored by the owners of jacked-up, four-wheel-drive pickup trucks. Three-foot-deep ruts in the black mud and empty Icehouse beer cartons are sure signs that mud-boggers have been here recently, driving endlessly back and forth through the mire simply because they can.

I step around the ruts, walking along the canal ridge past a stand of Australian pine with an understory of Brazilian pepper—both exotics—to where a piece of shore flattens out into a small point on Lake Washington. I see hundreds of dark ducklike birds forming a black line across the lake's surface in the distance, too far away to tell if they're gallinules or coots.

The lake is clear here and so shallow that a hundred yards offshore the water barely covers the feet of a white ibis that is standing in it. The ibis (*Eudocimus albus*) seems a model of flowing symmetry, S-ing its way down to the water from its orangish, curved beak through snow-white neck and body, to a set of spindly legs.

Its flight seems every bit as poetic, and I often see groups of birds flying in V formations, their distinct black wing tips marking them as adults. South Florida is ground zero for the white ibis population of the world, and when flocks of these birds make their way north, they usually do so along the corridor of the St. Johns. Once hunted for food by settlers as "curlew," the ibis seems common enough here in the basin. But that is only a regional function, in a place where enough habitat is still left to allow it to prosper: the white ibis is now considered a threatened species.

Writers of the wonderfully baroque nonfiction book *The St. Johns: A Parade of Diversities* reported that giant flocks of fifty thousand ibis would seasonally gather here at Lake Washington in the early 1940s to nest, at which time "their intake of daily food, in addition to countless grasshoppers, [was] estimated at 40,000 water moccasins." While it is true the bird will feast on snakes—along with small fish and snails and crayfish—I wonder if the writers weren't stretching a bit to make the ibis into more of a civic bird than it already is by portraying it as a fearless predator of heroic proportions.

I look down at the mud around me and see the distinct tracks of other wading birds, punctuated by the sharp, deep claw marks of a large gator. Nearby, at least one massive reptilian body has packed down the mud by repeatedly sliding in and out of the water.

The river channel north of the lake here was once full of little floating islands—bothersome "jams" of mud and weed. By the early 1950s, it had become for all practical purposes non-navigable. Local boaters, who were discovering the newly available joys of having outboard motors whisk them quickly wherever they wanted to go, took matters into their own hands: they dynamited the little floating islands to smithereens. Lake Washington, which had come to depend on the jams for its existence, promptly drained itself downriver.

Like little kids who break the cookie jar and then try to glue it back together again, the locals constructed a weir across the northern channel, careful to include a haul-over slot for small boats. The lake refilled itself again, assuming the proportions it more or less had before.

Washington is a gibbous moon of a lake, surrounded by low marshy shore with grasses and shrubs like elderberry, seeming more like a large swampy slough over a peat bottom than the deeper sandy-bottomed lakes I will find north of here. It is, at least, clear enough of submerged plants to be navigable by kicker-powered boats: I see one cutting across the water way off in the distance, watch another, lone fisherman anchored closer to the shore casting a net for bait. This lake is where the truly navigable channel of the river actually begins, or depending on one's perspective, ends. From here, one can canoe—or drive a kicker-powered boat—all the way to the river's mouth and back.

Like the lakes I have already seen, Washington—as well as Winder and Poinsett just to the north—sits neatly inside a fluvial plain, one that permits some bends and creative sloughing but generally shapes the lakes to conform to the river's flow.

The St. Johns here is still young enough to be easily understood: it enters the southern shore of a lake and flows more or less directly through to the northern shore, taking the lake with it. By the time it reaches Poinsett, it will have gathered enough energy from its mild gradient and current to began acting more like a river, asserting its way across the low marshy Florida terrain as a channel. By then, of course, it will have to, because there will be no reservoirlike lakes for miles to give it a hydrological boost.

Along this upper river, reclamation of a hearty chunk of the original floodplain was possible because adjoining marshlands hadn't been heavily gridded with roads and homes and schools. Here, Fellsmere not withstanding, it had seemed more logical in the days before air-conditioning to settle along the balmy coast than around the hellish, mosquito-ridden lakes of the upper river.

When I drive from Lake Washington past Winder, north to Lake Poinsett, along the very edge of the primeval river valley, I do so on the ferociously modern Interstate 95, next to travelers intent on making the most of the fast lane. The interstate does what Spanish explorers could not—it allows most anyone to see, and have access to, the upper river basin. But to no avail: the call of human-made Florida tourism has done its job well. And my fellow travelers whizzing next to me past the edge of the upper river valley today often don't have a clue that this vast natural landscape that stretches away from them to the western horizon is anything much but a place to get quickly beyond.

Just as Florida was first being introduced to the outside world as a tourist mecca in the late nineteenth century via the St. Johns, the nature poet and composer Sidney Lanier—who needed the money, as artists usually do—wrote a guidebook to the state for a railroad company. In *Florida: Its Scenery, Climate, and History*, the erudite Lanier included quotes from Chaucer, as well as a how-to chapter for visiting "invalids." In reference to the latter, those who came here seeking a cure from assorted wheezing and coughing illnesses were encouraged to exercise their lungs by playing the Boehm flute. When he was done with his guide, Lanier reflected on the St. Johns itself, writing several poems about what he saw and felt here—"A Florida Sunday," "The Mocking Bird," "The Dove."

As comprehensive as his guidebook otherwise was, Lanier described all of the upper St. Johns in just a few brief sentences as a shallow waterway where some travelers go on excursions from Lake Monroe, then the last bastion of civilization to the north.

Despite his brevity, Lanier still took time to remind his readers that the benefits to sportsmen down here along the warmer, more southern reaches of the upper river were astounding, with or without a flute. "There are many stories told," wrote Lanier, "of cadaverous persons coming here and turning out successful huntsmen and fishermen, of ruddy face and portentous appetite, after a few weeks."

I exit I-95 as soon as possible, ending up on a frontage road that parallels the interstate until, finally, it turns to dirt and veers sharply toward the river. The channel and its lakes are as close to the coast as they will ever get right here. For late-nineteenth-century passengers who wanted to make their way to and from Rockledge, just south of Cocoa on the Indian River, this was a handy bit of geography. It allowed them to hop aboard shallow-draft steamers on Lake Monroe. They would then ride the ships south, beyond the shallow lakes of Jesup and Harney and Puzzle to a busy wharf on Lake Poinsett, where they would off-load and then complete their journey aboard stagecoach or buggy, just a few miles overland, to Rockledge.

The vessels, with names like *Marion* and *Waunita* and *Astatula*, were seldom more than eighty feet, with small recessed wheels set into the sterns to guard them from snags. By all counts, these no-frills ships were not much to look at—"small, ugly and far from being sturdy," according to one observer. But these shorter, narrower boats could do something that larger, more luxurious steamboats of the middle and lower river couldn't: during periods when the rainfall was slack and the river was low, they could carry full loads in water no more than waist deep. (Because of their diminutive size, many of these same ships were also used to navigate the tightly winding Ocklawaha, a major spring-fed tributary far north of here.)

Although Lake Poinsett bustled thusly less than a century ago with its wharves at "Rockledge Landing," the sun- and rain-driven environment of Florida has a way of consuming abandoned wooden structures with foliage and rot and mud. There is little here in the way of treed swamp; most of the eastern rim of Poinsett is covered with sedges and forbs and grasses, giving way to an occasional sabal palm on a hump of higher ground.

From where I have driven, on a barren dirt road at the edge of the lake, all is lonely and quiet, except for the territorial shrieks of a limpkin that scolds me for trespassing on its territory as it pecks away at an apple snail. Rarely found outside the shallow marshes and swamps of the subtropical rivers here, the limpkin (*Aramus guarauna*) sports a curved beak like the ibis but is marked with the distinctive brown-and-white colors of a young fawn. While most wading birds have a call that is particularly fierce for their size, the cry of the limpkin is particularly so—far more blood-curdling than its meek appearance might lead you to believe. Yet meek is probably a relative term, and the limpkin would surely seem plenty fearsome if you were an apple snail.

Naturalist Billy Bartram first drew and described the limpkin after traveling the river in 1765–75, making this solitary wading bird seem every bit as animated as it appeared in his imagination. Billy didn't know what genus of European birds it belonged to, but that was understandable: although related to cranes, *Aramus guarauna* is in a family all by itself.

Audubon drew the limpkin, too, during his visit to the river in 1831–32, noting that most all of its kind were found in the "Everglades," and more to the point, "the flesh of the young is pretty good eating."

When they "owned" La Florida, the Spanish generally stayed out of the dense interior, preferring to rampage about on the coast in search of gold. But the newly founded United States of America was more retentive about its territory. Indians needed to be taught who was boss, and after ceding Florida in 1821, the military set out to do just that.

Before retreating deeper into the Glades, the Seminoles dug in along this upper river during the Second Seminole Wars of 1835–42. The U.S. Army, commandeering earlier versions of the smaller steamers, came in hot pursuit. Penetrating southward into the jungle of the upper river, soldiers traveled through the untamed lakes they "discovered" and named for their own—Harney and Jesup for two high-ranking, Indian-plummeting officers, and Poinsett for Van Buren's secretary of war. Ironically, the gentle naturalist Billy Bartram had penetrated almost this far on a small boat with his father, John, and a couple of other men a half century earlier, claiming nothing but the plants and animals they fondly sketched and described.

I quickly unload my kayak from the back of my jeep and, stepping around the dead cinders of a recent campfire, stick it into water just a few inches deep. Unlike narrow and less stable whitewater kayaks, these flatwater species are light, buoyant, and easy to lift and maneuver, and, most important, they let me get out on just about any part of the river I can see. They also sit me down a full head or so lower than I would be in a canoe, putting me in more immediate sensory contact with whatever arises on or from the water. It is the difference between bending down to talk to a small child and squatting to have an intimate, eyeball-to-eyeball conversation.

From here, I push away as quickly as possible to escape the hum of nearby interstate traffic, more or less aiming for a grassy island toward the middle. Alone, I try to summon up images of a steamboat, madly puffing black smoke from resin-rich pinewood, emerging from the edge of the tall bulrushes on the distant shore, invalid sportsmen aboard waiting to be ruddy and cured and hungry again. Instead, what greets me is a light rain, which gently dimples the water across the entire lake.

Rain can be tricky business when you are outdoors in the valley, not because it will get you wet but because it may be the precursor to a spectacular subtropical thunderstorm. Gators, of which I will later see very many, are perhaps the most feared natural threat along the river. But it is lightning that kills far more people every year than the shy alligators can ever imagine doing.

Common sense is usually the best guide: if it is the wet, warm season and the clouds are dark and brooding, something more than a light drizzle is being schemed. If it is, however, like today, when the great vast bowl above me is merely lightly gray from the touch of a routine winter Nor'easter, drizzles and light showers come and go with regularity, with no accompaniment from the great crashing timpani in nature's cosmic orchestra.

I gingerly work my way into my rain parka and then continue paddling out to the middle of the lake, out to where I can barely see the shore because of the drizzle. Alone here, I let the surface spit and gently hiss around me, the negative ions of the rainfall functioning like a waterfall, effervescing my spirits somehow. The dissolved oxygen released into the water from the action must do something similar for the fish, which seem more active now, swirling and puckering at the surface.

Although I will later encounter a number of artesian springs that help feed the flow downstream, it is rainfall from this humid subtropical coastal climate that drives the St. Johns at this point. And while it is true that the mean rainfall for the entire river basin is almost five feet, this southern region loses almost all but a few inches through "evapotranspiration"—a clever way of describing the cycle in which vapor returns to the atmosphere from both water surfaces and the moisture of plants.

Yet there is something else about all this that goes beyond the measurement of rainfall, lost and gained. I think of an observation once made by Father Thomas Berry, a ponderer of environmental spirituality, in *Dream of the Earth*. "Something more than the utilitarian aspect of fresh water must be evoked if we are ever to have water with the purity required for our survival," wrote Berry. "There must be a mystique of the rain if we are ever to restore the purity of the rainfall."

The abundance of rain overflows outside the channel and lakes here, creating wetlands that are "banked" by the gentle curve of north–south escarpments. On topographical maps, these modest scarps are identified by distinct "breaks" at the edge of the wetlands. In the ground truthing of real life, a botanist can mark the boundaries of these same wetlands by finding the place where the blackberry vine meets the swamp lily—where the community of upland plants ends and that of wetland ones begins.

But, of course, there are no maps or charts to measure reverence, except maybe how much is finally left.

By the time the clear but tea-colored channel of tannic water leaves Poinsett, it has been fed not just by the other lakes that came before but by streams that wander into them through marshes and swamps, creeks with names like Pennywash and Wolf, Cox and Crabgrass, descriptions that meant something once.

Here, not far from the place where it exits Poinsett, something dark and riverlike has taken form, ready now to wind its way far north with some certainty, like an indigo snake working its way through the tall rushes and reeds.

Marshlands north of Lake Winder are sandy, more likely covered with cordgrass than the wet marsh vegetation closer to the peaty-bottomed headwaters. As the low-lying floodplain fans out here, it becomes more frequently dotted with sabal palm tree islands. To anyone driving across the river on one of several highways that bridge this part of the valley, like SR 520, the St. Johns seems to be Old Florida incarnate, primitivistic in the way that only wet environments in the lower latitudes can be. But if they keep headed west, into the upland maw of Orlando and Altamonte Springs, they will soon find that the very same roads funnel them into some of the most urbanized congestion in all of Florida.

Of the entire river, water quality here in the rural portions of the upper basin remains the highest. The channel will later puddle up into the sluggish lakes northeast of the greater Orlando area, and there, storm-water sediments will wash their way into it from farm fields and paved streets and well-manicured lawns. But for now, it is still reasonably safe from civilization.

So far, this has been the easiest tract of the river for me to reach. It is a simple matter of pulling over to the side of the well-traveled SR 520, parking my jeep, and walking into the Lone Cabbage Fish Camp. Constructed of planked wood, worn and weathered into a fine gray, Lone Cabbage sprawls here at the westerly edge of the river as authentic looking as a fish camp can be. In a narrow canal behind the camp, I notice that an old tin roof that once sheltered a score or so of rental slips is beginning to collapse atop the dilapidated docks.

Inside, there is a country jukebox in the corner playing songs by guys with two first names, wailing plaintively of lost women and love and dogs. Behind the bar, there are stacks of preserved and varnished gator heads, compartmentalized by price and size—one stack with jaws large enough to gobble a hamster, another with mouths just right for a toy poodle. Next to the stacks are strings of gator-tooth necklaces, gator-tooth key chains, and, for the do-it-yourselfer, a box of just plain gator teeth.

There are also souvenir T-shirts and hats and rolls of Kodak film for sale, along with a menu suspiciously top-heavy with river critters—frogs and turtle and catfish and, of course, gator—all of which are available in any style, as long as it's fried.

I'm drawn outside to the deck by the distinct roar of an airboat engine; here, I position myself on a worn wooden bench facing the water, waiting. Soon, a giant custom-built airboat comes soaring around the southerly river bend, headed for the camp. But, it is not a standard two- or three-person boat like the scientists and sportsmen use. Instead, it is the minibus version of an airboat, with a broad sleddish hull fitted with four and five rows of padded, pewlike seats, half of which are now full with female tourists, some of whom I notice are wearing name tags.

Lone Cabbage, like other camps I will find on the river, is becoming gentrified, with just enough raucous good-ole-boy feel left to make it seem authentic, especially to northern tourists looking for tastes of the real Florida after mind-numbing doses of virtual reality at nearby Disney World. Airboat rides along the upper river have become a cottage industry, mixing doses of thrill-ride elation with exposure to a primitive environment. Gators—and the ornamental residue of gators—help sweeten the deal, making this a Mr. Toad's Wild Ride with real bumps and real cold-blooded reptiles.

Older Florida natives often bemoan the idea of ferrying tourists into the nooks and crannies of territory that was once solidly theirs alone. But this trend is actually history repeating itself: these buslike commercial airboats are the modern-day steamships, with the working outdoorsmen and their cargo replaced by visitors yearning for a glimpse of a rare place, like the early tourists who visited the river in the mid– and late nineteenth century.

While this surely introduces to the St. Johns River folks who a decade or more ago might have been dissuaded by the raunch of the "cracker" camps, it also creates startling juxtapositions when the new tries to conform to the old. From the bar, the toughest-looking member of the entire crew—a wiry, bearded, cowboy boot–shod, beer-swilling fellow—climbs off his stool, swaggers outside, and climbs aboard his Winnebago with New Jersey plates, wrangling it off into the horizon.

Back on my bench at river's edge, I sit quietly, basking in the silence as the airboat passengers deboard, sunburned and exhilarated. I chat briefly with the airboat driver, a big-boned man with a tan, a gold neck chain under his T-shirt, and a local drawl. He always takes his passengers south of here, he tells me, down toward Poinsett where it is wider and easier to navigate, instead of going north into the narrow channel under the low concrete bridge. I make a mental note of this for future kayak visits, as I seldom enjoy being confronted by a speeding airboat when I am in a vessel that sits not much higher than a flock of gallinules on the water.

I look to the opposite shore, no more than one hundred yards away, and see slivers of white sand at the base of the low grasses and shrubs; on this side of the river, the same low banks are more brownish. Near the base of the bridge, I notice a small flock of wood storks, standing there, self-contained and noble, looking more like Old World jabiru storks than anything of this hemisphere.

Atop their snow-white bodies are black, crinkled necks and heads that taper into a beak as pronounced as the peak of a witch's cap. For reasons that make great visual sense, natives call these birds "iron heads." Scientifically, they are just as well described as *Mycteria americana*—from *mykterismos*, which means "turning up the nose."

Until just a few years ago, one would have to go deep into the Glades to see many iron heads at all; but decades of drainage there have disrupted enough of their historic habitat to send them fleeing north into the valley. These iron heads often feed by sweeping their beaks through the water, rather than by stabbing or poking into it. For this to work, the water cannot be too high or too low, and, surely, there must be something there worth sweeping for.

Although it strikes me as odd that a wading bird that looks this primeval would be grazing here at the edge of a modern bridge instead of deep inside the unroaded Glades, ornithology is built on logic: the birds must find enough fodder and shelter to sustain them or they wouldn't be around. In fact, wading birds in the upper river basin are doing quite well overall. This is fine news because they are near the top of the food chain, and their presence alone is an indicator of particularly good wetland conditions. In fact, a recent study by the National Audubon Society here shows that ongoing marsh restoration in the upper basin seems to be "re-creating foraging habitat" for such birds. Surely, if you build it, they will come.

And too, what better indicator of health can there be than the desire to procreate? Nesting colonies of cattle, great, and snowy egrets, as well as tricolored, little blue, and great blue herons, have all joined the wood stork in its rebound. Some 7,500 wading bird nests were built in 1993—a figure that almost doubled in 1995, when 14,000 were cobbled together from straw and twigs and avian spit.

But there is another perspective, too. A wading bird like the iron head has been in Florida more or less since the peninsula emerged as a sandbar. If it reads the presence of cars and fish camps and people at all, it probably does so as a tiny blip on its genetic time line.

Perhaps these birds are just biding their time, waiting for us and our civilization to go the way of the giant sloth and glytopod and the Timucua with their chert-tipped arrows, so they can reclaim what was once theirs.

To the north, the St. Johns drifts under the concrete bridge at SR 520, through a terrain that is unscathed by development for twenty-five or so miles. On the easterly rim of the river, its sweeping wetlands are protected as "Canaveral Marshes Conservation Area" by the water district; and to the westerly shore, as the Tosohatchee State Reserve. Both serve as matching ecological bookends, preserving a vital, contiguous chunk of the river valley and related water quality here.

If you know public land only as "parks," with a crisply uniformed ranger stationed at the entrance and helpful interpretive signs to guide you to picnic areas and camping sites, then getting used to a "reserve" or a "refuge"—and surely, trying to figure out a "conservation area"—can be daunting. Signage is usually inconspicuous, if present at all, and trails often go widely unmarked, except on maps. Reserves are sparsely staffed, and conservation areas usually have no on-site supervision at all.

That's because the purpose of such public ownership is to maintain environmental integrity of the tract, either unto itself or as part of a greater whole—in this case, the St. Johns River. Visitors are usually a distant consideration, though, and—unlike parks—they often have to share territory at certain times of the year with hunters of deer, wild hogs and turkey, and, on the river, migratory ducks. As one guidebook advises, "During seasonal hunts, wear blaze orange." Large-caliber bullets can travel a long way across the marsh, and retorts can be startling to those not used to them, though, regardless of what you wear. John James Audubon, a superb marksman who first shot everything he drew and painted, might be right at home among fellow hunters, had he ever made it this far up the river, into this century, wearing blaze orange.

In places like this where there is little or no adult supervision, posting inviting high-profile signs at the edge of the boundaries might simply be too much of a temptation for poachers and vandals. Cloaked in obscurity, the land and water in such places is more or less "managed" by default. For enterprising naturalists, the upside is that such sites are usually more isolated and wilder—and during nonhunting seasons, less visited—than more popular parklands.

As elsewhere along the St. Johns, I find I do not have to be afloat to enjoy the rewards of this riverine system: there are sixty miles of hiking trails winding through the four-thousand-acre Tosohatchee alone, some of which lead to the marshy edge of the river, others winding through the pine flatwoods and oak hammocks.

Deep inside the reserve, where I appear to be the only visitor on this week-day, I park near the Jim Creek Bridge, looking beyond its edge to where some of the last remaining virgin cypress swamps in all of Florida still remain, as pure as the day they arose from the soggy earth. The territory here seems too big to be easily figured. A couple of days allows me only a massively condensed taste—like reading a Cliff's Review Notes of *Ulysses*.

From my visit, I learn this: the Timucua and those who preceded them enjoyed the *hummocks* along this stretch of the river, just as I do today. I know because a number of midden mounds rise dramatically from the woods like stupas, the residue of thousands of years of subsistence hunting and gathering.

But drama is a relative term, too, and when the valley is pancake flat, any-thing that's otherwise gets your attention. I come upon one mound that looks like a domed, ragged berm, and a well-forested one at that. I push my toe into a crumbly edge, and a few of the small freshwater snail shells tumble out, bleached white with age.

Bereft of a common name, these little gastropods are *Viviparus georgianus*, and they make up the bulk of the many mounds I will see along the river. Scattered here and there among them are the much larger apple snail shells, evidence of a lineage of wading bird fodder that extends far back into time. My anatomy of tiny, prehistoric femurs and skull bits has never been good. But I know from other studies of such mounds that I am likely to find a veri-table smorgasbord of local fauna if I look hard enough—including that of frogs, catfish, gar, gopher tortoise, rabbit, loon, alligator, and manatee. In other words, most anything that didn't move as fast as the hunter was fair game.

Thankfully, it is now a crime against antiquities in Florida to disturb burial sites anywhere—or even a garbage midden on public land—and the idea of filling roads with the contents of an Indian mound now seems tragic in con-trast.

The pre-Columbians who lived here in the river valley were, at one time, contemporary with the Maya of the Yucatan. If their presence here wasn't as well inscribed in limestone shrines and temples and pyramids as that of the Maya, it doesn't diminish the spirituality with which they lived their lives. I think of these vanquished Native Americans whenever I come upon mounds like this. From the earliest reports of the Europeans, I even have a graphic idea of what they looked like. Jean Ribault, the leader of the first French landing party on the river in 1562, described them as smooth faced, hawk-nosed and tawny, "all naked and of good stature, mighty fair and as well-shaped and proportioned of body as any people in all the world. Very gentle, curious and of a good nature."

As for the difference in the sexes, the men hid "their privates with breech-cloths of gaily colored deerskin"—and incised their skin with red, blue, and black tatoos—while the women modestly "draped their middle with Spanish moss."

Thought to be godless by the later Spanish, these pre-Columbians lived in a world in which nature and its forces were exalted, in an ancient prelude to the transcendentalism of Emerson and Thoreau. These beliefs, however, went far beyond mere philosophy. According to the Spanish priest Francisco Pareja, who made a detailed list of spiritual misdeeds that needed correcting in 1595, some tribes believed this about souls: that each person has three—one is the pupil of the eye, a second is the shadow the body casts, and the third is the image reflected in clear water. Upon death, two of the souls leave the body while the one in the eye remains. It is this enduring soul that is visited at the burial mound by those still living, a spirit to whom questions are addressed—and from whom counsel is received. In this way, the befuddled Spanish scribe reported, those who come to the mounds seeking guidance often learned things that otherwise could not be learned.

I am not sure what is left to be said of this process today, except that when I come to such places looking for peace, alone on the densely wooded, shelly hills, I am more likely than not to find it. In fact, to be in riverine forest like this on a fresh, crisp morning in late winter—when hunting season is over—is to feel nearly consumed by the promise Florida's wildness still offers. Shafts of sunlight filter through the moss-hung branches like illuminated pathways, leading me back to a time when parks or reserves or conservation areas weren't needed. Nature itself was sacred, and that was more than enough.

There are no wolves around me today like those historically found throughout the valley, and the "tigers" (panthers) Bartram once described have been worn down to a few score and chased south. But there are surely healthy populations of turkeys and bobcats, gray foxes and gopher tortoises, fox squirrels and white-tailed deer.

Being still for a while in one place doesn't guarantee you will see all these animals. But you will surely see more than if you are crackling like a madman through the brush. I position myself next to where a gopher tortoise has burrowed into the earth, leaving a heaved-up ramp of fine white sand outside its home.

Scores of other animals share these tunnels—from indigo snakes to burrowing owls—but today, the animal that rewards me for my patience doesn't emerge from the ground at all. It is a fox squirrel, a threatened species almost twice as large as the more common gray squirrel, and it fusses in the fallen leaves a hundred feet away for something nutty to eat. As it moves into one of my portals of sunlight, I see its coat is ablaze in a muted bronze, a handsome prince of a squirrel with the pelt of a fox.

State Road 50 marks the northern end of both Tosohatchee and Canaveral Marshes on the St. Johns. The next twelve miles of the river downstream is protected by another conservation area, one known as Seminole Ranch. Like other such preserves along the upper river, the aim of this one is to let nature do its work by filtering upland rainfall through the marsh buffers to the river. Nature, in turn, is generous. As nature fixes the water quality here, it also replenishes the wildlife.

Wading birds, a walking litmus test of clean water, range through the marsh, from white ibis to the occasional roseate spoonbill. White pelicans, which migrate east and west instead of south and north along the Atlantic Flyway, visit here too, gloriously massive birds too large to be geese and too small to be swan boats.

Before being purchased by the state under its Save Our Rivers program, this conservation area was a working ranch where beef cattle roamed freely up and down the riverbanks, trimming wild grasses to the nub and snipping the leaves off every low bough they could reach. Like cattle everywhere, the bovines created a nutrient problem, with each one leaving behind a daily average of forty pounds of nitrogen- and phosphorus-enriched cow paddies in or near the water.

It is here that the St. Johns becomes a navigational muddle, spreading out from the road bridge across as much marsh as it can reach, sloughing off from the main channel at Puzzle Lake into easterly lakes like Cone and Silver, Loughman and Salt. It is as if—like a high-spirited child—the St. Johns has tired of being confined to a single route and now wants to go virtually anywhere it can. By the time the river reaches SR 46 north of here, it will cross under that road at three different sites several miles apart, a sure sign of a river resisting its destiny.

Marjorie Kinnan Rawlings left her adopted home on Cross Creek one fine day and headed out for a trip downstream on the St. Johns not far from here with her friend Dessie to "get perspective." The women launched their open, wooden eighteen-foot boat at the side of the SR 50 road bridge "where the river was no more than a path through high grass." Although they were armed with a compass, the river tricked them almost immediately. Puzzle Lake, through which the channel runs, is full of hammocks and bars and watery alcoves, inscrutable enough all by itself even without its sister lakes to the east.

From their launch site, the women headed more or less northward, straight into a "labyrinth" of confusion, where the channel seemed to branch off "in a hundred directions."

"By standing up in the boat, I could see the rest of the universe," wrote Rawlings. "And the universe was yellow marsh, with a pitiless blue infinity over it, and we were lost at the bottom."

Today, the universe north of here is still yellow marsh, capped by a blue infinity. Except now, at the edge of SR 50, it is punctuated with a giant fiberglass alligator, which follows the shape of a low-slung green building, from tail to gaping, toothy mouth, forever open to accommodate visitors to Jungle World. On the other side of the bridge where Rawlings launched her downstream voyage, there is another, more modest and unadorned building—decorated with no tail or teeth at all—advertising simply "Air Boat Rides!"

If the river confused Rawlings at first, it also offered her a solution, one she found by stopping to watch the direction in which the floating hyacinths were drifting. It was a lesson that still holds today, one in which the slightest downstream current is bookmarked by anything that sits atop it. Later, she devoted an entire chapter in *Cross Creek* to the experience, "Hyacinth Drift."

"It was very simple," confessed Rawlings of the natural clues. "But, like all simple facts, it was necessary to discover it for one's self." If Rawlings thought the channel was confusing on this stretch of the St. Johns, she would have been stupefied by the science. That's because this is where relic salt water from a distant prehistoric epoch still remains, captured deep in the crust. Hydrologists call this water *connate*—for it was trapped under sand and shelly sediment when the land was under the sea.

Florida, at least in parts, has been flooded at least four times in the last 900,000 years, inundations that cover all but the highest terraces. The valley itself was most recently flooded 10,000 years ago; before that, 120,000 years ago. Relic sea water mixed with fresh water during those times, entering the upper aquifer, where it remains in places such as this today.

I go here now in my kayak, to see what difference it will make when seawater that may be hundreds of thousands of years old decides to seep upward into the bed of the river and its lakes. Instead of following Rawlings's labyrinthic descent, I have driven farther northward, to where the next highway crosses the river, and have ascended the river from SR 46.

Out here in this sprawling basin, with only sabal palm hammocks to provide definition on the distant horizon, I feel humbled, as solitary as the osprey soaring overhead—although far less self-assured. Reality is one single paddle stroke after another, and it has a Tao-like immediacy and harmony to it all. Although I have to admit I enjoy the rush of being in an airboat on the river, there is a be-here-now element to a self-propelled craft that naturally slows one down, replacing the dynamic of speed with one of introspection.

When I'm out on the river by myself like this, my thoughts often go to others who have tasted some of this experience over time, especially those who did so alone. Environmental pioneer John Muir, who once skirted the edges of the St. Johns during his walk across the state to the gulf in 1867, was as strongly connected to the wildness here as anyone who came before or after him.

"They tell us that plants are perishable, soulless creatures, that only man is immortal," Muir wrote after a reflective moment under a sabal palm in the river valley. "But this I think is something that we know very nearly nothing about." The palm, confessed Muir, ultimately "told me grander things than I ever got from human priests."

It is within this fold of the mind that I paddle for nearly three hours, during which time the sun rises higher into the cloudless subtropical sky overhead, simmering the marsh and me with it.

Thanks to earlier studies done here by scientists, I know what to look for—and it is not long before I find it. The salinity in some of the sloughlike lakes here is almost one-third that of seawater, a reality that has transformed the composition of the plant communities around me. Instead of bulrush and reeds and spatterdock, salt-tolerant halophytes like seaside purslane, glasswort, and cord grass (*Spartina* sp.) are now dominant. *Spartina*, from the Latin meaning "of broom," looks exactly that—as if thousands of brooms have been driven, handle first, down into the soil, leaving only the spiky, rounded bristles sticking up.

The smell these communities release under the warming sun is unmistakably that of a salt meadow, a distinctive, musky sea scent that I am used to finding amid the coastal Florida wetlands—but never this far inside the basin of a freshwater river. My very modern sensibilities are being brushed by a moment born in the sea, millions of years ago, wafting up now from where the sand and rock captured it so long ago.

Floating only in inches of water now, I stop for a granola bar and study the nearly dry patches of sand a few yards away where bright crystals of salt are sparkling like quartz in the Florida sun. Some ocean tides—if they get the right push of the wind behind them, and if the rain-driven water levels are low enough—can make it all the way into Lake Monroe in the middle river. Yet I am far enough south of there to be well beyond any tidal push or pull.

When icthyologist William McNair McLane extensively surveyed the entire river in the late 1940s and early 1950s for his doctoral thesis, he found this leg of the St. Johns to be "remarkable" for its marine influence. McLane's work was every bit as remarkable, in that it created a "benchmark" that scientists still use today to see what lives where along the St. Johns.

At the appropriately named Salt Lake nearby, McLane reported, salinities soared as high as 10,700 parts per million (ppm)—extraordinary when you consider that the ocean at the river's mouth contains 36,000 ppm of salt. An influence like that changes more than just plants: the dissolved salts help keep the marine fauna out of osmotic peril: McLane found five marine crustaceans, two marine worms, and nine species of saltwater fish. Most of them, said McLane, are actually breeding populations, and not just marine critters on a long sojourn from the ocean.

One night, McLane pulled a trotline he had set in Lake Harney, just north of here, and found fifteen southern stingrays thrashing on the hooks. At other times, he hooked small southern flounder there, 190 miles from the sea.

A few years ago, biologists with Florida's Freshwater Fish and Game found a rare—probably endemic—shrimp in Harney. It was a *Mysis*—of the order of Mysidacea—commonly known as the possum shrimp. Long and slender, the little *Mysis* feed on plankton on the bottom during the day and migrate to the surface at night, their characteristic shrimplike eyes glowing when light hits them. It is a testament to the incomplete nature of invertebrate knowledge along the river that this particular *Mysis* had never seen before—or since.

The most widespread bottom-dweller of all invertebrates on the river is the white-fingered mud crab (*Rhithropanopeu harrisii*), whose survival is also pegged to salt: it peaks in areas of the river with salinities between 6,000 and 10,000 ppm, doing as well down here in Puzzle Lake as it does east of Jacksonville.

While this connate seawater functions as an oasis, it also adds one more exotic element to the downstream flow of the river, leaking brackish water into a current that until now has been fully fresh. Downstream in the middle basin, the river will later conflux with the runs of more powerful artesian springs that carry relic minerals and salts to the surface, maintaining the allure to riverine critters with oceanic yearnings. It is a bit of a compromise, though: you can have the brine of the ocean, and the safe habitat of the river, too. You just have to settle for less of one to enjoy more of the other.

Surely, some marine creatures ventured into the estuary of the lower St. Johns and then simply kept going, blundering this far upstream with the periodic nourishment of isolated plumes of sea salts along the way. But both McLane and naturalist Archie Carr, who studied the St. Johns around the same time, figured there were other, quite astounding explanations for this phenomenon.

The sea animals may be here because they, like the inland dunes and sandy terraces, are relics of the ocean. "Perhaps the habit that these fishes formed was not that of ascending a river . . . to visit a spring but simply that of congregating in that spring when the river was a coastal lagoon," Carr once wrote. "And possibly the tendency was just held over from an even earlier time, when the St. Johns springs were under the sea."

Down here in the heart of the connate seawater belt, I can—given enough time and granola bars—paddle eastward, through tiny Ruth and Clark Lakes, down Snake Creek into Loughman Lake. From here, I can head northeasterly into Shad Creek, following it until it opens into Salt Lake. Along much of this route, I will see saltwater blue crabs and mullet sharing the same waters with largemouth bass, warmouth, and catfish.

This region also marks the southernmost point that naturalist and artist Billy Bartram reached on the river during his first trip here with his father on a cold January Florida day in 1765. The morass of the river confused him every bit as completely as it would Rawlings a couple of hundred years later. Just south of Puzzle Lake, Bartram and his father blundered finally across dry land in the form of a large Indian midden—today identified as Baxter Mound. After a night here, they ventured only a bit farther southeast before running headlong into nearly impassable vegetation. This was the dry season of winter, and the river may have been much lower then. Or they simply may have taken a wrong turn out of the channel.

If the river seemed impassable, Billy figured, then this indeed was the headwaters of the "grand and noble" St. Johns. Although Bartram erred geographically, he was at least metaphorically correct on another account, one of which he was probably not aware.

Today, we can think of Puzzle Lake and its westerly ponds as the marine "headwaters" of the river, the genesis of a rare inland sea of life, graphically reaffirming the prehistoric origins of a place that first came to life as a saltwater lagoon.

> Bear, deer and turkey are found in abundance, and the hunter may find
> a chance to shoot his rifle at a Florida panther. —*Into Tropical Florida,*
> *Or a Roundtrip on the St. Johns River*, a guidebook of the DeBary-Baya
>
> Merchants Line of steamships promoting the river in 1884

The Econlockhatchee River quietly slips into the St. Johns just north of Puzzle Lake, snaking its way out into the prairielike marsh as if it were just one more lazy bayou sluicing back to the easterly edge of the palm and oak hammock shore.

The Econ, however, is far more ambitious than a bayou. Arising from its own swamp some 36 miles from the St. Johns, the creeklike river flows north and then east across the fringes of the Orlando metropolitan area, draining some 280 square miles of terrain and confluxing with the Little Econ on the way. To do this, it runs under busy road bridges and through tangles of thick foliage and snags, making the Econ seem less alluring than it really is.

Of the three major tributaries to the St. Johns, the Econ is the one without the constant pumping of strong artesian springs to keep it steady and sure year round. It may also be the one with the least certain future, for the lower Econ has made the mistake of cutting down into the earth through upland hammocks and sandhills—high and dry land, as prized by developers as it is by gopher tortoises, who dig their burrows deep into the relic dunes.

Federal, state, and even county laws are already on the books to protect rivers like this. But all it takes is one local city with designs on an expanded tax base to make an end run around them all with creative exemptions. Thoreau once wrote that the preservation of the world is found in wildness. But if he lived in the basin of the St. Johns today, I wonder if he would have amended that to read "in the public acquisition of wildness."

I have entered the Econ at its mouth by a kicker-powered johnboat on earlier visits, following a gentle zigzagging series of curves that took a half hour to navigate across the marsh of the St. Johns. When the Econ finally revealed itself, it did so inside a series of wooded, sandy bluffs that clearly contrasted with the spiky bulrush and grassy maidencane at the edge of the larger river.

The Creeks, who moved down into Florida from Georgia and Alabama in the eighteenth century and became the tribe we know as the Seminoles, named this stream "earth mound river," or "mound river"—piecing together *ekana* for earth, *laiki* for site or mound, and *hatchee* for river or creek. Perhaps they did so for the prehistoric shell middens they found scattered along its banks, perhaps for the natural moundlike rises of its bluffs and sandbars.

Today, I meet the Econ some eight miles upstream, where the tributary modestly winds itself under a fancy new road bridge in eastern Seminole County, headed for the St. Johns. For reasons to do more with politics than ecological worth, the Econ is protected for less than half its length by a publicly owned buffer. This place where I stop today is squarely in the midst of that sanctuary, inside the Little-Big Econ State Forest.

I park by the road bridge and walk down into the steep ravine the river has cut into the terrain. Like the St. Johns itself, the Econ is a blackwater river, made so by the tannic acids dissolved into the water by the slow decay of leaves and wood. It is also a river that—under normal circumstances—takes its time to get to where it wants to go. Today, with months of dry winter season behind us, the root beer–colored water glides along gently at the base of its banks, sometimes dipping down deeper into a midstream swale, other times spreading itself only inches above a clear, sandy bottom.

I see a school of fingering bass hanging in the easy current, facing upstream, just inches from shore, watch as a red-bellied turtle flops off a log into the water, hear the cry of a red-shouldered hawk overhead. A blaze of red moves cryptically through the tallest oaks, and I see it is the large hatchetlike head of a pileated woodpecker. Deer and turkey visit here; so do sandhill cranes, with their distinct crimson head patches, and bald eagles.

Ahead, I hear a loud splash, then another. I stop and then move cautiously toward the noise. It is a family of otters, three of them, moving in and out of the dark water. These river otters are found nearly everywhere along the St. Johns, but their shy nature makes them less public than other riverine critters. It's always a delight to stumble upon them, for they seem truly playful, a reminder of the fun we humans ought to be having if we just weren't so darned evolved. As I watch, the three alternately roll around on shore, slide down a mud bank, and chase each other through the water, twittering in loud one-syllable chirps. When they finally hear me, they all freeze, little bewhiskered heads just above the surface, bright eyes searching the shore for any sign of a threat. Glistening from the water, they look more like large porcelain bric-a-bracs, of the sort you might find in a shop that also sells Garfield dolls with suction cups for feet and velvet Elvis tapestries.

This play, as some otter scientists suggest, may not just be for the sheer fun of it, though. As with other species, it helps to reinforce social bonds, even to hone hunting and fighting techniques. Still, it looks inviting enough to me.

The only truly amphibious members of the weasel family, otters use their stiff whiskers—called *vibrissae*—as a way to feel water turbulence by touch when submerged, a tool that helps them detect movement of their meals-to-be, which may include crayfish, frogs, crabs, fish, and even eel. Like most other river otters found throughout the world, these critters are members of the genus *Lutra*, a distant relative of the giant otter of the Amazon, which may reach six feet in length.

Next to the river now, I look closely at the concrete bridge pilings and see watermarks high over my head from where the last wet season brought the waters surging eight to nine feet above where they now are. Fed mostly by a floodplain swamp, this tributary is bound to be more given to ebbs and flows of precipitation than one that is not. But the Econ suffers more than its ordinary share of fluctuations: upstream on the branch known as the Little Econ, development has transformed wetlands, robbing them of their natural capacity to store seasonal floodwaters. As a result, heavy summer rains can cause flooding; a tropical storm may even send mild flash floods surging downriver, accelerated by pavement-channeled runoff.

I hike along the banks of the Econ for several miles, picking my way through muscadine grapevines and Virginia creeper hanging from the taller oaks, sometimes following a packed-down trail atop the higher banks, sometimes traipsing down sloughed-off ledges leading to the sandy lip at the edge of the low water.

Heavy trees and limbs crisscross in the tea-colored river like giant Pickup Sticks, formidable snags when hidden during a flood but easy enough to see and maneuver between now if I were in a canoe or kayak. As the river has crested around sharp bends during the wet season, it has cut steep banks into the high-energy "windward" shores, leaving behind piles of fine white sand on the inside "leeward" edges.

Scalloped by the light spring breezes, the sand heaps look for all the world like isolated, ocean-piled dunes, as if the land has memory and is trying to reclaim its prehistoric existence as an Atlantic beach once again. Never mind the soft pink phlox, the wild Carolina yellow jasmine, the red-tipped bromeliad blooming in the forest atop the tier a few millenniums above—down here on the dunes, I'm solidly back in time, standing on the nascent peninsula once again as it emerges from the sea. With this terrain-slicing energy, some deeper reaches of the lower Econ clip off the top of the shallow aquifer, allowing fresh water to leak up into the riverbed. During the driest times, such as these, that "leakage" helps maintain its flow.

I continue hiking, veering off from the river back into one of the folds of the land that, not too many months ago, was a feeder creek. As I stroll over the forest floor, I see more such arroyos, each veining off into smaller fern-lined gullies, a few with tiny rivulets of water still trickling over the bottom. Slender sabal palms crowd together here, competing for valuable light, bristling with ball moss and nursing watermarks that are chest level with me today.

I am here on a weekday, and in my stroll I don't encounter anything but solitude on this little river. But weekends tell a different story. Jet skis and their masters venture out on the Econ then, just as they have been doing on other peaceful tributaries up and down the St. Johns, often zipping around blind curves as if they are the only craft on the river. Although I try hard to be democratic about the use of a natural legacy that belongs, really, to us all, my understanding abruptly ends where the bow—and the wake—of the other person's speeding projectile begins.

The American shad (*Alosa sapidissima*) is an extraordinary fish, one that migrates more than two hundred miles upstream into the St. Johns from the Atlantic each winter on a spawning run. Shad do this in other rivers along the eastern seaboard; but they always begin their migration the earliest in Florida, in this river. Each individual shad, some say, is trying to return to the exact site where it was first born, genetically encoded to find that place of refuge where it knows its spawn will be safe. It is natural selection at work, a seasonal celebration of its own survival.

Although the shad often stray south beyond Lake Harney, sport anglers know that the core of the annual run won't breech the waters of the upper river in numbers large enough to be worth fishing for there. I have caught these shad northward from Harney, downstream to the mouth of Lake Jesup, in the crisp, premature spring that comes to Florida in January, casting from the shore or trolling tiny lead "darts" at the end of a thin line of monofilament from a small boat.

These shad journey here in a single-minded pursuit, seldom letting mortal needs like hunger stand in their way. When they strike the sinkerlike dart—which is usually painted red and white and improbably tipped with a snatch of dyed yellow deer hair—they are said to do so more out of anger than from a need to sustain themselves. The dart is an annoyance, something that comes between them and the primal need to find just the right spot where they can release up to thirty thousand eggs.

I know a gifted fly tier who innovates tiny bantamweight flies at his tying vise, assemblages of feathers and fur that imitate certain natural foods preferred by one species of fish or another. But when it comes to shad, he doesn't try to duplicate anything eatable or natural at all. Realizing the mindful obtuseness of the shad for food during its run on the river, he instead ties an imitation of a shad dart.

The shad that are the freshest from the ocean not only run hard when hooked but also jump often, the blue iridescence of the sea still flashing from their bodies on each brave leap. For the hundreds of sport fishers who each January pile into a fleet of small fiberglass and aluminum boats and search for the shad along this part of the river, the anadromous fish amounts to a poor man's marlin.

Unlike the bass and even the smaller bream and warmouth, which are commonly kept for food, the shad is a bony fish and is often released—unless, of course, one happens to have a yearning for the roe. Then, of course, cuisine triumphs over natural selection every time.

Harney is an immense wading pool of a lake that spreads out over a rural countryside for 9.5 square miles, becoming the largest water body so far in

this Welaka of a river. Beneath the surface, its shallow edges slope gradually down to a six-foot middle, making it seem more like a giant saucer than
a bowl. But I have come to visit at the end of an extended dry season. Heavy
summer rains and storms can swell the waters upriver, raising the seasonal
level of Harney by up to eight feet atop of what is already here, letting it
overflow onto the pastures and shallow marshes around its shores.

Harney marks the region where the still-rural St. Johns begins its distinct
jog westward, away from the coast, shadowing the spine of the Central
Highlands. The river forks into Harney just above SR 46 in a series of lazy,
watery tines, meandering past Jordan Slough and around Cow Island to do
so. Here, the St. Johns changes character, however subtly. The ancient sea-
driven terraces that hold the river sweep gradually to the west and tighten,
creating a more narrow valley.

Some geologists believe this "offset" section of the St. Johns may be older
than the upper river, perhaps laid down as long ago as late Tertiary time,
ending some three million years ago. With the basin of the upper river still
inundated by the sea, the headwaters for this westerly offset would have
originated somewhere east of present-day Sanford.

In these modern times, this is a dangerous place for a lake to be. Still sluggish from its low topographical relief, the river has limits on how much upland pollution it can flush from the massive pools of water it creates. Unlike
the upper river, which benefits from publicly owned wetlands to filter and
clean water, the middle river is more often than not surrounded by private
land. Here, the St. Johns depends on the kindness of strangers for its health,
and strangers have not always been so kind.

Harney is so far fortunate, not so much for what people have done to it
but for what they haven't done. Sitting low inside its floodplain, rimmed by
pickerelweed and bulrush and giant reed, the edges of Harney are wet and
far enough from the maelstrom of Orlando not to be easily peddled as prime
real estate. There are far more cows here than people. And while cattle are
locked within the horns of their own cow paddy dilemma, it is far less dam-
aging than what a paved and pesticide-drenched grid of tract neighborhoods
would be.

Because they are close to each other on the river and similar in size,
Harney is often confused with its sister lake, Jesup. But there are vast dif-
ferences, the most important of which is that the river enters Harney at its

southern tip and leaves by a northwestern one. As it does, it moves, ever slowly, beyond the tiny westerly peninsula of Gator Point and the easterly sloughs of Gopher and Underhill. There is enough of a current here to sweep Harney and keep it healthy; Jesup will tell another story.

Older scientific studies report small springs under Harney, discharging highly mineralized water with enough chloride in it to be tasted. But modern science is sketchier here than usual along the river. Usually, local fishers with fathometers can find the site of such springs by locating deep holes in the shallow bottom. But that is not the case here, and the artesian upwelling inside Harney takes the form of slow, diffuse leakages through the sand rather than in distinct springheads.

Here is what I know: it is the presence of chloride in water that most often imparts the taste of salt—normal taste buds usually don't detect chlorides below a level of 400 milligrams per liter (m/l). Just south of the lake, where the Econ confluxes with the river, the level of chlorides has been measured at well under that brackish threshold. But on the north side of Harney, where the St. Johns leaves the lake, it has been gauged as 570 m/l. And, like salt anywhere, Harney is tough on metal boats; locals report that their airboat hulls readily corrode after being immersed in the lake.

The saltwater Atlantic needlefish, a tubelike, silver fish with a tapering snout full of tiny needlelike teeth, has spent enough time in these reaches of the river that it has been known to breed here. A marine isopod, a primitive, thumbnail-sized crustacean related to the sow bug, lives here, somewhere. Inside the bucolic Harney, both join up with the southern stingray and the mullet, commingling with the freshwater bass and the bream, under a broad sheet of water rimmed with sabal palm hammocks and narrow sandy beaches and punctuated with the primordial heads of gators.

Although the Spanish virtually ignored the middle and upper St. Johns during their two centuries in Florida, John and William Bartram were fearless in their examination of it. In the winter of 1766, father and son explored Lake Harney by boat and camped somewhere on its southeast shore, before continuing downstream into Puzzle.

John was here as the royal botanist for King George to assess Britain's newest possession; his artistic son Billy was along for the ride. It was a ride that bound him to the river, drawing him back for a solitary second voyage a decade later, creating an original vision of the new American wilderness when captured in *Bartram's Travels*.

Nature and Indians in the St. Johns River valley were regarded by Europeans as both godless and unholy, in dire need of taming and civilization. But for Billy Bartram and other kindred souls who followed, the "great and noble St. Johns" and the aborigines who inhabited it were at the very center of the spiritual world.

"They appear as blithe and free as the birds of the air, and like them as volatile and active, tuneful and vociferous," wrote Bartram of the Seminoles he encountered. "Joy, contentment, love and friendship, without guile or affectation, seem inherent in them." As for the Native Americans, they wholly accepted this kind, inquisitive white man who incessantly collected flowers and drew pictures of plants and animals he found. They affectionately called him Puc Puggy, the Flower Hunter.

During the undeclared Second Seminole War (1836–42), when the United States decided to stake a claim on its new territory, federal troops commandeered early steamships and followed Billy's same route. Thinking they were blazing brave new trails into the interior, the soldiers named the lakes here for their white male war heroes: Harney, Jesup, Poinsett, Winder. It didn't seem to much matter that the Seminoles, who had their own names for the lakes, regarded this as their home.

This lake's namesake was Major William Harney, who dismissed the Native Americans as savages. Under his aggressive leadership, a series of forts were built along the middle and upper river as a first defense against the "rash tendency of the Seminoles to indulge in treachery and carnage." One such outpost was constructed on the higher western bank of Lake Harney and christened Fort Lane, for a soldier who went insane and ran a sword through his head. During the year it was occupied (1837–38), Fort Lane was famous for being the deepest foothold the United States had yet struck into the depths of the "treacherous" Seminole stronghold in Florida.

Abandoned long ago, the fort has since fallen into the nearly complete obscurity that blankets many of the former steamship landings, wharves, and pioneer outposts along the river. Today, all that remains of this once grandiose notch in the white man's territorial belt is found several miles away in the tiny block building of the Geneva Historical Society—a few pieces of wood, a shell casing, a military button.

As recently as 1964, the government scoured a five-foot-deep channel from Lake Monroe to Harney, perhaps more in recognition of what Harney once represented than what it had become. Today, any navigational channel that meanders out of Harney is natural, created by the upstream current gently pushing against the soft earth.

Maybe Puc Puggy's sublime wilderness has had the last word here on Lake Harney after all.

As it leaves Harney, the St. Johns eases past the mouth of Deep Creek, which winds for nearly five miles due north into Lake Ashby, snag-infested and difficult to navigate for most of its length. For the fisher—including those with long legs and feathers—the confluence of any creek along the river is notable for the way it interrupts the redundancy of the environment. There are new currents to be had, aquatic banquets rich with nutrients and floating animal plankton—eggs and larvae and critters too small to fight the flow. Such currents often dish swales from the river bottom and send eddies swirling over them. Stronger predators, like bass, can hang at the edge of the eddies and gobble what swirls past.

Topside, air-breathing predators can do the same, casting lures to the edge of the eddies or standing nearby with sharp beak poised for the kill. At nearly every creek or tributary mouth I visit along the river, I will find evidence that the food chain has been functioning like this centuries before the advent of Beetle Spin lures. And so it is at this site, a place where pre-Columbian Indians long ago acknowledged the local natural bounty by the act of sustaining themselves from it. In doing so, they fashioned palm fiber nets for fishing and sharp hooks from bones, accruing centuries' worth of shells into mounds that also doubled as foundations for their wood and thatch homes.

After the Timucua vanished, the Seminoles continued similar traditions, often in the very same places. By the early 1800s, this site was a busy village occupied by the Seminole chief, King Philip, and his son Coacoochee, known as Wild Cat. They called the stream here Ocoska, for Deep Creek. But by the time the Seminole Wars were over, the Native Americans who lived at the mouth of Ocoska and along the rest of the St. Johns would be either chased to the deepest Glades, shipped westward to reservations in Oklahoma, or killed.

By the early 1900s, with the original natives long displaced, the new "natives" of Florida were settling atop the same high and dry mounds along the river, such as this one. Like the Seminoles, early settlers sustained themselves from the environment. But, unlike the Seminoles, they didn't seem to know when to stop.

In 1916, on the former site of King Philip's village, ambitious loggers built the company town of Osceola. Here, they constructed homes enough for two hundred men, installed a sawmill, and mortared a fine brick vault, from which they paid workers in cash for helping to haul and cut up to sixty thousand board feet of cypress from the local swamps. Like other sawmills along the St. Johns, the Osceola Cypress Company was thorough in selecting the finest virgin cypress trees from the forested wetlands—some of which were as big around as a small room, and older in years than the time of Christ. There are few they missed; one they did has its own Seminole county park not far from here: it is a thirty-five-hundred-year-old tree, thickly buttressed and venerable enough to be given a name, the "Senator." Local history reports matter-of-factly that logged cypress trees were commonly this large.

The downside in consuming every last shred of natural resource one can get one's hands on in the valley is just as grim economically as it is aesthetically: there are virtually no such virgin forests left—either to exalt in the presence of or to cut into board feet. By 1940 the Osceola Cypress Company had logged its last tree. Today, I drive to the site, where industry was once built atop an Indian mound, and see that all that is left is the windowless brick vault, trashed and discarded at the side of a lonely country road.

Not far away, the St. Johns continues to wind its lazy trail through the hammocks and marsh, the only constant in a landscape riddled with forgotten dreams.

It is in this stretch north and west of Harney that the magnificent riverside bluffs first make their appearance on the river. Moving along now inside a more confined valley, the St. Johns seems to have gathered its scattered dynamics and—aided by the force of the flow from the upper river—has summoned enough energy to pitch alluvial sands on the outside lips of the sharpest oxbows. One of these cliffs is called Lemon Bluff, and it is locally famous enough to be depicted on an old colorized picture postcard from the 1940s. Lemon Bluff, so described for a grove of lemon trees that once grew here, rises fifteen and twenty feet above the river on one side, while falling away into the low, deep marsh on the other.

The St. Johns moves steadily westward here, sometimes sloughing into aquatic culs-de-sac like Mud and Mullet Lakes. Mullet, named for the silvery, blunt-nosed marine fish usually found schooling in tidal creeks and lagoons not far from the sea, disconnects entirely from the main river during times of longest drought. In doing so, it re-forms itself into a series of small, circular pools, fed by the same upwelling of connate seawater that makes Salt Lake so brackish back upstream.

Within a few miles of here, the river crosses back under SR 46 again, just as it did earlier on its way from Puzzle Lake to Harney. Here, to the casual motorist tooling down the road between Sanford and the coast, the lake once created by the river just south of the bridge seems omnipresent, a virtual inland bay that consumes the southern horizon in a broad, primitive sweep of cabbage palms and water.

This is Lake Jesup, and it is unique for several reasons—not the least of which is the fact it has been nearly abandoned by the St. Johns. Here, the river barely threads only the northernmost leg of this massive lake, allowing the main channel to pass it by without even much slowing down.

This tenuous link with the river was far less problematic in the last century. Steamboats journeyed out of the river down to at least four busy landings on Jesup, artesian springs gushed from its southern shores, and its waters were as pleasantly tannic and clear as any other lake along the river. There were then two small but open mouths on the northern edge—one that let the river in and the other that ushered it back out downstream. The dynamic created enough of a flow to circulate water clockwise, sending flotsam on a complete 360-degree journey around the rim of the sixteen-square-mile lake and then back down the river.

But the "Government Cut" navigational canal, built by the Army Corps of Engineers in the 1930s, and the SR 46 causeway built across the westerly exodus here in the 1950s effectively short-circuited the river's connection with Jesup. Today, incoming river water takes from 80 to 365 days to circulate in Jesup—compared with 10 to 21 days in Harney and upcoming Lake Monroe. In addition, decades of poorly treated sewage, leakage from septic tanks, and fertilizers from local farm fields have helped turn the sluggish lake into a sump. When a new 1.5-mile-long expressway link bisected the lake in the early 1990s, Florida's Department of Transportation took no great pains to shield the lake from the impacts the road would create. Jesup, it reasoned, was already out of the high-quality loop and no longer even navigable. That it was government causeways and lax permitting that helped make it this way was not addressed.

A local daily newspaper, the *Orlando Sentinel*, took a giddier view, editorializing that the new expressway could introduce countless legions of tourists to the once isolated lake. "Jesup has the potential to become a high-profile postcard setting for millions to see annually."

Bill Daniel is backing his airboat up to a hard-packed ridge next to an old logging canal on the southern shore of Lake Jesup, not far from where he lives. To unload the boat from its trailer, Daniel comes to a sudden halt, and the craft slides off the back with a loud thump. After he parks his pickup, we climb up in the airboat, with Daniel a couple of heads above and behind me at the controls in the aft seat. "This isn't Disney World," says Daniel, who makes his living as a heavy equipment operator when he isn't trying to roust public support for restoration of Jesup. "If you see a branch coming at ya, you need to duck or it'll hit ya."

And with that, we are off in a mighty metallic screech that takes the flat-bottom boat off the dry bank down into the water. Soon, we are breezing along inside the straight, narrow logging canal, dodging the fronds from the trunks of sabal palms that hang precariously over the water at improbable angles. Once, when I take my eyes off the path for just a few seconds, I feel a resounding thwack on my temple from a cluster of leaves at the end of a low branch of a bay magnolia.

Daniel is one of the hardy, individualistic souls who live in the junglelike Black Hammock community on the southern rim of the kidney-shaped lake. As I drove through the thickly canopied dirt road to Daniel's home, the sprawling hammock of palm and sweet gum and cypress did indeed seem dark, shaded by lush foliage from the light of the Florida sun.

Like others who coexist here with the subtropical wilderness, Daniel is content to endure periodic flooding, as well as the occasional alligator and rattlesnake in the yard, as part of the great compromise that lets him be close to the lake and the wildlife habitat it nurtures. What he won't endure, though, is the disregard others have shown for Jesup. While most of the river and its lakes remain tea-colored but clear, the pent-up Jesup throws routine fits of murky greenness. It is the pervasive blooms of microalgaes, fed by the same lake-locked nutrients that make grass grow, that do such work. When blooms die, the oxygen level in the lake plummets, sometimes taking sport fish down with it.

To placate Daniel and others like him who fight for the lake's restoration, the state legislatively created the Friends of Lake Jesup to serve as an advisory council for funding decisions that affect its health. (Although dissolved by the 1998 legislature, the council still continues to meet informally.) Daniel, who seems to have consigned anything ever printed about the lake for the last century to one rusty filing cabinet or another back in his basement, is the wild card in the deck, a tenuous grassroots advocate who intends to hold the government accountable for its misdeeds.

Jesup, which has some nine feet of bottom muck from years of bottle-necked neglect, can be restored, Daniel has told me. But rhetoric will have to be backed with the real dollars of funding. Public officials seem to agree, at least in part: beginning in 1984, the regional water management district has purchased nearly six square miles of floodplain around the edges of the lake to re-create the marshes that filter water, as they've done in the upper river. And in 1996 they bulldozed down a two-mile-long berm on the northwest shore, to reconnect historic wetlands there with the lake. Another plan, which computer models show working, has the lake benefitting from the cutting of a new channel near Hawkins Island.

Meanwhile, Jesup surely has its share of wildness left. Today, whitecaps are whipping up on the lake under wisps of wintery cirrus clouds, presenting the illusion of a place still not fully tamed. In the airboat, we stick close to shore, skirting in and out of islands of towering giant reed, thick as a cane brake, a dozen feet and more high. This is *Phragmites*, and while I will find it along much of the river, it is never as thick and awesome as it appears here on the shores of Jesup.

Off in the distance, I see the clump of foliage that is Bird Island. When soldiers led by Lieutenant R. H. Peyton explored the lake in 1837, they camped there. In a letter, Peyton described it as a "beautiful island of 200 acres with high grass in the center . . . filled with the nests of white heron, blue crane, and a red bird with a spoon bill called by the Indians *Hololo*, for the sound it makes." The *Hololo* was a roseate spoonbill. And while other wading birds still nest on the island, the spoonbill has retreated to the headwaters.

Although at a crossroads in its existence today, Jesup was healthy enough in its prehistory to have been an oasis for all manner of life. In 1987 a local homeowner dug a pit near the shore and discovered the bones of a now extinct giant ground sloth, a relic of the Pleistocene epoch. Deeper in the pit were the bones of an ancient whale, which likely swam through the deep saltwater channel that today is the basin of the St. Johns.

If the lake surface were flat today, we would see the snouts of at least a few of the ten thousand–odd gators Daniel says live here in Jesup, themselves living relics from the late Mesozoic era, 140 million years ago. On such days, Daniel has promised, we could summon a handful of gators to us simply by slapping our hands down on the water really hard—"like the sound of a raccoon or dog falling in the lake."

After the issue of restoration, gators are the hottest subject in the Hammock, as Jesup is said to have more of them than any other water body in Florida. Everyone, it seems, has a favorite story about *Alligator mississippienis*. Daniels has three: one tells of a six-footer running like a dog out of a small duckweed-covered pond in his yard to snatch an imported, mail-order pet rooster from his side; another tells of a ten-footer who tried like a mad dog to latch on to a tire of his wife's car as she entered the driveway; a third has a surly gator biting out the bottom of an inflatable kayak, much to the dismay of the kayaker inside.

Wildlife biologists say the only truly dangerous gators are those that, having been fed by people, have lost their fear of us and come to associate humans with food. But perhaps the sheer biomass of gators in Jesup has further rearranged the natural equation, allowing the naturally cautious and shy reptiles—perhaps tired of being hunted, skinned, and deep-fried into Gator Bites—to turn the tables.

After all, it was the old, gentle naturalist himself, Billy Bartram, who first sent back chilling accounts of gator attacks along the St. Johns in 1765–75, when gators and not people were preeminent. Surely Bartram's worst gator day was the time his small wooden boat was surrounded on all sides by roaring, snapping reptiles, leaving him "expecting at any moment to be dragged out of the boat and instantly devoured." Then again, Billy was as poetic as he was scientific: he sketched his tormentors as virtual dragons, blowing smoke from their nostrils as they charged. Surely, there is room for poetry in great tale telling.

At any rate, the chances of spotting an alligator on a day like this seem remote. So instead, we cruise , looking for an opening in the giant reed that will lead to a natural alcove in the densely wooded shore. When we find it, Daniel cuts his engine and points to a depression in the earth where a creek once ran. This was Wharf Creek, one of the prosperous steamboat landings that included a store and several buildings in the 1800s. Today, the community of Wharf Creek has disappeared as fully as Fort Lane back on Lake Harney, leaving a fretwork of cypress and baywood in its place. "This place used to really be something," says Daniel, shaking his head at the richly departed Florida past.

We are on the far eastern edge of Jesup now. Between us and the distant west side, the shores are defined by soggy outcroppings of land and fingers of water that help bring character to this seemingly boundless inland bay. Jesup is a huge gulf of a lake, and to be in the middle of it is to be an aesthetic victim of its hugeness. But to cruise around its margins—beyond islands called Seevee and Hawkins, sloughs named Marl Bed, and creeks mapped as Carr, Phelps, and Bonn—is to touch it, a tactile experience that allows intimacy.

Shorelines are important for aquatic animals, too, because they provide nooks and crannies of habitat, places to hide, feed, replenish their numbers. Because of this, critters like gators aren't inventoried by the acreage of the water volume but by the length of the shoreline. (In Jesup, biologists working with the Florida Game and Freshwater Fish Commission have counted twenty-one gators per shoreline mile—making it the sixth densest population in Florida.)

In an earlier trip to Jesup, I hiked next to Soldier Creek, a tiny westerly vein that feeds the bulging headlike cove on the prone, horizontal body of the lake. Soldier, named for those intrepid Seminole War veterans who once camped on its banks, is home to some towering, venerable cypress trees that would have made any logger's day, and it was good to see them still alive back there in the swamp.

Yet Soldier Creek held another surprise: under its clear waters, I had seen symmetrical, tire-sized craters scooped out of the sandy bottom. They puzzled me until I stood quietly, watching. As I did, a blue tilapia, a wide-bodied tropical fish with a metallic bluish hue, swam back over each bed. Also known as Nile perch, the tilapia (*Tilapia* sp.) is an African freshwater cichlid that grows a foot or more in length. Although they are herbivores, tilapia are bulky, brutish-looking fish that move into shallow habitats like a herd of aquatic buffalo, crowding out native bass and bluegill.

Introduced in 1961 by the game commission as a prospective "sport fish," the tilapia has provided more embarrassment than sport for that agency. It is a benchmark that today not only makes them carefully question any exotic but encourages them to police actively the importation of any aquarium fish that might accidentally get loose and go on a tilapian rampage. I ate a tilapia once, and it tasted exactly like grass—which, given its diet of plants, was not terribly surprising.

Back on dry land, I say goodbye to Daniel and drive my jeep slowly over a series of canopied dirt roads to the site of nearby Clifton Springs. As I do, I watch carefully for any of the locally deranged gators that might seize the moment to rush out of the edge of the swamp to chew my tires, but all I see are a couple of wild turkeys strutting along the road's shoulder.

Clifton Springs, the site of another steamboat landing, appears at least a bit more tangible, with a few modest low-slung country homes and, in a little cove at the end of the spring run, the wood and tin-roofed ruins of a defunct fish camp. The spring itself is tucked away in a woody glen, where small pools of bluish white water gather up in earthen bowls bristling with the rare great leather fern before flowing off down a short creek into the cove. There are four distinct springheads here in all, pumping a little more than a million gallons of highly mineralized water a day up from the aquifer through breaks in the limestone and sand.

In 1837 Lieutenant Peyton reported this as a set of "remarkable sulfur springs which give rise to a large and rapid current that empties near an old Indian village, said to have been the residence of Euchee Billy and his band." The village, built on a fifteen-foot-high midden, once held twenty lodges, occupied by one hundred Native Americans. As springs go, Clifton is a modest one compared with others I will later find along the river. But it still embodies that mysterious quality of creating a flowing, softly gurgling subtropical tableau where there otherwise would be none, a fairy tale of an environment where one can imagine some elfin magic having just been concocted or waiting to begin.

Because the temperatures of such artesian springs hover around seventy-two degrees Fahrenheit, they often become biological "islands" along the river, protectively incubating plants and animals in a way the seasonal fluctuations of the St. Johns cannot. Studies of all the springs—and the caves that lead down from them to the aquifer—are piecemeal, with more work done on the water flow of hydrology than the critters of biology. Endemic animals and plants, those that don't exist outside a single place, are most likely to be found in aquatic, thermal islands like this along the river.

And so it was here, in the waters of Clifton Springs—formerly known as White's Wharf Springs—that an ichthyologist in the spring of 1940 identified a killifish that existed nowhere else in the world. He named the minnowlike fish *Fundulus bartrami*—*Fundulus* for the genus of killifish, and *bartrami* for the romantic naturalist himself, who once camped here.

But *bartrami*, if it still exists, is not alone in its endemism: in the white sand and soft grasses at the edge of the spring lives a two-inch-long, porcelainlike snail with its whorls split by soft, fine lateral lines. It is the Sulfur Spring aphaostracon (*Aphaostracon theiocrenetus*).

Ironically, the presence of both it and the killifish seems to be a well-kept secret. Neither is a high-profile, charismatic species, like the West Indian manatee or the Florida black bear. And the idea of a club such as Save the Aphaostracon or Fix the Fundulus seems doomed to quick failure. Yet developers have their eye on this spring-fed chunk of the Hammock now. And the singularity of Clifton Springs may disappear before it is ever fully appreciated, taking who knows how many as-yet-unidentified such critters with it.

From Jesup, the river continues its westward meander toward Lake Monroe, traveling through marsh, past sabal palm hammocks, stands of cypress, and thick forests of water oaks.

It is late February now, and this is the beginning of spring in the valley, a subtle seasonal transformation marked by the soft presence of light green on the bare deciduous trees and at the base of grasses, reeds, and ferns of the marsh. There are more insects on the crawl, more brightly colored butterflies on the fly, more snails and worms and crustaceans on the squirm in the sun-warmed mud. In response, birds and animals are actively prowling, chirping and preening and grunting, satisfying their own eternal urge to renew. Blossoms, like the delicate wild iris known as purple flag, are on the verge of bursting from their pods. All of nature on the river seems to be in heat.

Author Marjorie Kinnan Rawlings, who traveled by motorboat up this same leg of the river on her brief excursion away from Cross Creek, remembered this as a special time, "when the cypress bursts from gray bareness into a dress of soft needles and the swamp maple put out young passionate red leaves."

Despite the recharged activity, Rawlings was careful to note that changes here are still more subtle than those in the North, and if we don't pay close attention, we can surely miss the quiet drama of it all. After all, she reminded, this is a place where "the seasons move in and out like nuns in soft clothing, making no rustle in their passing."

It is in this season, on this leg of the river, that I climb aboard a large pontoon tour boat piloted by Captain Bob Hopkins. I do so not just to see the St. Johns as it unfurls through the terrain here but to see how others regard it. Hopkins runs one of several "eco adventures" on the St. Johns. By doing so, he introduces the river to tourists, some who are seasoned naturalists, some who regard Busch Gardens as the very heart of Amazonia. Personably stoic and endlessly patient, the wiry Hopkins is a native who's betting that the concept of nature-based tourism might finally have found a place to bloom in Florida, if visitors would just put away their TV-clicker sensibilities long enough to pay attention.

It is midmorning on a Saturday, and twenty-six of us are leaving the dock on Hopkins's boat from the Sanford Boat Works and Marina, where the high Osteen Bridge crosses the St. Johns at the easterly mouth of Lake Monroe. As I look around, I see most of my fellow passengers are sunburned, perplexed, still swooning from the theme park experience of nearby Orlando.

To get here, I drove from downtown Sanford, out beyond the southerly rim of the lake on rural Celery Avenue, winding past now fallow farmland that a century ago helped make Sanford among the most prominent towns on the entire peninsula. As we move out into the channel and head upstream, I unfold a brochure promoting the nature trips. I can't help but notice the same descriptive snippets that have appeared in one form or another ever since the earliest steamboats visited here. On this St. Johns, I can "See the Nile of the Northern Hemisphere," take an "Everglade Cruise," and venture down "Florida's Original Tourist Route," all at once. As hyperbolic as it sounds, it is also true.

Channel markers, shown on most maps, don't appear on the St. Johns until Lake Monroe, and we are headed south from there today, in the unmarked meander of bayous and channel between here and Lake Jesup, twelve to thirteen miles away.

When the river waters warm later in the spring, the massive aquatic mammal known as the manatee ventures down here from Blue Springs and other runs to the north. On good manatee days, we could see as many as thirty-five of them near the marina, chomping water hyacinth, rolling at the surface in some ancient blubberous rite, poking their forlorn-looking, whiskery snouts out of the water to breath. On occasion, the gentle herbivores will stray southward as far as Harney. But adult manatees are big, lumbering animals that need a deeper channel through which to move their giant, sausagelike bodies, and the more shallow waters south of here usually don't provide it.

From his helm at the stern, Hopkins provides a running commentary on natural history, replayed with a casual, local spin. Early morning and evening are the best times to see wildlife on the river—especially during a weekday when the go-fast sport boaters that are now zipping around us are safely toiling away somewhere else. Under better conditions, Hopkins told me, he recently shepherded a boatload of Auduboners out here for their annual bird count; they returned with a visual bag of 170 species after just two hours.

Nonetheless, Hopkins has a sharp eye and even on this busy weekend alerts us to a number of wading birds, along with a ring-billed gull, a pied-billed grebe, and a belted kingfisher, a bluish, agile songbird with a spiky head plume that routinely makes its living diving for small fish.

There is subtext to this identification. When we pass a common white egret, we learn the bird was almost hunted out of existence at the turn of the century for its prized plumage—back when its feathers were "worth twice the weight of gold." We learn that the pointy-billed anhinga drying its wings on a snag just above the water uses its sharp beak to spear fish, while its cousin in the water turkey family, the cormorant, has to be content with grabbing its dinner with its shorter, more crumpled beak. The vultures circling overhead, we are told, must fly lower in high winds like today because they use smell more than sight to target their dinners-to-be. We are advised to look closely at the circling pantheon of these carrion eaters because bald eagles are often among them, and the noble-looking raptors are just as happy as the vultures to find something splayed out inert on the ground.

With the water level well below its seasonal highs, the upstream current our bow cuts into is almost negligible today. Yet, when the river peaks after weeks of rain, the current can soar—sometimes as much as six knots or more—as it eagerly rushes out of the lowlands toward its eventual climax with the sea.

We leave the main channel, puttering into Indian Mound Slough, up to the edge of Jesup, and then back through another slough called Brickyard, aquatic back alleys created when the river generously spreads out over the low terrain. Although, at one point, the map I have brought along shows us to be in the middle of a broad lake called Thornhill, we are instead inside a narrow channel defined by green walls of maidencane and gator grass and pennywort, studded with the two-foot-high "bull hyacinths" that have toughed it through the winter. After all, this is Florida, and given the chance, water plants will overwhelm a terrain as quickly as terrestrial ones. In fact, the flow of the river and its bayous change so fast here, Hopkins tells me, that it's hard for a map even to keep up.

I think again of Rawlings and her realization of how the drifting hyacinths define the river's flow, and it makes me more fully appreciate how vital common sense is to navigation out here, on one of the world's flattest waterways.

On board, the captive audience seems receptive, if a bit befuddled. Most sit quietly, heads turning from one side of the boat to the other when wildlife appears, like fans watching a tennis match. At least a half dozen passengers are preoccupied with capturing each moment from the other side of their video cam viewfinder, instantly distancing reality into an experience safe enough to take home.

When we pass a herd of lazy cattle grazing in a riverside pasture, one passenger wonders if these are the wild Florida cows he's heard about. Another asks if the vultures feeding in the field nearby are wild turkeys. A third asks if the fox squirrel we see is a hybrid between a fox and a squirrel.

Hopkins fields the questions without once condescending and then tosses back one of his own. Since by now we have seen several of the imposing great blue herons along the river's edge, Hopkins wonders if we care to guess how much these wading birds with the six-foot wing span might weigh. Answers come in fast and furious, at thirty, forty, and even fifty pounds. "Five pounds!" says Hopkins, to a collective sigh of disbelief. "He's all feathers!"

And then there are the gators, downsized dinosaurs that sink like a forgotten memory into deeper waters to escape if we approach too quickly. When one ten-foot bull gator hangs in the water like a line of jet black rubber tires placed end to end, nearly everyone moves to the gator side of the boat, straining to see this terror of B movies. In response, the gator shudders almost imperceptibly, a shrug of millennia, and disappears into a crest of bubbles.

Although Hopkins could exploit this opportunity to scare the bejesus out of his passengers, he instead reminds them all that gators are more threatened by humans than we are by them, repeating the warning about how feeding changes their behavior. "We've only had nine people killed by gators in Florida—in fifty years," he says, correctly. "On the other hand, ninety-three people died from insect bites in less than a year." It is easier to get hit by lightning or attacked by a shark than by the reptile the Spanish called El Lagarto—"The Lizard."

Yet the alligators of the St. Johns remain wild and primitive and fearsome looking, intractably capturing the imagination of everyone. Never mind an insect bite—*these guys are big; they can eat you up*. Waves of titters wash over the boat whenever one appears.

By the time Hopkins putters back toward the marina, *lagartos* seem to be materializing everywhere: minicams pan excitedly over the river—to the black clump of dead hyacinths, to the black muddy log, to the black fat body of a coot. It is a hunger, it seems, that begs fulfillment. And we didn't even go into Lake Jesup.

Much later, back at the marina restaurant, I see a former passenger focusing his minicam on his platter of fried gator steak, zooming in for the kill.

Toboggan Slide, Spring-boards. Diving Stage. Shower Bath. 46 Dressing

Rooms. Dance Hall. Amusements. Woodland Park is in a class by itself.

—From a brochure advertising the long-abandoned Woodland Park,

operated from 1891 to 1920

*L*ake Monroe marks the very distinct place where—for most of the world—the St. Johns moves from the unknown and the unseen to the highly available. If the river upstream of here is a mystical Gregorian chant, then Monroe is Montavanni, as easy to find as an AM radio station.

A lone, stern-mounted paddlewheel steamship from the Hart Line spit and smoked its way to an extended wharf at Sanford here for the last time in 1929, ending an era of riverboat service to the town that first began in the 1850s. Today, the only working smokestacks to be found on the lake are those poking up from two electricity-generating plants, one on the north shore near the site of the once thriving resort of Enterprise, the other where the lake constricts itself back into a river again at its downstream confluence.

Although it is bulkheaded at Sanford today as if it were a giant swimming pool, the fifteen-square-mile Lake Monroe once swashed freely at the edges of its southerly shores, nurturing soft sandy beaches with stands of cypress, sometimes notched with the canopied, funnel-like mouths of local spring-fed creeks like Cloud Branch.

When Billy Bartram and his father traveled upriver through here in 1765, they camped on Stone Island at the lake's northeasterly rim. They did so atop burial middens where twentieth-century archaeologists would later excavate three four-thousand-year-old skeletons from the Late Archaic period, aborigines who predated the Timucua, a tribe with no remembered name. During the time of the Bartram visits, they surely knew the lake as Valdez, for that is what the Spanish had named it. But the Seminoles had a name for it, too, Wepolokse, for round lake. Later, land surveyor John Eatton LeConte mapped the river, calling it Monroe, in honor of the fifth U.S. president.

By the 1870s, several rail-mounted wharves stretched a thousand feet and more from the lake's southern shore into deeper water, and small-gauge trains chugged over them, taking out winter vegetables and citrus packed in Spanish moss, shuttling in excited vacationers eager for a look at this "Gateway to South Florida."

On the north side of the lake, the village of Enterprise was Sanford without the industry, an elite outpost devoted to upscale tourism, a place one observer described as the "Palm Beach of its day." Around the lake, Carolina parakeets nested in the cavities of cypress trunks and flocked together in the branches, small birds with yellow heads, amber faces, and bodies of forest green, fizzing madly back and forth across the water like little Technicolor skyrockets.

Ulysses S. Grant, after two terms as president, journeyed here in 1880, Harriet Beecher Stowe ventured down from her home at Mandarin, and artist Winslow Homer, an avid sport fisherman, spent parts of seven winters at the luxurious Brock House hotel in Enterprise, a resort built around the sparkling "White Sulphur Springs." All of them arrived by steamboat. Like the savvy artist he was, Homer knew how to mix business with pleasure: the eleven oils he painted here depicted what he loved most about the river. Usually, that was men fishing at the edges of lotus lilies, backlit by towering cypress draped with moss, all rendered in muted harmonies of gray, blue, and green. In letters to friends, Homer described Enterprise and its surrounding wilderness as "the most beautiful place in all of Florida."

Grant, a good linear-thinking soldier, took a look at the messy, vine-woven mosaic at the edge of civilization and pronounced it ready for exploitation. "When her swamp land is cleared of the timber," said Grant of Florida's interior, "there will remain the choicest kind of a rice country."

Sidney Lanier, who never got this far upriver but wrote as if he had in his railroad-sponsored guidebook, briefly described the two ambitious villages here at the edge of the "head of navigation" on the St. Johns. In passing, he also praised nearby Upsala, a colony of Swedes imported by General Henry Sanford in 1871 to maintain his local groves of citrus, avocado, and figs.

Although the Swedish colony—now assimilated into the community—is frequently mentioned by local historians, few remember that Sanford turned to the hardworking Swedes to replace an earlier camp of black grove workers whom local crackers had terrorized, beaten, and even murdered, a prelude to the twentieth-century Rosewood massacre on Florida's gulf coast.

Terrorism isn't good for tourism, of course. But even without it, sustaining the allure to fickle vacationers is tenuous business, with loyalties and trends shifting every few years. It is only the most corporate of theme parks, the ones that analyze market trends and then set out to fulfill them bloodlessly, that seem to thrive today, and they do so far from the banks of the St. Johns. Sanford, which once prospered simply by being the last major riverboat-serviced town squarely on the fertile, agriculturally friendly shores of the noble river, figured its luck would last forever. Without a trace of irony, it called itself "the City Substantial."

By 1891 a thriving tourist attraction, Woodland Park, was even built on a massive Indian midden on the southwestern edge of the lake, advertising itself as "A Real Playground Where the Mound-Builders Lived." It was the archetypal Florida theme park, with diving towers and water slides and a giant, tabby-walled swimming pool, filled in the morning with fresh artesian spring water and emptied at night. It was Wet 'n Wild before its time, a fenced-and-gazeboed place where "rowdyism" was not allowed and a "self-playing orchestration" was the hit of the dance hall. As many as twelve hundred people flocked here on a single day. They paid five cents apiece to get in.

Sanford and Enterprise and the "Playground" of Woodland Park were a mom-and-pop of a dream, the same one to which all the roadside Monkey Jungles and Indian Villages of the 1950s would later succumb. By the time the bulkhead was built in the 1920s to show the world Sanford was serious about itself, farming was relocating to the newly productive muck lands created by draining the Glades in south Florida, and tourists were being funneled off to the coast by railroads and highways. On the north side of the river, Enterprise floundered, the Brock House was torn down, and, on the south side, the city of Sanford finally went into bankruptcy. It was a one-two punch from which the "Gateway to South Florida" seems to have never been fully able to catch its breath.

I drive down Lake Shore Drive, a quiet, two-lane roadway that shadows the north shore of Lake Monroe under an arching canopy of cypress and oaks, passing the site of the Brock House and its once famous White Sulfur Springs.

Scattered pilings at the edge of the water hint at wharves that once were here, but otherwise Lake Shore Drive gives no indication it once hosted anything as grandiose as a resort; a hydrological report on the river doesn't even show a spring here anymore. To the east, I drive over a causeway to Stone Island, its middens now covered with expensive country homes. Somewhere here in a small creek, the *Fannie Dugan*, one of the last steamers to visit Enterprise, was abandoned, left to sink and rot into the detritus.

Back on the south side of Monroe, I follow U.S. 17-92 as it winds beyond a busy marina around the bulkheaded shoreline. I see the remnants of Cloud Branch Creek today, which empties into the lake from inside a concrete pipe, bringing enough sediment with it to create a small peninsula of sand, now covered with elderberry. As the only real shore inside the southern bulkhead, the few square yards here are precious to wildlife: wading birds roost at night in the low branches, surrounded by gator snouts—I have counted up to seven—waiting patiently at the surface for one skinny bird leg to take a false step.

Today, because it is at the end of a dry season, the lake laps near the bottom of the bulkhead, six feet below where I have seen it. If I were careful to stay out of the modest channel, I could virtually walk across the entire lake.

Yet heavy and extended rains from the upper river basin will fill the bulkhead to its brim, and strong winds will send whitecap spray over the edge. At such times, locals—who momentarily forget that their lake is connected to a larger ecological system upstream—question why Monroe continues to fill, even after the rains have stopped. It is the spongelike wetlands of the upper basin that do this, slowly releasing saturated waters into the channel for days and weeks after the last raindrop has fallen.

The southern bulkhead is also a place where straw-hatted cane polers sit patiently atop camp stools and lawn chairs, fishing for speckled perch, blue gill, and even the herbivorous mullet, a far trickier proposition. Mullet don't strike as much as they graze, gumming algae and weeds like aquatic sheep. It is no wonder the scientific description for the black mullet is *Mugil cephalus*—"sucking helmet-head."

To catch a mullet on a hook often requires chumming, in which balls of fish meal are scattered on the waters and the mullet, hardly able to resist the siren's call of the pungent chum, dutifully swarm in, lips puckered like a goldfish. One mullet angler who specializes in Lake Monroe has even authored a self-published manual, "The Mullet Mystique," in which she offers angling tips with a certain Zen-like flair ("You have to enter into *strife* with the mullet").

Although Monroe is 160-odd miles from the sea, low water and high winds sometimes conspire to "push" tidal currents this far upstream into the shallow four- to seven-foot-deep lake. As it moves southward in this way, the tide sometimes commandeers sea critters with it, briefly introducing saltwater sport fish as large as four-foot-long tarpon and thirty-pound redfish to this distant inland lake, bewildering anglers used to having palm-sized panfish tugging on the other end of their line. Because the reds and tarpon are particularly sensitive to cold, they often seek sanctuary in the thermally heated plumes of effluent next to the power plants, just as manatees do, here and elsewhere in the rivers and estuaries of Florida.

For well over half its length, U.S. 17-92 is also bordered by a hardwood swamp, which descends into a wet, green swale of duckweed and ferns, punctuated with mahogany-colored cypress knees. Here, on a few higher acres of land, is the Central Florida Zoological Park, the only such zoo on the St. Johns, as alive as the nearby Woodland Park once was.

Back at the edge of the swamp, I spend one afternoon slogging about in the mossy woods, searching for the foliage-hidden site of the older park, ducking under swags of giant webs spun by golden orb spiders and stepping gingerly around cypress knees. I enjoy not just the solitude of such places but the fantasy of being transported to some Devonian epoch where the green of newly evolved plants and ferns is dominant and mammals are still in cosmic incubation. It's uncommon, even rare, to encounter venomous snakes in wetlands like this—and whenever you do, they try their best to get out of your way. Yet the dreaded specter of a *snake-infested swamp*, even among natives, has helped sustain the solitude I find today.

When I finally stumble onto the site of Woodland Park, abandoned since the early 1920s, I discover that its gazebos and dance hall are long gone, disassembled and moved, or rotted into humus. Two sides of the tabby-walled pool rise from the floor of the jungle, burnished with reddish lichens and dark algaes, like an old Spanish fort. The rusty pipe that once filled the pool with its artesian flow is broken off near the ground; I look down inside and see still water, without enough energy to rise. The exuberance and gaiety that once drove the place is vanished, gone to that same place as the spirit of the mound builders, swept away with the river itself.

Back out in Lake Monroe, the St. Johns takes its own strange biological turn: the river entering and exiting the lake is cleaner than the water inside it. Severed from most of its wetlands by roads and bulkheads, Monroe functions as a giant retention pond where sediment—washed in from asphalt and parking lots and lawns—actually settles out on the muddy bottom. Nonbiting blind mosquitoes, or midges, swarm here during warmer months like biblical plagues, enticed by the out-of-whack water quality, blanketing windshields and creating unlikely paradigms. The Midge Patrol, a city-run, pesticide-spraying truck that tries to control the insects, appeared in a recent Christmas parade in Sanford, to great applause.

Although the health of Monroe is not as good as most other lakes in the chain, it is far better now than it was when the city actually channeled storm water and raw sewage through shared pipes into the lake in the 1960s, just as other "point sources" of pollution once did at Palatka and Jacksonville.

There is hope still for a renewed Lake Monroe, and someday it will actualize, perhaps when local leaders come to appreciate the resource as much as the cane pole fishers do.

The St. Johns moves out of Lake Monroe under the towering Interstate 4 bridge, back into the confines of its northerly channel, which by now is heavily wooded, more tree-lined swamp than open marsh. As it does, it seems to stutter briefly, creating the DeBary Bayou under I-4 nearly two miles from its exit, affording southbound motorists two expansive views of Lake Monroe, perhaps confusing them more than necessary about the intentions of this river they may have first encountered back at Jacksonville on Interstate 95.

Between here and Lake George, the banks of the St. Johns become higher, and the river narrows, cutting deeper into the earth. Water level fluctuations become less drastic.

Although one might expect the current of the St. Johns to quicken its pace here, it instead seems to gain some sort of equilibrium, albeit a lazy one. A 1981 U.S. Geological Survey (USGS) measuring the "velocity" of the current just north of here found it to be 0.3 mph, the slowest of any of the thirteen major coastal rivers of Florida.

The St. Johns is not just laconic in comparison with northern rivers that rush down to the ocean from inside mountain furrows. It is laconic even among its own, a fact visitors have been observing for a long time. "The sweep of the current is slow and grave, so that, apparently, there is a curious fixity and permanence about it," wrote Margaret DeLand in "Florida Days" in 1889. "It is without the hurry and noise of the little running rivers of the north, and it has none of their light-hearted intimacy."

The Army Corps of Engineers, that omnipotent government agency that once helped pull the plug on half the historic wetlands of Florida, toils today to keep the St. Johns navigable. To that end, it periodically dredges the river from Monroe to its mouth, carving a twelve-foot-deep channel from here to Palatka, deepening and widening it beyond. Nautical maps clearly illustrate the path of the channel, not just depicting the bottom depths along the river but showing where each of the stunted red and green navigation markers that bookend the channel is located.

Ospreys, big black-and-white raptors that catch fish in their talons, often construct huge stick nests on these same markers, raising entire generations of offspring here atop these odd geometrical trees, surrounded by water. They return to the nests each year, like eagles, enlarging and improving on their homesteads. For me, there's great irony in the markers being shared in this fashion—by intelligent, civilized humans who require maps and compasses and even Global Positioning System (GPS) receivers to relocate the very same marker that a "dumb" bird finds year after year, all by itself.

As for dredging, there is plenty of compromise in that. For the pollutants that are quietly asleep in the benthic murk, a bottom dredge is an abrupt wake-up call for them, one that suspends them again in the water column, perhaps redistributing them over vital submergent river grasses in shallow water and suffocating or even poisoning shellfish and other critters there.

The mollusks that make their living filtering nutrients from the water are among the hardest hit, not just here but in other rivers where they must be content with "breathing" the residue of pesticides and herbicides, PCBs, even toxic paint sloughed off the hulls of boats. In fact, freshwater mussels, with their distinctive oblong shells shining like mother-of-pearl on the inside, are the most endangered family of animals in the United States. Ultimately, a disappearing mussel population means more than just fewer mussels; it also results in fewer of the animals who feed on them.

Yet if the channel is not periodically scooped out, larger boats would simply not be able to go much farther south beyond the natural tidal main-stem grove that ends somewhere north of Lake George. Dredging is still, well, a cloudy issue, and locals who live and do business along the river say the government's channel maintenance below Palatka is sporadic, anyway. In fact, it is the stout-bodied, deep-hulled tugs that routinely push oil barges up and down the river from this point that take up the slack, scouring the bottom anew with each pass of their props, whether they want to or not.

Artesian springs begin to appear with more regularity along this part of the river, most of them bursting to life on the western edge of the St. Johns—sometimes even under the river itself. They arise from the west for the same reason water flows down a hill: the relic marine terrace known as the Central Ridge is there, a dwarf of a mountain at three hundred–odd feet above sea level. When rain falls here, it percolates down through the fine, sandy soils of the ridge, dissolving and enlarging cracks and fissures in the limestone below with its slightly acidic touch.

As it does, it creates vast, forever-dark underground rivers and reservoirs, watery veins contained inside the porous limestone "karst," aquifers that supply Floridians with 90 percent of their drinking water. As the weight of the water above—the hydrostatic pressure—builds, the water below seeks faults in the rock where it can escape, surging out through these vents at the bottom of the ridge as natural springs. Perhaps if the terrain atop the ridge were hard instead of soft, rain would simply fall on it and run off to the east in little rivulets down to the St. Johns—rather than seeping in and exuding back out in a genesis that is far more mysterious and hidden, a subdued reflection of the topography.

One contrary exception is Ponce de Leon Springs farther north of here, which flows into the river from the direction of the Atlantic coast. Another is Gemini Springs, a gusher of far less magnitude that meanders through DeBary Bayou into Lake Monroe.

Magnitude is a relative word, of course. Hydrologically, De Leon pumps nearly 20 million gallons of water a day out of the ground, compared with Gemini Springs, which has a velocity of around 6.5 million gallons. For hydrologists and others who rate things in the order of how powerful they are, Gemini would be close to the bottom of the list.

For me, however, each spring is vital in its own right, spectacular enough by virtue of bubbling to the surface of the earth at all, a special occasion in which the science of underground water flow confluxes with something akin to natural magic. I saw it earlier at the modest Clifton Springs at Jesup, entranced by the wonderland the upwelling creates. And I will see it later—

will taste it, in fact—from inside the limestone crevices below other spring-heads, including the one at the 120-foot-deep bottom of the immense Blue Springs.

Just as the Timucua and earlier tribes settled along the St. Johns because the river provided readily available food and water and a pathway along which they could travel in their dugouts, they also camped around the runs of these springs for the same pragmatic reasons.

But I doubt they missed the magic. After all, the Timucua also worshiped the sun. And on the dawn of each vernal equinox they placed a stag's head decorated with wildflowers on a post. When the sun's rays fell on the deer, they bowed together in prayer. I wonder if the rise of cool water as clear as the air from rock in the ground could have been any less sacred to them.

Here, on a fresh early March afternoon during midweek, the county park around Gemini is virtually deserted, and it doesn't take me long to discover that the spring is descriptively named: Gemini is, in fact, a pair of "vents" in the aquifer. I walk up to the fenced edge of one, a woody alcove that falls off into the springhead, and look down. Several yards below, I can see water surging out from under a limestone lip, watch as a turtle the size of a child's palm darts about the edge of the earthen bowl, scattering the gam-busia, the tiny dartlike minnows also known as mosquitofish. A voracious feeder on swimming mosquito larva, the gambusia has the distinction of also being one of the first fish to be sold and kept as aquarium fish decades ago.

Not far away, the other twin spring does similar work, helping to create an outflow that gathers up into a circular swimming hole behind a walled dike built in the early 1970s by the former owners. From here, the water surges over a chutelike concrete weir, quickly loses its clarity in the muddy turbu-lence, and begins its run down to Lake Monroe through a corridor of bul-rush. I scan the run with my binoculars and identify a lone wood stork, a kingfisher, an immature glossy ibis. The seldom seen ibis is mostly black and, when the sun hits it, as opalescent as the inside of a freshwater mussel shell.

At the edge of the run, I notice a stumpy cornerstone for the historic es-tate of Count Frederick DeBary, the ambitious river promoter who built a winter retreat nearby in 1868 and in the process became the namesake for a town, a mansion, and a once thriving steamboat line, two of which still endure.

Like a handful of other springs in the basin, Gemini was held captive by private landowners, who kept it out of the public domain until recently. Here, in the surrounding pine and oak forest, the former owners raised a cattle hybrid called Santa Gertrudis, sort of a boutique version of a cow, one valued for its hardiness in warm climates. The cattle, which chewed the understory of the towering longleaf pines down to the nub, had a distinct advantage over luxury neighborhoods around other private springs—such as those that now occupy the gated Sanlando Springs system off the Little Wekiva River: they need little infrastructure to support their lifestyle here on earth. When this county, which is Volusia, acquired the 210-acre farm from its private owners in 1994, it was a lot easier to herd the Santa Gertrudis out the gate than it would have been had each built itself a giant brick-and-wood nest and learned to drive a BMW.

By twilight, I slide a canoe into the clear, spring-fed waters of the Wekiva River with a friend and from the stern push off downstream, headed for its distant confluence with the St. Johns. In little more than an hour, the hardwood swamp around us is fully dark, forcing us to slow down and take cautious strokes in the dim light, sometimes braking as the current pushes the canoe faster than we want it to go.

Although fed with rainwater from its own floodplain, the Wekiva relies mostly on its nine major springs to sustain its flow—including Rock Springs, which nurtures its own clear-water run. As a tributary, its outflow is far more constant than that of the Econ but somewhat less than that of the Ocklawaha, which not only is fueled by its own springs but—as I will later find—also rises from a far more distant and mysterious past.

The Wekiva, though, has its own share of mystery, especially at night. Soon, the full moon rises above the thick canopy of trees and lights everything with its pale, unworldly glow. Deep in the swamp around me, the cypress trees dance in the muted light, becoming anything you want them to be, trees with a secret life.

With a drop of 1.6 feet per mile—almost twice that of the St. Johns—the Wekiva is one of the steepest rivers in all of Florida. With its gradient and its steady artesian upwelling, it may also be one of the swiftest.

It is full spring here in the basin, and that season is distinguished even at night by the exuberant sounds of wildlife and the scents of renewal—the fresh fernlike cypress needles, the wild jasmine blossoms, the newly cloaked

tree canopies, raging with chlorophyll. Large unseen mammals—deer, bob-
cat, bear?—crash periodically through the woods, wading birds and barred
owls chatter and call endlessly, and each frog seems determined to consume
the night, ribbet by happy ribbet. From somewhere inside a pod of spatterdock lilies comes a deep throaty croak, and I know it is either a gator or a
pig frog. By day, I would see the gator; at night, I can only guess.

Near a tree island, a limpkin—probably caught in the midst of preparing her seasonal nest of twigs—lets out with a territorial warning in the form
of a high-decibel shriek, the kind of sound I'd expect to hear in a tropical
rainforest. The Native Americans, always descriptive, had a name for the
limpkin, as Billy Bartram first reported: "There is inhabiting the low shores
and swamps of this river . . . a very curious bird, called by an Indian name—
Ephouskya—which signifies in our language the 'crying bird.'"

In other trips on the Wekiva, I have watched these elegant limpkins wading in the shallow waters in their stealthy search for apple snails, heard them
conversing more casually in a ratchetlike clacking, and, by summer, seen
young fledglings stumbling about an island rookery like giant clumsy duck-
lings, covered in a light down. Ephouskya is a Wekiva bird, a river bird, and
it belongs to the St. Johns Basin and to Florida; to come upon it each time is
a pleasant surprise, like running into an old friend.

In fact, you can think of this Wekiva as a microcosm of the entire St.
Johns. This is an area of "biological transition"—where the range of temperate zone plants meets and overlaps the margin of tropical ones. The
warmer spring waters crank up the thermal factor a few more notches, miti-
gating the northern winter winds and intermittent cold fronts.

As a result, the biodiversity of both plant communities and the critters
who live in them soars. Along the thickly wooded riverbanks are threatened
plants like needle palms, butterfly and water orchids, and the Florida shield
fern. In the branches and understory, at least 178 different species of birds
are found, including wood ducks, ruby-throated hummingbirds, and the
yellow-billed cuckoo, which cryptically sings its song of deep clucks back
in the swamp.

Turtlewise, there are some ten kinds here—although the Florida red-
bellied are most often spotted sunning themselves atop logs, each with a leg
or two in the air for balance, like some freeze-framed reptilian arabesque.

Because it is mostly spring-fed, the waters of the Wekiva are usually glassy clear. This opens up a whole new window of wildlife observation, much like looking through the sides of an aquarium. In this manner, I have watched largemouth bass hunkering under lotus lilies, seen schools of yard-long spotted gar cruising like organic missiles, even watched dumbfounded as a small saltwater "stingaree" glided by, undulating his wings as if he were flying in the clouds instead of swimming over the eel grass.

Although they are secretive and seldom seen, this sub-basin has the largest single population of Florida black bears (*Ursus americanus floridanus*), a subspecies that is now threatened with extinction. Like the white-tailed deer found here, it is smaller than its northern cousins, scaled down into three-quarter-size adults by adapting to a peninsular world that simply has less of itself to offer.

Considered an "umbrella species," the bear ranges over territory shared by other critters as well, including threatened animals like scrub jays and the Eastern indigo snake. It is one giant canary in a coal mine, for when the bear goes, so goes the unfettered wildness that cradles all manner of flora and fauna—the same wildness that, if we are lucky, arises to stroke a resonance in our own souls.

In hikes near the riverbanks, I have seen signs of this small bear: the deep claw marks on tree trunks, the scat at the edge of the trail, the large padlike imprints of its paws in the soft earth. There are bears up in the Ocala Forest, too, and the natural corridor of the St. Johns will wind beyond their home there. But in a state that has only fifteen hundred left, the Wekiva, with its population of forty to sixty of them, is surely bear central.

Oddly, some folks argue the sport hunting of bears should be allowed, on the grounds that humans have speared, clubbed, and shot the Florida black bear for thousands of years. It is true the bear was consumed—and idolized—by the Native Americans and that even Bartram regarded the bear and its fat as a handy source of food and grease. Yet there were well over twelve thousand black bears roaming the state two centuries ago, and their habitat had not yet been fragmented by roads and shopping malls.

This same junglelike corridor along the Wekiva that still makes the river attractive to bears appeals to animals that are far stranger and less native: on a recent early morning canoe trip, my partner pointed to an unusual, animated presence high in the branches of a sweet gum, something way too big and clever to be a squirrel. It was a rhesus monkey, and it eyed us as curiously as we eyed it, each of us trying to figure out what in the world the other was doing here.

Back in the 1920s and 1930s, colonies of these sharp-witted little primates were stocked at Silver Springs as backdrops to the Tarzan movies filmed there, and their descendants have since claimed the wild banks of the Silver River. Lately, I'd heard of more adventurous monkeys migrating northward from the Silver, up along the forested buffer of the Ocklawaha to the St. Johns. Now, at least a few of them have made it upriver, down to the reaches of the Wekiva, where they swing among the wild muscadine grapevines, just like Tarzan used to do.

While I have to admit it's a bit of cheap thrill to spot a wild primate along the shore of a Florida river, the little rhesus are exotics that—like feral hogs and starlings—can crowd out natives and, if given half the chance, munch the natural environment into tiny bits. Since monkeys are more humanlike, they may even be as thorough as we have been about this business.

Wekiva is a Creek-Seminole word, meaning "waters of the spring." But there is a twist to it, in that it is spelled in two different ways, ending in either a "va" or a "wa," depending on whether it is the spring or the river. Purists, who would have everyone calling it Wekiwa, at least get their way at the site of the springhead, which is surrounded by a state park of that name, while the Wekivas have the rest of the tributary for themselves.

The Timucua also had a name for water, *ibi,* and it covered almost every manifestation of that element—from river to ocean, rain to dew. If that was so, then Ibi was the name for the Wekiva, for the St. Johns, for the Atlantic, for the moisture that drips off the edge of the bay wood leaf.

All we know of such things today is that the little seventeen-mile-long river was a mecca for aborigines like the Timucua—there are at least eighteen midden mounds along its banks, all holding pages of history still unread, assembled from snail shells that once came to life in the sweetness of the Ibi.

There are endemics present, too, with two mollusks, the Wekiwa hydrobe and the Wekiwa siltsnail, found nowhere else in the world but here, safe inside the temperate womb of the spring waters.

And there are other secrets still being uncovered.

One was the identification of an entirely new spring in the late 1980s, one discharging 834 gallons a minute from the ground. Unreported by either the Florida Bureau of Geology or the USGS, the boil was found near the run of the Little Wekiva, a mostly rainwater-fed tributary of the larger river.

Another discovery was more complex, with a human twist.

When in the late 1970s the owner of the Wekiva Falls resort near SR 46 sank two large concrete pipes down into soft mud that had been gurgling water, he tapped into the limestone caverns of the upper aquifer. By doing so, he created a geyser of an artesian spring, with a daily outflow of twelve million to fifteen million gallons a day—nearly one-third the magnitude of the headspring itself.

It was not unlike drilling an artesian well and then leaving the faucet continually open. Conservationists, already worried about a 20 percent loss in the outflow of the two main springs along the river between 1969 and 1983, saw the newly divined falls as hydrological plunder from an aquifer that was not infinite.

A judge agreed in 1990 and ordered the owner of the falls to turn off his megafaucet. But when he complied, the aquifer experienced a reaction not unlike a flash flood: the force of the newly contained geyser tried to burst back to life elsewhere through ancient faults along the bed of the Wekiva. As it did, it blew open at least one prehistoric, silt-encrusted sinkhole, uncovering the tusks and bones of mammoths and mastodons that once roamed here, up until the end of the last ice age.

Sometimes when I am on the Wekiva in a canoe or kayak, I think of these animals and how they would have looked at the edge of the river, trunks and wooly heads bent over for a long drink, and wonder what grunts and roars they would have brought to the darkness.

Like other tributaries along the St. Johns, the Wekiva has been used by Europeans since they first learned of it. Soldiers camped here during the Indian Wars, and later, in the 1870s, a little steamship called the Mayflower made semiweekly trips all the way up to the headsprings, then a busy landing called Clay Springs.

This Wekiva may be one of the most protected rivers in all of Florida: some fifty thousand acres are publicly managed as the Wekiva Geopark— a series of state parks, forests, and reserves that stretch along its banks and back around the tall forests of longleaf pine that still thrive here. With the exception of a few older homes and cottages already in place, a five-hundred-foot-wide natural buffer must be kept on private land between the river and the buildings of people who live near it.

Much of this is the doing of a nonprofit, grassroots citizens group, the Friends of the Wekiva River, which mobilized in the early 1980s around the same time real estate developers were on their own lockstep march to the riverbanks. It is a good lesson in riverine civics—with rare exceptions, elected officials in Florida seldom rise to the call of preservation, unless pressured to do so.

The Friends have circled the wagons around the Wekiva, helping to make it the most intact Florida wilderness river still found within a short drive of a large metropolitan area. Still, their fight is not over, and while the Wekiva is a biological microcosm, it is also a political one, too. Indeed, the Friends helped lobby for the Wekiva River Protection Act, a state-mandated law that in 1989 promised to keep the 180 square miles of land immediately around the river "rural" in character. Although both Orange and Lake Counties honored the intent of the law, Seminole commissioners—who made no bones about their personal friendships with local developers—approved twenty-four hundred new homes in the area in the decade after the law was passed.

Uncontrolled growth has also been accompanied by an indirect impact that goes far beyond the more obvious issues of traffic, noise, and loss of wildlife habitat. That impact is storm water, runoff from heavy rains that washes sediment and nutrients into the Wekiva from densely developed urban uplands, forming sandy bars and culturing nitrogen-loving plants like cattails atop them. For this reason, the Wekiva I paddle today is in some places less than half the width of the one navigated by the Mayflower, and it will continue to shrink and shoal as long as storm water continues to run freely into it.

But early in the evening on the river, this is not what I am thinking. It is a few days beyond the vernal equinox, and, as if in celebration, the chuck-will's-widow is singing its plaintive two-note refrain back in the woods, the spring peeper frogs are happily chattering, and the mullet are splashing over the surface like stones skipped by a child.

By night, the Wekiva seems as if it has reclaimed its historic territory once again, becoming a jungle where one can truly lose him- or herself—can even, in fact, get wonderfully lost. In appreciation, we put our paddles on our laps and drift wordlessly in the gentle current, like a very large leaf on a rill, letting the whims of the nocturnal river carry us into the subtle romance of the river night.

Just north of the mouth of the Wekiva, the St. Johns takes a spectacular dip southward, bending as classically as any oxbow ever has before deciding to continue north again. Oxbows are common when a slow current runs head-on into an obstruction and, instead of bulling through it, goes back and starts again, imitating the curving, U-shaped frame that binds the head of oxen under a yoke. Back when efficiency wasn't nearly as important as it is now, riverboat captains and their passengers on the St. Johns experienced the scores of each oxbow fully on the river, deckmen with long poles often pushing away from the tight corners, bows crunching against the underbrush.

Today, though, there are at least thirty short, canal-like "cuts" made by the Army Corps of Engineers along the river, connecting the serifs at the top of each oxbow "U" to make navigation easier, as it does here at the "Wekiva Cut." Most were dredged between the 1880s and the 1930s. Since Indian middens had virtually no value during that period, it wasn't uncommon for a dragline to slice neatly through a pre-Columbian mound, leaving fragments of shell, pottery, and even bone to gurgle in the newly dredged mud.

If the cutoffs are well maintained so the current flows through them, the original oxbow corners will eventually become shallow and thick with snags, providing aquatic labyrinths in which to poke about. Given enough time, some may even separate themselves entirely from the river, natural retribution for being bypassed and ignored.

Yet it is not only engineers who alter the channel; they just do it more quickly. A river like the St. Johns follows the path of least resistance, changing course inside its floodplain when it needs to do so. The lakes themselves were created in such a way, perhaps when some prehistoric logjam drifted into a shoal on a much wider river, accumulating sand and floating islands of aquatic grasses until the water pooled up behind it. Some geologists say these sediments may have even been deposited between several different rises and falls of the prehistoric sea, when the basin was still estuarine.

At any rate, the river I see today does not flow exactly where it did when Bartram first saw it more than two centuries ago, or even when Lanier rode atop it a century later. Because its shift is gradual, though, we think of its path as a permanent fixture forever welded into the terrain. It is an illusion that fools us, makes us forget about where the river has been.

The poet Linda Gregg thinks that poetry is found rather than written, that the substance and theme of a poem already exist before it is put into words. That is a fine description of how a river flows as well, determining its shape by a historic collection of tiny nuances, long before its course is ever revealed to us mere mortals—who are isolated by the presumption of the *now*.

Elongated, eel-like shards of water begin to appear in the landscape here. Sometimes they eventually reconnect to the river channel, like Hontoon Dead River. Sometimes they are stranded in distant prairie lands to the west, like the Banana River. Almost always, they follow the north–south topographical contours of the land, mimicking the nascent path of the marine lagoon.

Because the channel is deeper and easier to navigate here, motorboaters frequent it more regularly—although far less so on weekdays. As a result, canoe and kayak guidebooks to rivers in the Southeast usually ignore the St. Johns altogether to protect their readers from the danger of churning wakes. Yet the backwater streams and sloughs that accompany the channel can be delightfully peaceful sojourns for small, human-powered craft. Any good map that shows the depth and configuration of waters is a gateway to those sojourns, with *shallow* and *narrow* providing the keys.

I am finding that those who usually travel on the St. Johns via combustion engine are a widely eclectic lot—from those with little river experience who rent pontoon party boats for day trips, to houseboaters on vacation, to sport fishers. Depending on how serious they are about fishing, the last group drive small john- or V-hulled aluminum boats with modest kickers— or wrangle high-powered, fleck-painted, bullet-shaped craft that rooster-tail their wakes, like kids burning rubber on their hot rods. The latter seem less inspired by the *Compleat Angler* than the Daytona 500.

The environmental sensibilities are just as eclectic, and one of the best ways to measure the responsibility factor of each is by watching how they handle the "no wake" zones set up to protect the endangered—and slow-moving—West Indian manatee. Some throttle down as the law requires, but others breeze by at top end as if shooting the bird to the zone and the manatee inside it.

I used to think that all people who enjoyed being outdoors understood the finite, even sacred potential of that experience—that they in some way appreciated the chance for connectedness between themselves and nature, the opportunity to distance themselves from the techno-transience of our contemporary world. And this is true of many who visit the St. Johns. But there are increasing numbers who simply enjoy traveling at high rates of speed on a medium that just happens to be water; others seem to relish the notion of chemically numbing themselves while the riverine environment plays a sort of natural background Muzak for the experience.

Consider this: Boat collisions are the leading cause of mortality among manatees in Florida. What's more, Florida also leads the nation in boating deaths of humans—in which speeding and drunken boaters plummet one another with bows and hulls and props. Although moderation would seem a reasonable course, there is a persistent campaign to lift or relax speed zones, engineered chiefly by a few who make money selling, renting, or berthing boats. Even one writer of a self-published boating guide to the river demands the easing of extensive manatee zones because of the "inconvenience" to boaters. Those who disagree are labeled, in advance, "extreme environmentalists."

Funny, when I think of myself at all when it comes to the St. Johns, it is usually as a fisherman, because that is what I was, long before I became a conservationist, extreme or otherwise. I suppose if I were more honest, I would admit that my fancy graphite fly rod and hand-tied flies are sophisticated props to open the door to the connection Edward O. Wilson describes so well, to satisfy my own biophilia. Without it, I would be left to stare endlessly into the water, gripping nothing.

It helps me understand why Bartram and Homer drew and painted what they saw here, why Lanier and Rawlings wrote so poetically of their experiences. They, too, entered into a gentle strife—if not with the mullet, then surely with the river—and it absorbed them, gave them a reason to exist. What would they have been without their pens and quills and oils?

Fishers, probably.

The St. Johns is layered with textures, and these textures change not only every few miles as the river meanders through its floodplainbut also with season and perspective. Boating or hiking on or near the river by day provides one perspective. Living *atop* the river for a few weeks provides another.

To explore this last texture, I set out to experience the St. Johns between here and Green Cove Springs by rented houseboat. Aboard the craft, I have packed kayaks and scuba tanks, both of which I plan to use to ease me back into the aquatic alleys and geological cellars of the St. Johns, outside the mainstream. I have never associated the idea of a houseboat with finesse, but that is what this lumbering thirty-eight-foot-long, single-prop vessel I am now at the helm of demands. Unlike smaller craft that simply go toward the target one aims them for, a houseboat requires one to think at least a few moments ahead, to start a turn before that turn is required. Because its sides are steep and boxy, it is also vulnerable to wind, not unlike a sailboat would be.

During my own sluggish learning curve, the boat lazily zigs and then zags on an eccentric course back and forth across the channel for a day or so until I learn the ropes. Other than that, my temporary home is much like a camper trailer mounted on a huge pontoon—or, to see it another way, a fancy raft with a steering wheel and a fathometer and a gas grill. In fact, I like seeing it the other way, as it puts me in cahoots with Huck Finn himself, who once remarked of his journey on another river, a monstrous big one: "There waren't no home like a raft, after all. Other places do seem so cramped up and smothery, but a raft don't." If the inside of my raft becomes too smothery, I simply walk outside or climb a little ladder to the roof.

As I cruise downriver, I become more sympathetic to the concept of the navigational "cuts" that have been sliced through some of the oxbows. They are simply easier to navigate than the convoluted natural twists. Yet I also know the most intriguing places I have ever found on land are at the end of the worst and least-traveled roads. The cutoffs are little turnpikes, good for making time but not too much else.

Today, I am following the current northward, above where the St. Johns weaves around N. Emanuel Bend, beyond the aptly named High Banks, through the oxbow cuts that take me past other bends mapped as Dutchman and Florida and Coxetter. The last was named for Lewis Coxetter, an early steamboat captain who used his ship *Starlight* to run Yankee blockades in the Civil War, leaving it finally scuttled somewhere back in Lake Monroe. I anchor near the backside of the Snake Creek cutoff. Snake Creek itself winds northwest of here, more or less paralleling the river until it becomes a trace of itself, confluxing finally with Hontoon Dead River. In between, the nautical map shows it as "unnavigable," a virtual bayou with a little branching cul-de-sac of its own mapped as "Negro Slough."

Unnavigable always means what it says for motorboats. But if you happen to be in a kayak or canoe and don't mind ducking under low-hanging branches and pulling your way atop snags hidden under a few inches of water, the concept of "unnavigable" may vary depending on seasonal dryness and your personal sense of adventure.

Just south of Snake Creek, there are at least three horizontal "logging canals" that link the channel with Hontoon Dead River. I will find several other "dead rivers" along the St. Johns, and they are only *dead* nautically because they terminate somewhere off the channel; aesthetically, they may be some of the most pristine stretches of water in the entire valley. Hontoon has something else, too: the old logging canals were here for a purpose, and that purpose was to cut the biggest and oldest cypress trees the loggers could find.

I paddle up one in the kayak, back here in a matrix of leaves and vines, and see the remnant stumps of what must have been massive, ancient trees. Loggers, who first went into the swamp in the late 1800s, "girdled" the cypress by chopping a deep groove around each tree a season or so before they planned to fell it. The grooves bleed sap—the death knell of a thousand-year-old tree. When the loggers returned to finish the work, the giant, sapless conifers would float instead of sinking and thus could be towed down the river.

I look closely at several hollow stumps—each large enough for three or four people to climb inside—and see the marks of ax girdling, still in the wood, below the top of the stumpy rim. Scientists know that trees actually give off warning signals to other trees when they are being attacked by insects; what such cues would a millennium-old cypress emit when it was girdled, and for how long?

It is May and full spring now. Along with fall, it is my favorite time to be on the river, since the air is cooler and the mosquitoes and deerflies and no-see-ums are still at bay. Other insects, though, are beginning to stir, and they are the ones I most look forward to seeing. Some are from the order Lepidoptera, others from the family of Lampyridae—wings of colored feathers or lighters of lamps. By day, this means butterflies; by night, fireflies.

Back in the channel, from the deck of my boat, I am pleased to see that the tiger swallowtails are beginning to emerge from their chrysalis, their great lacy yellow wings edged with black, looking like some Rorschach test colorized and come to life. I sit on the stern, watching one doing its little butterfly dance, gliding from above the ever closed yellow bud of the spatterdock lily, up into the leaves of the willow and hickory. Later, I will see the muted blue spring azure and then the black swallowtail, pure ebony spotted with white and blue, a distinctive frilly tail dribbling at the bottom of each ink-blotted wing. By fall, monarchs will move down across Florida in their long migration, stopping to rest on twigs and leaf edges, pumping their little wings like arabesque fans from a Victorian parlor.

The St. Johns is as good for butterflies as it is for birds, and for many of the same reasons: there is tender leafy food for the larvae, wildflower nectar for the adults, and—along public stretches of land—few pesticides or herbicides to poison them. There are insect naturalists, in fact, who routinely identify and count butterflies, just as the Audubon Society does with birds, and I imagine rivers like this must be dandy staging grounds for such things from the spring through the summer.

By early evening, the fireflies emerge in that cusp of time between early and late. I often hear people in Florida say they see few of these lightning bugs nowadays, and perhaps that's a function of several things—from too much artificial light in their neighborhood to simply too much neighborhood. But biodiversity holds true here for fireflies as well, as there are fifty-six species in the state, more than anywhere else in North America. Maybe we don't see as many anymore because we don't take the time; but sitting on the stern of an anchored boat on the St. Johns surrounded by dark riverine swamp at night surely gives you back that time. Here, I watch for these little sparks of bioluminescence to flicker on and off at the edge of the river, never fully sure where they will flash to life next, always guessing. It is a sort of visual fishing, without the props.

Scientifically, the biochemical sparks of the fireflies are the clues of sex or hunger—males courting females, or hungry females of a different species enticing unsuspecting males into becoming a snack. But for me, the displays are far more, part of that grand connect-the-dot picture pieced together to illustrate the natural river experience, the tiny flashes surprising me each time with wonder, a serendipitous break from my ordered human-made world.

Blue Spring is ground zero for manatees along the St. Johns. Whenever the temperature of the river begins to drop well into the sixty-degree-

Fahrenheit range, the warm-blooded mammals flock here, to the thermal womb of the springs. From forty to sixty return here to these springs each year, much like northern vacationers revisiting their favorite Florida motel or campground.

A great, lumbering beast, *Trichechus manatus* may weigh up to three thousand pounds and measure fifteen feet from head to rounded, flipperlike tail. (Average sizes, though, are closer to twelve hundred pounds and eight to ten feet.) Bulk like this requires fuel, and manatees get it solely in the form of plants, at a rate of sixty to one hundred pounds daily—water lettuce, hyacinth, and other vegetation.

Although it can move at a fair clip when it cruises laterally underwater, the manatee does not do nearly as well when it drifts to and from the surface, which it must do to breathe. As a result, lots of manatees get run over by boats, which seems to kill more of them than anything else. The noise of a boat motor carries a surprisingly long distance when you are underwater, and manatees, which have come to know what this means, have been seen visibly cringing when they hear such sounds. Those who don't succumb can live as long as eighty years.

Jacques Cousteau and his divers visited Blue Spring when it and the Indian mound surrounding it were privately owned back in the late 1960s. The documentary that followed helped galvanize support for the public purchase of the land here, one of the favorite winter habitats of the West Indian manatee in all of Florida.

There are people who complain about too many laws, and I am sometimes among them. But before the docile manatee was protected, animals had been found with pitchforks embedded in their backs, initials carved into their bodies, and bullet holes in their blubber. At Blue Spring, Cousteau found manatees with rope burns, where harnesses had been attached by brave adventurers who rode them for sport. Even today, with criminal penalties for harassment and "no wake" zones, every manatee I have ever seen has a grid of prop scars on its back. It is how researchers have come to identify one from the other, to distinguish Brutus from Phyllis, Lucille from Lenny.

I have seen manatees underwater, have had them actually approach me when I've been snorkeling, as some manatees—like people—are simply curious. We have hung there in the clear water, briefly studying each other, and I have been struck with how human the animal's eyes seem, each a pensive pool of brown recessed inside a starburst of skin wrinkles. It is almost as if there is a person inside all that insulation. Perhaps the animal thinks like-wise of me, that there may be a manatee in there somewhere, behind the blue eyes, underneath all that neoprene and rubber.

Billy Bartram was among the first to ever describe Blue; he visited here twice, the first time with his father in 1765, and the second time on his soli-tary journey up the St. Johns in 1774. Fascinated as he was by springs, Bartram described it as *diaphanous*, in which "entire tribes" of fish and alli-gators are easily seen from the surface. "They appear as plain as though ly-ing on a table before your eyes," he wrote, "although [they are] many feet deep in the water."

As for the springhead, "it boils up with great force, forming immediately a vast circular basin, capacious enough for several shallops to ride in and runs with rapidity into the river three or four hundred yards distance." There are other springs in the St. Johns Basin that blow out more water than Blue, but no large ones that do so this close to the river channel itself.

The romantic poet Samuel Taylor Coleridge never laid eyes on the river and its springs. But he read Bartram's *Travels* before toking on his opium pipe. And literary historians believe it was Billy's engaging descriptions of the springs that inspired *Kubla Khan*:

> In Xanadu did Kubla Kahn
> A stately pleasure-dome decree
> Where Alph, the sacred river, ran
> Through caverns measureless of man
> Down to a sunless sea. . . .
>
> A mighty fountain momently was forced:
> Amid whose swift half-intermitted burst
> Huge fragments vaulted like rebounding hail,
> Or chaffy grain beneath the thresher's flail.

Coleridge was likely inspired by Bartram's specific description of Salt Springs, upcoming in the Ocala National Forest; but there's no escaping the naturalist's fascination with all the springs of the river, where tiny chunks of limestone rebound in the crystal upwelling like hail.

By my arrival, the warmer river waters of May have coaxed the mana-tees out of the spring, and its run today is filled with snorkelers, entire tribes of them, their skin goosefleshed and puckered, here among the mullet and bass, gar and tilapia. I watch this panorama from a boardwalk at the top of the earthen basin encircling the boil, see a deep eternal blue pulse from down inside, shimmering with the electricity of the earth itself.

Along with a dive buddy, I gear up with scuba tanks and, after a strenuous slosh against the strong upstream current of the run, fin out from the shallow bottom to where the water seems actually to boil, over the gaping diaphanous maw. Just below the surface, I navigate through the forks of two immense fallen trees, giant Y's wedged against each other. Below me, the hole plunges sharply and then angles gradually back into the limestone, for at least 120 feet.

Now that I am inside it, the bottom of the spring doesn't seem as much blue as it does stark black. I fin down, pushing against an upwelling of ether, some seventy-seven million gallons of distilled water that pours out of the upper aquifer daily, from inside unseen labyrinths of limestone and dolomite. The cool current presses against my mask into my face, and countless bits of shell and sand and fossils swirl around me.

I inhale deeply from my regulator, exhaling gradually in a loud rush of bubbly air. In the few scant seconds between my own respirations, I listen for the voice of the spring in its own exhale from the deep earth. As I do so, I imagine I can hear something that sounds like a freight train roaring. But it is more likely the whoosh of water simply surging into and around my body.

I am sinking into the cellar of Florida, descending past ledges protruding from the rock, walls sculpted like gentle, vertical waves by a prehistoric water flow. I bump into one ledge, and as I push off it with my hand, I feel the softness of it, more marly clay than hard rock. The force of the spring, bottlenecked inside these narrow walls, is compressed, too strong to give much refuge to fish. Fresh from its long journey inside the earth, the water emerging directly from the rock is also low in oxygen, not nearly as desirable as the spring run for most critters who staff the great organic food chain.

But there are other constraints, too, those special to us higher mammals. Darkness and pressure and depths underwater can be particularly tricky for those of us used to breathing surface air. And for this reason, there is a sign posted at sixty feet, where the light first disappears, warning divers without special training to go no farther. It reads, "Prevent Your Death," and it is not hyperbole, as men and women without such skills have died here.

I have been trained in the precautionary redundancy-laden behaviors of

cave diving, so I turn on my underwater light and let its beam pull me downward, tethered by its narrow, dim shaft of illumination. The water I swim
against is impressive in its magnitude, cool enough to chill me inside my thin
wetsuit. I take my regulator out of my mouth and gulp a small mouthful,
swallowing. It is pure, with the taste of innumerable eons of shell fossil and
ocean bones, fresh water soaked for centuries in calcium created once by
the sea.

Like other springs, Blue is recharged by rainfall seeping down through
soils and rocky cracks and crevices upland from here. But the journey is not
a straight or easy one, and the delay between the time water falls from the
sky and emerges from the limestone vent may be wondrous. Elsewhere along
the river, hydrologists have examined spring water to determine age using
a carbon 14 process. At Croaker Hole, a dark, river-bottom vent I will later
visit just north of Lake George, the water has been trapped in the rock for
3,900 years; at Salt Springs, 7,000 years. Generally, the deeper the vein the
water comes out of, the longer it has been in the ground.

Perhaps the rain I taste now once fell when the earliest Native Americans
who inhabited the river valley were still alive, even fell on and around them,
all of it now a part of the *ibi*, cooling and everlasting.

At 120 feet, the water pressure surging out of the limestone is enormous.
Even if the cave entrance here were larger, the force alone would keep me
from penetrating any farther. I hold on with both hands to a boulder near
the darkest hole and let the pressure coming from it blow my body away and
up, suspending my torso in the swirling ether, moving my legs and fins like
some unseen puppet master in the rebounding hail.

I am deep inside the diaphanous magic now, my exhaust bubbles becoming part of the upwelling roil of Alph that swells and finally drifts away to
the surface. Off it flows, this confluence of spring water and poetry and ex-
halation, past the tribes of humans and fish, down the spring run to the river
and toward the sea.

The St. Johns is a tropical river of the dreamy kind; its beauty does not . . .

strike you, but rather steals over your senses slowly, as moonlight steals over

the summer night.—Constance Fenimore Woolson, writing in a January 1876

issue of *Harper's New Monthly* magazine on her trip upriver.

The dark tea that is the river curls around the east side of Hontoon Island, beyond the clear creek of Blue Spring. As it does, it takes a bite out of the southwesterly shore of Lake Beresford before continuing its sullen seep northward.

Beresford appears before me as a great, shallow swath of water, gridlocked by woods, canopied thick like broccoli. There were once two busy steamboat landings here, each with a wooden wharf and frame storage house at its end. An old photo from the 1890s shows the opulent paddlewheeler, the *City of Jacksonville*, moored at the end of the dock of one, crates of freight stacked along the wharf, waiting to be loaded. It is a brief snapshot in time of river life, now fully as vanquished as the Timucua.

Jacksonville was the flagship of the DeBary-Baya line, and it commonly hauled bales of locally grown cotton, boxes of oranges, and timber out of the interior; sometimes, it even carried barrels of salted fish, crates of pineapples, kegs of syrup, gator hides, and pelts of otters and raccoons. The three-decked ship had thirty-two carpeted staterooms with marble washstands and mahogany-trimmed mirrors for its passengers. From bow to stern, it measured more than half the length of a football field. In the Grand Salon, passengers sat in plush red armchairs, drinking lemonade. On local moonlit runs, which cost fifty cents, they were serenaded by "Prof. Baratta's orchestra." For longer trips, from Jacksonville to Sanford, each paid three dollars, which included all meals. Beresford was a stop along the way.

Named for a Lord Beresford who owned an immense indigo and sugar plantation here in the late 1700s, the lake was charted in the early 1800s as

"Barefoot." During his second voyage up the St. Johns, Billy Bartram was chased ashore here in his small sailing dinghy by a violent summer tempest, "tumultuous clouds" spitting purple flames overhead in a "frightful chaos." Although I will find plenty of natural clues first described by Bartram along the St. Johns, Beresford holds the hope that I may even find residual evidence of something human-made from that distant era.

Billy was regarded as a bit of an odd duck, even in his time. A failure as a merchant and farmer, he was a gentle Quaker who seemed to take great pleasure in going off on solitary odysseys, drawing exquisitely detailed pictures of both plants and animals. In them, the birds and the fish, even the plants, acquired an almost humanlike quality of expression. Under his pen, the passion flower appeared as a bloom dancing atop a body of leaves and buds, the leggy sandhill crane as a gentleman out for a stroll, the shellcracker bream as a fish flushed with astonishment. They were more than animals and plants; they were his friends.

Bartram was not just the first American botanist to explore the St. Johns fully; he was our first spiritual naturalist, one for whom nature and the Native Americans who lived in harmony with it were to be respected instead of exploited. His detailed and stylistic descriptions of his experiences can be read not just as reportage but as poetry, immutations bound by one man's delightful affection for a place he regarded as "sublime."

Looking through binoculars from my houseboat on Lake Beresford, I had sighted the canopy of a gigantic live oak tree ashore where the plantation once stood, dominant among the young sabal palms, Florida elm, and water hickory. It was a good landmark for the Beresford manor house, as oaks of this size still left today along the river were often planted or nurtured as young trees to provide shade for homesteads, even when the rest of the ground was cleared for fields.

I hoist my bantamweight kayak overboard and paddle ashore on the calm lake here, to a natural alcove where the thick subtropical jungle opens just enough to let me in. Here, I carefully pick my way through the thick tangle of green, scattering the anoles, little lizards busy puffing up their red throats to impress other little lizards, for conquest or copulation. I brush aside the serrated leaves of a woody bush of native lantana bristling with bright yellow-and-orange blossoms the size of a half dollar. Nearby, I look closely at a clutch of frilly knee-high weeds and see they are indigo, wild now and rebirthing themselves from the brood stock of crops once cultivated. The foreign indigo is joined here in the otherwise native woods by ancient orange trees, their fruit sour now from too many freezes over too many years, and a giant stand of bamboo.

Under the massive, spreading canopy of the live oak, I see an unusual rise in the flat hammock, covered with humus. It could be a small midden, but it is not. Instead, under a thick cover of leaves, I find geometrical blocks of hardened red clay, handmade and fired into bricks long ago, perhaps for a foundation of a wooden manor home or for its fireplace. The entire pile seems to be made of them, and most are covered with a patina of forest-green moss.

It appears to be all that is left of the manor house, the place where Billy Bartram sought refuge. I linger here holding a single brick in my hand, waiting for the image of the plantation to reform itself in my mind, allowing the solitude and the indigo and the touch of the hard clay a chance to do their sublime work. But there is only the wisp of a spring breeze in the tallest pines and oaks overhead and, down here at ground level, the dim bronze-green ambient light of a subtropical forest in the business of fully reclaiming itself.

Back in the channel, I steer my floating home into a slip in front of the ranger station on Hontoon Island State Park, not far from where a small state-run pontoon boat ferries visitors across the river to the 2.6-square-mile island.

The Owl Clan once lived here; perhaps the Otter Clan did, too. To mark their territory with the spiritual protection of their icons, craftsmen in each tribe carved totems and mounted them at the edge of the island so other tribes would know who was doing the protecting. Near the ferry landing, there are two totems, fiberglassed and painted but nonetheless good replicas of the originals, which are now preserved in the Florida Museum of Natural History.

Not far from one of the totems, I meet Bill Dreggors, sitting alone on a picnic bench. With his long, flowing white hair and beard, black suspenders over a denim shirt, Dreggors seems a vision from another century, a stuck-in-time persona who maybe stepped on a river steamboat in the nineteenth century and then stepped back off a hundred years or so later. "My family came here from Georgia in 1866," says Dreggors, from under a suede hat with embroidered leather brim, clear eyes burning like the fireflies on a St. Johns night. "I've spent a lot of time on the river, fishing, hunting." Later in his life, he started collecting old hand-colored penny postcards from the St. Johns. The long-gone scenes reminded him of how special life along the river had once been and how important it was to remember every bit of it he could.

Today, Dreggors has become a fountain of history about the St. Johns, especially the halcyon days of the steamboat, when every high bank on the river had a busy wharf on it, just as Beresford once did. A few of those wharves evolved into villages—like Welaka or Astor. But most simply vanished when their time was up. "They're mostly gone today," says Dreggors. "The place my Daddy was born, St. Francis, is just a wide spot in the river."

I will pass this St. Francis site later and will put my kayak overboard there, navigating around a set of weathered pilings jutting up out of a field of water hyacinths, like bookmarks of old pages of history. There had once been a hotel and newspaper on the riverbanks here, along with a factory where a Captain L. H. Harris, a doctor who settled St. Francis in 1875, made patent medicines. I will paddle for several hours past those gray pilings up into the St. Francis Dead River, a quiet, winding tributary stream, spotting an anhinga and a pair of otters in the water and, in branches above, a tiny marsh wren and a yellow-crowned night heron. Other than what lives in the mind of Bill Dreggors, they are all that I will see inhabiting St. Francis.

Dreggors is only too aware of the transience of it all; where we are sitting today had once been a pioneer homestead of William Hunton, a Seminole War soldier. It had also been a boat yard and even a cattle ranch before the state bought it for a park in 1967. Long before that, though, Hontoon had been other things to other people: here, amid the pine flatwoods and cypress swamps, pre-Columbian Indians lived for more than three thousand years. By the time the first Europeans arrived, the Native Americans along the river had become known as Timucua, and in addition to trapping fish and turtle and hunting deer, they cultivated squash and collected wild grapes, fern stems, acorns, and the tender inner shoot of the sabal palm.

Of the Timucuan language, there were said to be at least ten different dialects, spoken by competing tribes, each with its own territory along the St. Johns. Each tribe had its own name, which was also that of its chief. But the tribal names left in record today were ones passed along by the Spanish and French, phonetic remains of words used by the Native Americans themselves. Just saying them out loud revives the feeling and rhythm they had for the place, the flow of the vowels sweeping timelessly against the bend of the consonants: To-MOOK-kwa.

The particular Stone Age tribe that lived along this stretch of the river is described today as the Mayaca. What little is known of them was pieced together by archaeologists from the University of Florida in the 1980s who excavated portions of the two fifteen-foot-high middens left behind. From this work, they found that the upper tier of the middens—created around the dates of European arrival and afterward—revealed a dramatic 70 percent increase in stone "points" over earlier, deeper levels of time. But such discoveries asked as many questions as they answered. Did the abundance of points mean the Mayaca had simply found a new way to hunt—or were they trying to defend themselves from the often brutal encroachment of the Spanish?

Despite the diligent work of the archaeologists, no single artifact they uncovered was as spectacular as the totems, which were more or less blundered upon during river bottom dredging. The owl came up during the digging of a canal in 1955 near where the mainland parking lot for the park is today; a pelican emerged in 1978 after a barge repairing an underwater utility cable snagged what workers thought was a muddy log in the river. When the log revealed itself as a pelican, divers then searched the bottom and found another wooden icon, an otterlike animal holding a fish. They are the only North American totems found outside the Pacific Northwest.

Wood is the first to go in warm and wet environments like this one. It was only the soft anaerobic mud that preserved the icons, their designs carved in relief by sharpened shell, chert, or shark-teeth tools and still clearly recognizable as a set of owl ear tufts, a pair of animal eyes.

But why were such totems only found here and not elsewhere on the St. Johns? Are there still other wooden symbols, buried in the river bottom or wetland mud, perhaps totems of biota as thoroughly removed from the river as the Native Americans have been, maybe panthers or wolves or wooly mammoths? And did anyone else see that animal with a single horn on its head, drinking?

It is something to wonder about, sitting here with a man who looks a bit like the river itself might look if it ever took human form, rivulets in the creases of his smile lines, pools of deep blue in his eyes, a steady, unhurried current in his manner. Dreggors is over seventy now and won't be on earth forever. What else does he know, this teller of lost river tales? I could spend days here exploring the past, but we both have to leave, pulled back to the present by the ever ticking clocks that still give us our cues. Finally, as he stands to go, I ask Dreggors one last question, wondering what it is, after all, that makes a person a historian, a keeper of vanished river time.

Dreggors brightens, straightens the brim of his hat, and flashes me a big smile, a suggestion of something far beyond brooding contemplation. "A historian," says Bill Dreggors, "is the oldest living person who still has a memory."

The opening to the modest Mud Lake passes to the port, a shallow, linear slough that trails off southward into the narrow Shell Creek, leading from depths of two to three feet into eight to ten before finally trickling off into thick woods surrounded by parkland. The river bottom often defies common sense like this, for I would expect the trailing, disappearing stream to be far more shallow than its entry, rather than deeper.

Back on land, a diminishing trail usually stays diminished until it disappears. But this is terrestrial reasoning, logic that doesn't allow for confluxing streams to transport alluvial sediment to the mouth of their confluence. Somewhere south of here, Snake Creek has a vitality, earned from its contour in the wetlands, perhaps even from upward groundwater "leakage." But when it ebbs into Mud Lake and then the St. Johns, the history of its vitality accompanies it, piling up there in the form of banks and shoals, mini-deltas of eroded earth. (Later, on the southernmost banks of Lake George, where the channel is thread-thin, I will run aground on similar river-driven shoals, imitating a blunder that steamship captains routinely made long before me.)

Northward, the St. Johns dips around an islet mapped as "Drigger Island," and I smile as I remember Bill Dreggors earlier describing it to me, complaining good-naturedly about the misspelling of the site named for his uncle, who was the first tender of the river bridge near Fort White in the year 1926. "That's how it got on the map, as *Drigger*," said Dreggors, "and it'll be that way from now on."

As the channel winds beyond Dreggors's namesake, it passes the bluff named "Happy Hill" and then gets serious again, coursing down through a nearly straight leg that bites into the earth, at depths of fifteen to thirty feet. The St. Johns is no longer a river one can walk across, in any fashion.

Fish camps and marinas appear and then disappear along the middle St. Johns, some changing names every few months, some closing down, others living on as they've been for years. Often sited on higher ground or bluffs where many of the old landings were located, the marinas sustain the best of the time-stuck river ambience, often lagging a pleasant decade or more behind the tides that wash over the rest of the world. Some have gas, berths for boats, a launch ramp, maybe some fishing or even nautical gear. Almost all have ice and fishing bait, dead or alive. In some places, the live bait— usually the cyprinids called "shiners"—swim about in concrete vats or tanks that are tightly enfenced. The fencing is not to keep the giant silvery minnows from running off but to discourage herons and egrets, even gators, from dining on them.

Often, riverside marinas will feature little oddities hardly found anywhere else in the entire world. One of these is a small metal, horizontal barrel, labeled "Super Scaler," which I have seen mounted on the docks at three different locales, painted a bright orange. To operate this particular machine, the angler deposits a coin and a fish, steps back while the little motor-driven barrel whirls and scales fly, and—Viola!—gets a scaleless, if slightly battered, bass or bream. Truly, it is an invention only another angler could have dreamed up.

Because of all these things, marinas more often than not tend to slow me down, to make me realize there is more to life than full throttle. In this way, visiting a marina on the St. Johns River is a bit like fly tying or fly fishing, in that it is nearly impossible to make the activity go any faster than natural grace would allow. And it is simply hard to be too serious when one's catch of the day is spinning about inside a bright red barrel, spitting scales out like confetti.

After a spat of such diversions, the river braids itself through the forested landscape, doubling and even tripling its natural course, re-creating itself in a series of vaguely parallel creeks. Each seems like a photocopy of itself, just a bit more faded on each incarnation. From here to Welaka, above Lake George, the entire westerly shore of the St. Johns will pass beyond the boundaries of the Ocala National Forest. A national forest is far less than a park: it allows private, albeit limited, property ownership; permits logging;

and, in a designated zone in Lake George, even has a practice bombing range for the U.S. Air Force. But, as I will see, it is also far better than no protection at all: there are vast undeveloped areas here, mostly of scrub pine, countless sandy-bottomed lakes unconnected to the river, and a number of artesian springs—which have a very decided link to the St. Johns and its flow.

From here, if my boat drew less than three feet and the season was a wet one, I could leave the main channel at Highland Park Run and navigate through the easterly Norris Dead River, a serpentine maze of twists that empties into the southerly rim of Lake Woodruff. Just north of the circular spot of channel known as "Revolving Bend," I can make fine use of my kayak by exploring two splendid culs-de-sac. One, on the east rim of the St. Johns, is the narrow Honey-Harry Creek system, which seems to want to head north to Woodward but loses its train of thought along the way and dwindles off into the swamp; the other is the St. Francis Dead River, where Bill Dreggors's daddy was born.

I anchor at a channel marker near the mouth of the St. Francis and set my kayak down in the water here, paddling south. It reminds me of the spring-fed Wekiva, except that there are no public or private ramps about and the natural seclusion is nearly complete. I stop to rest under the fronds of an old sabal palm, its trunk leaning nearly sideways over the creek. As I do, a small bright green anole plops from a frond onto my head, tiny wide-open reptile eyes regarding me from inside millions of years of aplomb. From its vantage point, it hesitates only briefly before performing a dandy swan dive into the water, thrashing a few frantic feet back to shore, far more startled than I for the experience.

There are Styrofoam floats the size of fat softballs in the river; I have been passing them every so often since Lake Monroe. These floats are attached by rope to wire fish traps on the river bottom, and each is marked just a little differently, colored red or blue or numbered, to distinguish the ownership of each. These are not sport anglers who have set these traps but commercial fishers who make at least a portion of their livelihood from the waters of the St. Johns. From the traps, they empty catfish and eel and blue crab. I will see small trawlers pulling outrigger seines to net shrimp farther downriver, but these traps are strictly for those benthic species that wander about on the river bottom, looking for something inert and tasty to eat. Because it is long and relatively deep and has a diversity of critters in it, the St. Johns is the only freshwater river in Florida to support a major fishery.

Although fishing commercially is a physically difficult, repetitive, and uncertain way to make a living, there is still a certain romance associated with it. Perhaps the artists have made this so, portraying workers bending over gunnels at the crack of dawn, or floats and nets rakishly hung between weathered wooden docks. Maybe the anthropologists have helped, reminding us that this is the last manifestation of the hunter-gatherers, humans still going *mano a mano* with nature itself, a continuum in time that stretches back to the earliest riverside dwellers. Whatever the reason, nautical motifs are pervasive in the valley of the St. Johns, just as they are elsewhere in Florida. Yet the farther removed such decor is from the actual hardscrabble fishery itself, the more fanciful it becomes. In Altamonte Springs, a concrete strip mall of a town outside Orlando, I have eaten dinner in a restaurant chock full of spanking new traps and buoys and nets—fishing gear that will come no closer to water than that found in a glass, with ice.

It is harder than ever to make a living fishing on the St. Johns, and that has to do with the reality that fish stocks everywhere are declining. Part of this is caused by overfishing; but a larger part is caused by the loss of natural habitat for the fish and a decline in water quality. There is a bitter conflict now between sport fishers and their commercial counterparts throughout the entire state, with recreation anglers blaming the working fishers for the loss of fish. But because they usually do not hunt for the same species on the St. Johns, there is less strife, more of a tolerance between the two user groups here.

In fact, one of the critters that is a mainstay of the fishery isn't much appreciated by sport anglers at all. It is the American eel, *Anguilla rostrata*, and it is perhaps one of the most fascinating aquatic animals under the surface of the river. What makes the eel so special is that it leaves the St. Johns to travel great distances into the ocean to mate and spawn—sort of the flip side of what the anadromous shad does. The adult *Anguilla* begins its long run out into the ocean during the darkest phases of the moon sometime between late summer and early fall. Convening in the Sargasso Sea southwest of Bermuda with eels from other foreign rivers, the fish mate, spawn, and then die, leaving their eggs behind to continue the cycle.

After the tiny, transparent larvae emerge from the eggs, they drift about in the sanctuary of their oceanic birthplace for more than a year and then, after acquiring fins, begin the long swim back to the continent, where their progeny spent most of their lives. Upstream in a freshwater river like the St. Johns, the eels grow and mature, becoming yellow-greenish in color. Snorkelers in springs along the river are most likely to encounter them then. When they do, a flipper-thrashing race often ensues to distance the human snorkeler from the harmless eel, for *Anguilla* is a slender, undulating fish that for most simply spells *snake*. It is this same "yellow eel" that cave divers commonly see, deep inside the dark caverns of the spring systems. It is the animal's highly developed sense of smell that has led it back there, searching for insects, even crayfish, in a place where most fish would simply be lost.

Although some have been known to stay in the river for up to forty years, most "yellow eels" begin their spawning trek back to the ocean after about a decade. To do so, they began a final metamorphosis, developing special osmotic cells to help them deal with their upcoming saltwater journey. In doing so, they sport a metallic purple-black sheen, becoming "silver eels." They are ready for their long swim into the sea. And so goes the eel saga— unless, of course, the animal's sense of smell betrays it, leading it inside a fisher's wire trap on the river bottom. In that case, its only journey across the sea will be inside the hold of a cargo plane, as the eel is in high demand by gourmands in Europe and Japan. It is not uncommon for a quarter million pounds of eel to be harvested in this way in a year on the river.

Shrimp from the lower river estuary and blue crab are more valuable commercially. But the eel remains, inimitably, a critter of heroic, serpentine odysseys.

Downriver, the St. Johns sprawls indolently through the landscape, supine in the way of southern blackwater rivers. As it does, it sluices through one of the largest publicly protected stretches of swamp, marsh, and uplands along its route, the 97.5-square-mile Lake Woodruff National Wildlife Refuge. Still less than a park, a refuge is a few giant management steps above a forest, in that no one but animals live in it. In fact, it is "managed" in just such a way, more for the benefit of wildlife than visitors. Sandhill cranes live here; so do bobcats. Almost two dozen species of migratory ducks and geese have been seen overwintering in the refuge, including fulvous whistling ducks, ring-necked ducks, and hooded mergansers.

Now that it is spring, the wood ducks (*Aix sponsa*)—the only duck to nest in the swamp—are busy feathering their homes here in tree cavities and in small wooden boxes made to replicate those cavities, mounted by people who care about such things. Indeed, as cypress trees have disappeared from the river, so has the wood duck; tree boxes are helping to revive them. The male is one of the most distinctively marked ducks in the world, with its large wedgy head tapering into a slicked-back crest, like a greaser from the 1950s. Its plumage is scored with black, white, purple, green, and chestnut, and sometimes, when the light hits it just right, it almost seems to glow. Wildfowl carvers say they love to whittle male wood ducks because their features are so dramatic, so easy to distinguish.

Less grand, the females are dull brown with a white, horizonal teardrop mark around each eye. Unlike other nesting avifauna—including songbirds, wading birds, even raptors—baby ducks are good to go within hours of hatching. Out of the nest they come, taking the one giant step down to the river, where they shadow their mother.

But *Aix sponsa* isn't the only exotic-looking bird of flight about. No less spectacular is the glossy ibis (*Plegadis falcinellus*), the darkish wading bird with the opalescent plumage, which begins to appear in greater numbers at this point on the river—thanks to the surrounding wildness of the refuge. It was hunter and artist John James Audubon who first illustrated the glossy, and he did so during his visit to the St. Johns in 1832 in search of new birds to shoot, sketch, and paint.

Although Audubon added several plates to his collection from the birds he found here, he was gravely disappointed with the St. Johns, apparently unable to reconcile the swampy, buggy environment with the expectations of a glowing tropical paradise he had long carried with him. Of his two journeys to the St. Johns, it was the first—made overland from the Atlantic coast—that was far more agreeable. On this expedition, Audubon traveled with friends from the coastal plantation of John Bulow, riding an Indian pony on an ancient path known as Kings Road. "It was," reported Audubon, "the wildest, most desolate tract of pine barrens, swamps and lakes that I ever saw."

Tucked back into the forest at the end of the trail was the bucolic "Garden Spring." The spring is mapped today as Ponce de Leon Springs, a second-magnitude artesian vent from which nineteen million gallons of water a day surge up out of the limestone. The St. Johns lies far westward, reached by a series of streams and lakes in the entangled landscape. From Garden Spring, reported Audubon, the travelers boarded a small dingy and rowed westward, to Spring Garden Lake, and then along the winding Spring Garden Creek to "Woodruff's Lake." Audubon spotted gallinules and anhingas and ospreys and alligators. Somewhere between Lake Woodruff and "Dexter's Lake," farther west, they stopped for lunch amid the fragrance of a "sweet little orange grove island" where the artist saw a ruby-throated hummingbird. The naturalist's host, a Colonel Orlando Rees, named the site "Audubon's Isle" in his honor.

Although Audubon admitted to a certain enchantment with the island, the primeval, moss-draped terrain of the St. Johns Basin seemed only to confuse him. It had, he confessed, "a tendency to depress the spirits." "It would have been a perfect paradise for a poet," wrote Audubon of his experience. "But I was not fit to be in paradise. . . . I felt unquiet, too, in this singular scene, as if I were almost upon the verge of creation, where realities were tapering into nothing."

For most, the name Audubon seems to indulge a fiction; like the owl and otter totems, he has become an icon, a character so far removed from reality that it's hard to imagine him in flesh-and-blood form. But to be surrounded here in the wilderness of Woodruff is to be reminded that not only did Audubon—and Rawlings and Bartram and all the others—exist, but he was a vital and complex human who once stood on the same ground and rode on the same waters where I am today. Audubon was also a superb marksman who, in a time predating photography, first observed and then shot everything he drew to study it more completely. Like a good sportsman, he wasted little. Once, after shooting a great blue heron at the edge of the St. Johns, Audubon cut it open. Inside was a freshly swallowed, whole "perch"—likely a crappie—which he promptly cooked and ate. At other times, he feasted on "young gator" and possum during his journey on the river.

The narrow run of Alexander Springs sneaks into the St. Johns from the westerly national forest, rimming the thickly wooded northerly shore of Kimball Island as it does. I slow long enough to see a bright yellow tiger swallowtail butterfly darting there amid wild hibiscus blossoms near the confluence, folding and unfolding like a tiny set of bellows. Some fifteen miles back up the spring run, in the heart of the Ocala National Forest, lies the beginning of Alexander. I have been there on other trips, scuba diving down into the twenty-seven-foot-deep spring basin, where white sand lies on the sides of the limestone walls like snow on a mountain cliff. The powerful spring rises up through a small bedroom-sized cave at the bottom of the basin, a place just dark enough to give a hint of the labyrinth buried deeper in the rock.

Inside the cave, looking carefully into the darkest crevices with an underwater light, I once saw a solitary albino crayfish scuttling about, its pigment gone from its exoskeleton in a life bereft of sun. Crustaceans like this are not only troglodytic—cave dwelling—they are extremely rare, often even endemic to the individual cave system. In their netherworld, they are joined by tiny amphipods, shrimplike relatives with neither color nor carapace. If the science of underwater life has lagged far behind that of the terrestrial world, then the knowledge of underwater cave dwellers is even more, well, in the dark. Scientists who study such critters say the blind animals have a low metabolic rate that allows them to live in the food-deprived cave darkness. They are also finding that such animals, which once free-ranged throughout the river system, are speciated by individual cave systems, custom-molded by centuries of exposure to minerals and darkness and a near constant temperature.

Besides providing case studies in evolution, the existence of such animals sheds new light about how life unfolds. For instance, the diminished needs of the troglodytic environment slow the aging process: some scientists believe these little crayfish may live for twenty-five years or more, growing no bigger than my thumb, downsized like the aged, stunted tree islands I saw back on the upper river. Surely, a quarter-century-old crayfish is a life form to be reckoned with. Undoubtedly, when brand-new discoveries are made along the river in the years to come, most will likely be from such caves, where evolution quietly makes its natural selections in the soft darkness.

Just northward, the river passes the mouth of Stagger Mud Lake, rounding Dexter Island to the right, and to the left, the historic tip of land known as Idlewilde Point. This is where Bartram once camped, where he was besieged by alligators in a place he dubbed "Battle Lagoon." It is also a spot revered by fishers for hundreds of years, where the natural confluence of several bodies of water brings nutrients and plankton and bait together in a stew. The Native Americans called this place "the Striking Ground" because of the way large predators voraciously struck at insects and smaller fish near the surface. As recently as 1939, when Bartram scholar Francis Harper traveled here, he reported that the site was still locally referred to as the Striking Ground.

Archie Carr, who admitted to turning to Bartram when he had a question about the original Florida landscape, also pondered the Dexter phenomenon. Carr had a name for it, too: he called it a "jubilee," an unexplained but intense feeding frenzy he had seen among aquatic critters in rivers and creeks elsewhere in Florida and the Southeast. Perhaps the confluence of waters had something to do with such things, Carr figured. But, mostly, it was a mystery. ("Being alive," wrote Carr, "wild creatures are unsettlingly prone to behave as they please.")

I know an ichthyologist in Florida who studies the sounds fish make underwater. On certain times of the year, say, during spawning or on full moons, those sounds—the clickings and gruntings and moans—dramatically increase. The Native Americans who lived near the water learned to listen for those muted sounds. When they discovered sites that were clamoring with fish chatter, they pronounced these as sacred places, for the critters who made those sounds were a vital part of the broader chain of life. Perhaps the Striking Ground was just such a site for them.

Tick Island lies not too far east of here, a place where the land rises ten to eighteen feet above the low swamp, partly earthen, partly in a tedious accumulation of shell and bone. While there is evidence that nomadic bands of hunters and fishers seasonally camped along the river as long as ten thousand years ago, archaeologists say Tick Island is one of the first places the pre-Columbians known as the "Early Archaic" actually begin to settle, from four thousand to six thousand years ago. What distinguished these people from all those who came before them was their social evolution from a roving, restless people in constant search of food to villagers—who had food at their doorsteps. While the Ice Age began winding down ten thousand years ago, the thaw that followed shook the natural boundaries of Florida for the next several thousand years.

It wasn't until the most recent Holocene epoch of five thousand years ago that the climate and sea level began to resemble what we know today: the sea rose, the coastline retreated, and the basin of the river we call the St. Johns became inundated, less a river and more an extended, linear chain of lakes.

The ecology of this new place proved to be enriching; there was plenty of food to be had without searching all over creation for it. By settling into one place or another, the people had more time on their hands. There was space now to imagine what their gods were like, space to grow crops and to create pottery to cook in and to eat from. Thus, the St. Johns River valley became one of the first places in all of North America where such ceramics came to life. Soon, pots acquired a peculiar crisscross pattern, called St. Johns Check Stamped, which varied in design according to what tribe made them and when. Gradually, this cultural art became more sophisticated, revealed in wood carvings with owls, wading birds, panthers—icons to celebrate the spiritual power of animals, to create links between the natural and super-natural worlds.

It was the shift in the environment that made all this possible. Radiocarbon dates of ancient Tick Island midden shell tell us that. What we can hear in that data, if we listen closely, is the sounds that fish make when they aggressively feed, of a sacred place coming to be.

It is late afternoon now, a perfect time for me to pay attention, to see what still remains of these Striking Grounds. In my kayak with a light spinning rod, I toss a silvery, spinning lure into the water at the edge of a pod of lotus lilies and retrieve it slowly, with motions I am sure are irresistible to any fish. From the flat green pads, I hear the sharp reports of stealthy predators feeding on bugs at the surface, hitting them so hard with their mouths that the water actually resounds with scattered "pops."

On my third cast, the lure stops dead in its tracks, my rod tip bends down like a bow, and something shakes and pulls hard on the other end, running and then jumping. I see it is a largemouth bass, modest by the standards of professional fishing tournaments but a fine specimen for my delicate rig. After a minute or so of this it tires, and I reel it to the side of my little boat. Usually, I release fish I catch for sport. But I have decided to camp here ashore at a midden on the edge of this sacred site, and I want to have my bass for dinner, just as others have been doing here for a few millennia.

Paddling to the edge of Idlewilde Point, I notice the snout and armored back of a gator nearly the size of my nine-foot-long kayak hanging nearby.

Ashore, I quickly pitch my tent several yards back from the water atop hard-packed midden shells under a cover of magnolia and sabal palms and gather dry wood for a small fire. It is early evening now, and the fire glows here on the ancient mound.

I cut the head off my bass, and as I do, it makes a sound from deep inside, a sad, ineffably final moan. I squeeze the juice of a wild sour orange I have found over the fish, just the way the Native Americans did. After letting its flesh turn flaky white over the fire, I eat it here alone in the settling darkness. Around me, the night sounds build into a crescendo of ancient crackles, screams, and croaks, the chatter of wading birds and frogs and gators, as wild as anything I am likely to hear on this continent. I climb inside my tent, given over to the timelessness of it all. Before I fall into a deep sleep in my bag, I hear manatees surfacing to breathe yards away in the river channel, releasing air in great mournful exhalations, until the entire river night is full of the manatee sighs.

I am 130 miles from the river mouth, just north of where the channel leaves Lake Dexter and continues its solemn crawl to the sea. Saltwater white shrimp have been caught this far upriver, but the environment I am passing through remains fundamentally freshwater and will continue to be so until I am farther north, at the mouth of Lake George. The St. Johns is mapped here as a nearly straight channel for three or four miles, one single corrugation that stretches to the bend in the river at Astor. But straightness is relative and consigned to maps. Even without the serious twist of an ox-bow, I am headed constantly around corners, passing the ruined pilings at Bluffton, a nonplace charted ironically as "Manhattan," a smallish island called Lungren. Each new tree line falls away, replaced with a promise of what lies beyond.

Dwellings along the St. Johns appear and disappear, personal statements of how each owner approaches the notion of a river coursing through his or her backyard. Boathouses often rise from stilts at the edge of the water. While some are wooden and quaint, others are more grandiose, mounted with motor wenches and little cranes and powerboats. As for the homes, there are grand, sweeping lawns, studded with birdbaths and little shiny globes and pedestals and plastic flamingos. There are also ramshackle, low-slung "cracker" homes, the sort of places I can imagine Rawlings passing on her trip upriver in the late 1920s. Wooden Adirondack chairs appear and disappear, places for people to sit and sip iced tea, watch the parade of the river unfold, one float at a time.

Astor approaches on the west bank, a once lively landing that is now a monument to lost ambition. Named for the famous financier William Astor, who purchased a large grant of land here in the 1870s, Astor was expected to boom and prosper as a winter resort. And for a while it did, with its namesake building a railroad link to the town, a telegraph line, and a string of hotels. But when steamship traffic slowed, Astor settled back into a sort of low-key obscurity. All that shows ambition today is a brace of residential canals sliced back off the river, dredged spoil hidden under the lawns of modest ranch homes.

During Florida's brief British occupation, Astor was also the site of the southernmost trading post along the St. Johns, Spalding's Upper Trading Store. When Bartram made his trip back upriver during his second visit, he stayed for several months at Spalding's, sorting his notes and the plant specimens he collected during his solitary expedition.

I tie up at a fish camp here called Hall's Lodge, a place where a thin blond woman is skinning commercially caught catfish on the dock, hurrying them along one at a time, between the whole fish stage and one in which they become filleted, reddish meat packed in ice. I wander over the dock and out back, beyond the trailered airboat and the sign that advertises "Fresh Gator Meat." There is a narrow road here that bridges the river, and the far side of the road holds what I am looking for. It is a venerable live oak tree, about the size of the one I saw earlier back at Beresford, and it has several markers posted under it, a tree with status. Dried clumps of resurrection fern grow on its shady, nearly horizontal limbs, waiting for a good rain to be reborn. In an overgrown field nearby, a contraption that looks like a cross between a tractor and a pontoon boat sits quietly, posted with its own sign, one special to the river: "Water Weed Harvester For Hire."

Under the tree, there is a distinctive slate-gray metal marker on a post, and I can see from a distance it is a Bartram Trail sign, like a half dozen or so others placed along the river by a federation of garden clubs to remind us Billy Was Here: "William Bartram, famed naturalist, classified flora and fauna for shipment here at Spalding's Upper Trading Store, May and June 1774." A fondness for gardening, of course, does not restrict one to cultivating a little enfenced patch of petunias. There are higher aims afoot in the basin, a grander view that embraces the historic and ecological links of the place. Plants, old explorers, big trees, fish camps, blackwater rivers. We're all in this together.

The fact that we are is brought home by the other marker. Embedded in a tabby rich with midden shells—like the wall of the defunct pool back at Woodland Park on Lake Monroe—the plaque reports this to be the site of a Mayacan Indian mound. There is hardly a sign in all the state erected just to mark a midden, regardless of how ancient it might be. And so it is with this one, which also informs me of a European site here, built atop the mound about 1667, a Spanish fort and mission called San Salvador de Mayaca.

The peninsula of Florida, particularly the interior defined by the St. Johns, was a tricky proposition for the Spanish. They came here not in search of a fountain of youth but in search of gold and silver, the same reason they went to Mexico and Peru. But with neither mineral treasures nor a state-level central chiefdom to exploit, they bided their time with lesser things. If there were many fiefdoms to be controlled, then each would get its own mission for that purpose. If the tribes of Timucua couldn't deliver gold, they could be taught to farm around the mission outposts in exchange for trading beads and trinkets. In this way, the produce of La Florida would at least feed hungry conquistadors with maize, beans, and squash from fields, and figs, citrus, and grapes from groves. The fertile soils of the St. Johns Valley became the garden to fuel the New World warriors and its proud Timucua, the gardeners.

In return for saving souls, the friars banned Indian dances they considered pagan or obscene, outlawed a soccerlike ball game, and urged the Timucua to move from a naturally centered, subsistence life—which was rife with "idle" time—to one that produced surplus crops that could be exchanged for clothing and material goods. This mission period lasted some 140 years, from when the earliest Jesuit missionaries set up shop in St. Augustine to when both the outposts and the villages built around them were destroyed by the British and their Native American allies. San Salvador de Mayaca was at the very tail end of that period, surviving longer perhaps because it was farther upriver than the others.

I stroll back to the fish camp, into a cluttered room where cane poles, rubber worms, and red-and-white plastic bobbers seem to have commandeered every square inch of space. I ask the fellow behind the counter, an older gentleman for whom the term *taciturn* may have been invented, if he's ever heard of anything to do with a Spalding's Upper Trading Store. "You're standing on it," he replies, speaking as many words in a row as I figure he probably ever will. The man's name is Ray Lucas, and his daddy used to run the old drawbridge right here, before it was replaced by a newer, higher crossing. Surely, he must have known Bill Dreggors's father, as the drawbridge tender fraternity on the river couldn't be that broad. But before I can ask him that question, Lucas becomes more loquacious. Spalding's, he heard tell, used to sit atop an Indian mound right here, a mound as tall as the roof of this shop.

When he was a boy, Lucas remembers workmen coming to cart off piles of the mound in trucks, scattering pieces of Indian skulls, bones, arrow points in their wake—all of it tinted a dark sepia by the tannins of river time. I wonder where these untold chapters of history could have ended up, but I know the answer even before the words are out of my mouth. "Road fill," says Lucas. "It's underneath all the roads here in the county."

Back on my boat, I start the engine and putter away from the dock, continuing downriver. But I remember a need for ice, so I pull over at the very next marina. It is Blair's Jungle Lodge, a place that seems plucked from the 1950s. On its exterior, I see a painting of a very large and apparently very happy cartoon catfish, grinning the way pigs grin when they are depicted on barbecue signs throughout the South, giddy with the prospect of becoming someone's dinner. I realize stopping for ice was just a ruse, an excuse to set foot in a place so devoid of guile. On the dock outside, next to the orange Fish Scaler machine and vats of live shiners, there is one sign warning "No Bait Allowed in Rental Units" and another advising "Only Authorized Jungle Den Personnel Allowed to Dip Bait." Visions dance in my head of anglers sleeping next to their live shiners, which they've surreptitiously dipped from the live bait well.

I am still in the throes of this vision when a motel room door swings open, and there I see, atop the brown formica bureau, a bait bucket of shiners and a screened box full of madly chirping crickets. The occupant gives me a sheepish look and kicks the door shut with his foot. I have no choice at this point but to submit, to enter the restaurant, find a booth next to the window, order a fried catfish dinner with hushpuppies and a tall glass of iced tea. The St. Johns flows soundlessly by outside, and inside, to the strains of country music, the waitress calls me "Hon," using two syllables to do so. It is delicious, all of it, and I grin like a catfish ready for the batter and deepfry.

"For the last word in procrastination," conservationist Aldo Leopold once wrote, "go travel with a river reluctant to lose his freedom to the sea." And so it is here, at a place where the St. Johns seems undecided about whether it wants to empty itself into the six-mile-wide-by-twelve-mile-long Lake George at all. After flirting briefly with the notion of acting like a deep, ambitious river, it now launches itself into a stupendous series of swampy-edged switchbacks, beginning at Morrison Bluff and climaxing right beneath the funnel-like mouth of the lake itself at the "Volusia Bar." In between are creeks mapped as Hitchens and Payne, Axle and Blue, as twisted as serifs on Old English letters. Each of them seems ripe for exploration by kayak—sloughs and streams and aquatic swales that go nowhere in particular but do it extremely well. Most of this shoaling is alluvial foolery, sediment from miles of upriver conveyance piling itself up below and even in the mouth, like long queues of tourists bottlenecked at a thrill ride gate at Disney World.

When it finally reveals itself, Lake George is a force that demands my full attention. At seventy-two square miles, it is a deep, elongated bowl, so well defined that geologists say it was likely a hollow in the sea bottom, scooped out in that time before Florida arose as a sandbar from the ocean. It is no wonder that dolphins sometimes make it this far upriver to hunt in the coves, maybe answering a pull stronger than any tide.

After Okeechobee, Lake George is the largest lake in Florida. In his 1791 *Travels*, Billy Bartram described it in fearful reverence: "Behold the little ocean of Lake George. . . . I cannot entirely suppress my apprehensions of danger. My vessel at once diminished to a nut shell on the swelling seas." Marjorie Kinnan Rawlings crossed this same little ocean some 150 years later on her own trip downriver in a small boat, every bit as respectful as Billy had been. Before entering the lake, she and her companion, Dessie Smith, stopped at the riverfront home of an old Clyde Line steamboat captain to solicit advice. He advised crossing in the morning, with care, before the sun warmed the great expanse of water and the wind lifted up off it. The safest course was to hug the westward shore.

Although the women left especially early from their overnight camp at "Volusia Bar," they had "no intention of hugging the safe shore," wrote

Rawlings. Their adventurous spirit got them caught in a frothing, white-capped sea across which it took them almost two and a half hours to navigate. As I launch my own crossing, it is a bright, cheery spring day with a sky full of puffy cumulus—so benign it looks like a scene from a preschooler's storybook. Just for this moment, Lake George appears before me as a great pussycat of a lake, a flat mirror that sparkles from one horizon to the next, prisms of sunlight dancing over its vast surface. My boat is much larger than those of my literary predecessors, equipped with a protective cabin and fancy gear. I have maps, radios, fathometer—even a microwave oven—what could go wrong? I am, understandably, overbrimming with confidence, with absolutely no intention of hugging the safe shore.

Fencelike wooden jetties that funnel outward from the narrow southern entrance to the lake are the only tangible sign of menace, for they mark the way through the famous sand and mud shoals known as the Volusia Bar. Steamboat captains routinely grounded here, forced to wait for another paddlewheeler to come along and pull them off. I aim for the middle of the channel on the approach, not fully appreciating the presence of the sandy shoals until an errant wind hits my houseboat broadside and I drift a few feet off course. As I do, my depth-finder drops almost immediately from a reading of twelve feet to something akin to scrapping bottom. Within seconds, my speed drops from five knots per hour to a zero, and I realize I am hope-lessly grounded, fathometer, microwave, and all.

It is midweek, and there is no other boat in sight to tow me off, let alone a sympathetic steamship captain. But I am lucky enough to have a friend aboard for this leg of the journey, and between tossing out the anchor and retrieving it in some giant tug-of-war, we are able finally to pull ourselves free of the bar's famous treachery. By the time we are done, the flat lake is corrugated and lightly whitecapped, which gives the hull a gentle rock as it plows easily through the water.

The lake, named for England's crazed King George III when Florida was British, is the last great expanse of wildness on the middle river. Its higher western shore is rimmed entirely by national forest, while a forty-square-mile chunk of state-owned conservation land surrounds Willow Cove on its lower, swampier easterly edge. Most of the rest is owned by private timber companies.

Ospreys have been with me on the river ever since my first airboat visit to the headwaters. It is always a welcome sight to see them, for they are impressive raptors, steely and cautious hunters as well as ambitious builders of twig nests the size of bushel baskets, nests they build larger each season. On Lake George, they also seemed to have modified their standard practice of fish snatching. In most places, that practice relies on using their deadeye visual acuity to spot a single fish from the air and then dropping like a missile, talons first, to snatch the unfortunate specimen out of the water. Here, though, ospreys actually troll the surface of the lake with their talons for hundreds of feet at a time, hoping to nab some hapless, surface-feeding critter. It is more of a shotgun approach to feeding, instead of a single, well-aimed rifle shot, but it seems to work very well.

Lake George also marks the appearance of another larger and more endangered raptor, the southern bald eagle, *Haliaeetus leucocephalus*. Because eagles feed mainly on fish—either directly or by stealing them from ospreys—they build their own nests no farther than two miles from the water. And Lake George has nothing if not lots of water. Bald eagles, which were almost wiped out in this country because of hunting and DDT-damaged eggs a half century ago, are making a slow but steady comeback, and Lake George is a staging ground for this revival. There is more great irony here: although this elegant raptor is often pictured in dramatically mountainous settings, there are more bald eagles in swampy Florida than in any other state except Alaska. Within Florida, the greatest concentration of nests in any single area is the Ocala National Forest, where fifty-six were reported in a wildlife study in 1994. With binoculars, I see two eagles near the lake today, one soaring over with giant twigs for her nest; the other dive-bombing an osprey to get the smaller bird to drop its freshly caught mullet.

When Sidney Lanier visited the lake during his trip upriver in 1875, he reported even then that Lake George was noted for its birds, including the flocks of forest-green "paroquets." But Lanier hinted at other secrets here as well. "I am informed," he wrote in his Florida guidebook, "that some notable mineral springs have recently been discovered here." The "paroquets" have been gone for a while. In their place are more modern, exotic birds—fighter planes that use an extensive bombing range covering one-fourth of the eastern side of the lake. Dummy bombs are said to be used in this practice instead of live ones. But *dummy* is surely a relative term. And the prospect of having planes roaring over, spitting neutered rockets about inside one of Florida's great freshwater wilderness areas, doesn't strike me as particularly rational way to care for the riverine environment.

There are no bombs being dropped today. But as I chug along through the lake, I notice nature has its own volatile surprise in store: the scattered, gentle whitecaps I saw not long ago have grown in proportion to my distance from the shore. It appears that the sleeping pussycat of a lake is waking up and is a bit grumpy to boot. A strong wind is now blowing toward me from the opposite end of Lake George, delivering watery tannin hills with it that hiss with spindrift.

In no time, Bartram's little ocean becomes just that, with baby whitecaps metamorphosing into large, angry waves that crash repeatedly into the bow, splashing over onto the deck. The boat lists at a dangerously steep angle, drawers slam open and shut, glasses crash onto the floor, and I stagger at the wheel like a drunken sailor, holding on for dear life. My vessel has metaphorically shrunk to the size of a nut in the vast churning seas, just like Bartram's once did. I look anxiously for a shoreline and see none, just acres and acres of whitecaps and waves. While a small part of my mind tells me there's a certain historic symmetry in all this, a much larger part tells me to *get off the lake*.

Symmetry trailing in my wake, I aim for the opening to Silver Glen Springs on the distant westerly shore. As I approach the lee of the tree line there, the water calms. Looking closely, I see the lake's surface transform from muddy to clear, a sure sign of the spring-fed plume moving outward from the mouth of Silver Glen's run. I look back at the still-frothing lake. The sun is shining, but the great puffs of cumulus are scattered across the sky in brushlike streaks, torn by the wind. Locals say, by winter, a good gray northeasterly storm will send six-foot-high waves rolling across Lake George, and I don't doubt them for a second.

6 *Juniper Springs to Croaker Hole*

The sluggish flow of the river tends to encourage and maintain wetland habitats throughout its length, thus preserving the natural appearance of much of the river corridor.—From the state's "Florida Rivers Assessment" report of 1989

*O*f the "notable mineral springs" Sidney Lanier once reported along the river in his guidebook, the three most powerful emerge from the hilly karst terrain of the Ocala National Forest. They seem spaced, territorially, along the western shore, each with its own hydrological fiefdom: Juniper to the south, Silver Glen in the middle, and Salt to the north. Geologically, all arise from the limestone and dolomite of the Ocala Uplift, sedimentary bits of sand and coral and shell laid down as sea bottom in the Eocene some forty million to fifty million years ago.

Juniper is a thin, enchanting scribble of a clear creek fed not just by its namesake but by other spring boils along its run, including Fern Hammock and Sweetwater. It is a canoeable place, a narrow respite from the overwhelming largeness of Lake George. Salt, ensconced at the end of a shallow five-mile run through a lush green corridor, arises from four separate vents inside a limestone basin. Although owners of larger boats complain that the outflowing run is too shallow for them, it is precisely this shallowness that keeps the shoreline of the creek as undisturbed as it is. Eagles nest here above, bluegill below, the fish scalloping out rounded underwater beds from the sand with their tails.

Salt Springs is aptly named: ancient, deeply embedded veins of connate seawater hot-wire the chloride content of its outflow, at a rate much higher than any other spring in the region. Compared with Juniper, Salt carries four hundred times the dosage of chloride; in contrast to Silver Glen, three times. There are no "salt beds" the water passes through to make this so, as is popularly believed. Rather, its brackishness is the result of relic seawater entering the aquifer in distant geological time, when Florida was nearly covered by the ocean. It is no wonder that a submerged marine grass (*Haisa marina*) found nowhere else along the freshwater river grows here in profusion, no wonder that a four-foot-long blacktip shark was recently spotted, swimming upstream, in the run of Salt.

In Bartram's time, the force of the upwelling at Salt was so strong that it was described as "a continual and amazing ebullition where the waters are thrown up in such abundance and amazing force as to jet and swell up to two or three feet above the common surface." Today the surface is nearly flat, showing only ripples of a mild boil. Perhaps well pumping in the fast-growing city of Ocala to the far west has increased at the same time recharge areas have declined. There is simply less *ibi* to be had, a sign of finite hydrological power defused.

The 625-square-mile national forest here surrounds the most extensive scrub environment in the world, one marked by sand hills and rolling scrub communities, covered mostly with sand pine and the stunted Chapman and myrtle oaks. Locally, the forest is even called the "Big Scrub." Admittedly, this does not sound like much—a big scrubby forest?—until you realize it implies the presence of a unique diversity of plants and animals that have learned to survive in desertlike conditions. It is hot and dry here, and the relic inland sand dunes of sugar-white quartzy sand readily drain rainwater down into the limestone below like a sieve. As a result, fauna and flora, such as Florida scrub jays and sandhill cranes, Florida mountain mint and fall-flowering ixia, have learned to adapt. And they have done so in a rarefied place where the aquifer is also revitalized. The result is a sunny, natural xeric landscape above and a clutch of forever dark underground rivers below.

Because high and dry also means geologically ancient in Florida, the region now covered by the forest was among the first places in the interior to be settled by humans. *Ocala* itself comes almost directly from an old Timucuan name, Ocali, which implied many things bucolic—fertile soil, green, fair land, abundant, even big, hammock.

The artesian springs here were often the oases for such settlements—from the Native Americans of the Early Archaic period up through the twentieth century. An archaeological survey that covered just one-third of the entire forest recorded more than five hundred sites, from an extensive eight-thousand-year-old snail shell midden to Spanish camps and early historic "cracker" settlements. I ease my large boat up the half-mile-long spring run along the midwestern shore, toward the natural bowl of Silver Glen.

Somewhere off this run is another spring, one so tiny that it is not even reported today on hydrological surveys. It is "Jody's Spring," so depicted by Rawlings in her opening chapter to *The Yearling* in 1939. Naturalist Archie Carr, also enamored with the artesian vents of the St. Johns, later visited Jody's Spring. "There is no one big, river-making outpouring," said Carr, "but instead a scattering of gentle little geysers of crystal water and snowy sand bubbling in the bottom of a shallow pool surrounded by evergreen hammock. . . . Some of the boils are no bigger than your fist, some are the size of a washtub."

With veteran cave cartographer Eric Hutcheson, I've received special permission to explore the underwater system beneath Silver Glen itself. Hutcheson, an easygoing native who lives nearby in Ocala, has traveled worldwide to map similar karst environments, sometimes journeying back for miles under the earth to do so, using aquatic scooters and highly technical diving gear. In the depths of Silver Springs, near the headwaters of the Ocklawaha, he once led a special expedition that not only produced the first map of that cave but also collected rare, endemic crayfish and shrimplike amphipods for the Smithsonian Institution.

Like other spring runs I encounter along the river, Silver Glen protectively nourishes the flora with its presence, turning it into a community classified as a "hydric hammock"—a soggy, ever moist jungle. Heat, combined with lots of water, is what makes any good jungle. And this spring run has both, with wild grape and Virginia creeper vine braided in the foliage, and epiphytic mosses, lichens, and wild orchids hidden in the crooks of nearly each branch. There is also a marked difference between the heights of trees, shrubs, and herbs, which are layered like a rainforest canopy.

The waters of the run itself are as clear as air and, because of its recent odyssey through the limestone, alkaline enriched. Sunlight penetrates more fully through these waters than through the oblique, tannic-stained river, a reality easily experienced with just mask, snorkel, and flippers. To go into a spring run in such a way is like stepping through to the other side of the looking glass. Just inches under the surface, I now have a mask-sized perspective of a giant, well-stocked fish tank. Except I am the one inside the glass, and everything else is outside. Around me, entire pastures of eel grass

(*Vallisneria americana*)—the river's most common underwater plant—flourish here, helping to anchor a fecund and diverse food chain.

Water clarity is a factor scientists use to determine how bountiful any section of the river can be. Studies clearly show the link between thriving "submerged" vegetation and the presence of all manner of wildlife, from apple snails to limpkins to largemouth bass. But when storm water–driven sediments enter the river and join the humus-bred tannins to darken the water further, bottom plants—fresh or estuarine—die from lack of sun.

Topside, I look in vain for a royal palm, a tropical, less cold-hardy variety of *palmae* with pinnate fronds much softer than those of the brittle sabal and saw palmetto. These trees, with tall cement-gray trunks rising out of the canopy, once thrived along the St. Johns, as recently as the time of Bartram's visit. Botanists speculate that a series of hard freezes between then and now drove the palm away, for the closest wild groves are now two hundred miles south.

Silver Glen is unique in the valley in that its run is short, deep, and easy to navigate. Unlike Blue, its basin is not a manatee sanctuary with restricted entry. When I reach its source after just a few minutes traveling across its creek, I see a springhead gently churling up Windex-blue water inside a natural amphitheater, one framed with towering cypress, backgrounded with a blufflike Indian midden. There is a rare natural aesthetic here, one birthed by the unique hydrology of the river valley. Archie Carr tapped into this aesthetic as well as anyone. Here he is in 1975, describing such phenomena: "Each spring is different from all the others," observed Carr, "but in the intensity of its grace and color each is a little ecological jewel in which geology and biology have created a masterwork of natural art."

People have been living around geysers like this on the river for at least eight thousand years—perhaps visiting them even longer. That's because the artesian upwelling at Silver Glen was pure and consistent—back in a time when the St. Johns itself was still shifting, intermittent, unsure. The spring sustained all manner of life, surely. But it also sustained a promise, too, a natural sensibility into which cultural magic could be woven.

Yet promises can be transient in a place like Florida. And Silver Glen has a reputation not just as a pristine alcove of water and land but as a place to *par-dee, dude.* In this way, weekends and holidays transform the spring into a floating, gunnel-to-gunnel bacchanalia where the raison d'être seems to be showing off one's boat, playing music at impressively high decibel levels, getting half naked, and entering a state where you can't much tell a bullhead from a Budweiser—and don't much care, anyway.

It is Monday, and the party is mostly over, but as Hutcheson and I motor into the basin, there are still a few stragglers about. One is a rather smug, cigar-smoking middle-aged sybarite who has moored his sleek fiberglass craft from bow to stern alongside the floating line stretched outside the immediate springhead, blocking much of the view. As I putter in, he briefly stands on the stern deck of his boat with his pedigree pit bull, under the colorful collegiate banner he has hung there, and ridicules my navigation skills. Then, he goes back inside his air-conditioned cabin. Later in the day, as I prepare to dive into the cave, I will see this same fellow floating over the spring in an inflatable lounge chair, still smoking his cigar, yammering. The spectacular artesian phenomenon of the spring and the sublime nuances of all it has created here seem to have been consigned by him to the ranks of a very large swimming pool.

Silver Glen may be the biggest lesson in *access* I've yet to find along the river. It clearly illustrates the classic argument between national park service advocate John Muir and Gifford Pinchot, architect of the U.S. Forest Service—between the closely supervised preservation of wilderness and unlimited public use on demand. It is an argument historically paralleled since the earliest days when Europeans first ascended the St. Johns, each of them pleading to appreciate it or clamoring to exploit it. There's little doubt where my sympathies lie. Whenever in doubt, I turn back to Muir, who hiked across the lower river basin in 1867, for solace. "I have precious little sympathy for the selfish propriety of civilized man," wrote Muir then, "and if a war of races should occur between the wild beasts and Lord Man, I would be tempted to sympathize with the bears."

It is with that perspective that I welcome the underwater side of Silver Glen, an aquatic door through which I can instantly distance myself from Lord Man. I do so by strapping on scuba tanks and descending at the edge of the spring basin with Hutcheson. Around me, entire fields of the flat-bladed eel grass undulate, textured whitish by the geohydrology: it is carbonate, rained down from the water as the bicarbonate of the limestone-bound upwelling is first exposed to the air. Through these pastures, schools of striped mullet swim in unison, moving like one very large and graceful aquatic animal, dozens of smaller parts instantly acknowledging a greater sum.

Of the two cavern entrances at Silver Glen, one is reached through a symmetrical well-like hole that plunges down into the limestone; the other, via a narrow horizontal slit in the rock. The well is chock full of giant silvery "stripers," five- and ten-pound striped bass, which circle endlessly, like caged animals, cold-blooded animals enamored by the relative warmth of the spring. Classified as *Morone saxatilis*, they are nothing like a freshwater largemouth at all. Normally, they are anadromous, seasonal visitors from the sea, like shad and sturgeon. Except in this case, the stripers have become so enamored by the thermal allure of the springs that they no longer go back to sea, as they do elsewhere along the entire eastern seaboard. In Florida, they can grow to mammoth sizes: in 1979, a state record was set for a striper at 38½ pounds.

As I gently free-fall, flippers first, down through the center of the well-like vent, the stripers swim a wider circle to let me pass, and then close the circle above me after I do. In the dark cave at the bottom, the sand beneath me moves as I put my gloved hand on it. I look down, startled, and see a tiny, palm-sized saltwater flatfish skittering away, both eyes vigilant from atop the same side of its head. Both gulf and southern flounder range far upstream in the St. Johns, but this is more likely a sole, *Trinectes maculatus*, a flounder cousin that Archie Carr once found living in spring environments along the river.

Unlike the stronger-swimming tarpon and snook and shark, which can journey between the river and the sea, smaller, sedentary fish like this sole may even be marine relics, consigned by time to the mineral springs. Have they been speciated yet by the experience, reshaped by the insular environment like Darwin's finches in the Galapagos? It is a good question, one that a molecular biologist or an anatomist may some day even answer—indeed, it was an inquiry posed by Carr in the 1950s.

After some cursory poking about at the base of the well, we resurface and fin over to the other nearby vent for a real cave penetration. As Hutcheson and I sink deeper, the cave mouth appears before us in the side of rock as a dark, crescent-shaped maw. Hutcheson fights his way in through the narrow opening first, and I follow, scraping my tanks on the limestone ledge and pushing my mask down into the white, shelly sand, both wiggling with my body and grasping rock to pull my way with my hands against the tremendous outflow of water.

On the other side of the maw, back in the darkness, I see a gargantuan blue crab, nearly a foot wide from tip to tip, waving its claws at me in territorial menace. In the white sand bottom, I pick up fragments of a fossilized clam, a sea-bottom relic, both shell halves welded together for eternity. Earlier, Hutcheson told me he had found an entire bed of breadbox-sized clams in the depths of the Silver Springs cave, a bivalve swept into extinction long before humans evolved to name it.

Both cave vents intersect and trail under the landscape for well over two football field lengths, before culminating in a massive room one hundred feet high by ninety feet wide, an abyss Hutcheson has mapped as "Assum Pit." Some seventy-two million gallons a day course out of Silver Glen, nibbling away at the limestone for thousands of years, carving caverns like this from the soft rock in the cryptic darkness.

Back on the walls of Assum Pit is a yellow lichenlike growth that one cave-diving biologist dubbed "iron bacteria." Eels, those critters with the great sense of smell, travel all the way back to the pit, feeding on the patina of troglodytic yellow growth there, fulfilling an ecological niche that raises more questions than it answers. Along the way, they pass the large freshwater *Macrobrachium* shrimp, pigmentless, slender claws waving in the dark.

At the bottom of the pit, the cave narrows and plunges, deeper down into the aquifer, well beyond 160 feet, a territory yet unseen by humans. Technical divers like Hutcheson are just now exploring the outside limits of places such as this. What they find will help us better understand not only how large these mysterious unseen reservoirs are and what lives inside but what kind of hydrological links occur between upland recharge areas, surface pollution, even sinkhole formation. Decisions allowing growth and development in Florida are often based on surface water flow—indeed, that's why the five water management districts are each set up around a major river system, like the St. Johns. But the subterranean realities of a system like Silver Glen are forces to be reckoned with. They affect any land use equation, whether they are factored in by Lord Man or not.

Still, there is something more here to be considered. There is discovery-era art afoot, too—wilderness maps captured from the brink of exploration by cartographer Hutcheson. Like the earliest Le Moyne prints of five centuries ago, it is art that illustrates a reality few have ever seen, a first draft of history that shows others the way.

That such "voyages of discovery" occur within yards of some of the most raucous topside displays of known civilization along the river is, indeed, nothing if not *assum.*

Lake George is doing its quiet, glass-flat imitation again this morning, perhaps hoping to entice some foolhardy souls out onto its middle so it can batter the bejesus out of them. Ecologically, the wind-driven chaos is actually welcome, as the waves churn the surface, oxygenating the waters below in a way the barely flowing channel never could in a lake this large.

I spin the wheel to take me and my boat north, beyond the truncated peninsula mapped as Yellow Bluff and the outflow of Salt Springs run, tucked back inside the westerly dilation of Salt Cove. As I do, a large, brownish animal materializes from the woods of the cove. Watching it through my binoculars, I see it is a white-tailed deer, a tawny doe, and it has come from the forest to drink, head down in the blue-flowered pickerel weed at the lake's edge, an animal with no horn at all.

Drayton Island looms before me as a giant, forested hammock. At three miles by one mile in breadth, it is large enough that—if I didn't know better—I could slip around its westerly shore without even realizing it was an island at all, passing an outcropping called Rocky Point and a smaller island mapped as Hog. Yet the map shows the deeper navigational channel flowing along the *easterly* rim of the Drayton, helping to create an island in the shape of a large spatulate leaf.

There are only three public ferries left on the entire St. Johns, and one of them connects the mainland with Drayton here. It is a flat, wood-planked barge of a floating platform that holds two cars maximum at any given time and runs on a schedule that—as far as I can figure—is pegged to certain moon phases. Less, surely, is better for the handful of people who live here, and the only way to guarantee this minimalism is by the slimmest thread of access. Or, as one guide to the river notes: "Drayton Island is privately owned and very wary of outsiders."

Le Moyne, on an exploratory journey upriver from Fort Caroline, was one of the first white people to see the island. Then, it was called Eldelano, for the Timucuan chief who ruled it. It was thick with live oak trees, rich with nuts, fruits, and berries, and so full of wild game that Native Americans fought over who should have the privilege to hunt them. The French artist was smitten. It was, he reported, "the most delightful of all islands in the new world."

Two centuries later, when Billy Bartram stopped to spend the night atop a pile of soft Spanish moss under the protective canopy of one of the ancient oaks, the island was uninhabited. But, he noted, it "appears from obvious vestiges to have been once the chosen residence of an Indian prince." Bear, turkeys, wolves, and wild cats lived here, said Billy, along with "many curious shrubs," including the lantana, several species of wild hibiscus, and morning glory. As the botanist made his bed under his chosen oak, "the tender warblings" of a painted bunting in its branches sang him asleep.

Neither Bartram or Le Moyne are commemorated on Drayton. But Zephaniah Kingsley is. The southernmost tip of the island is named for him, Kingsley Point, and somewhere there are the remains of his plantation—one of a chain of farms, in fact, built between here and Fort George Island east of Jacksonville between 1803 and 1821. Kingsley, a maritime merchant, shipbuilder, and slave trader, owned some three hundred slaves and prided himself in his egalitarian treatment of them, establishing training courses to teach them job skills. His wife, Anna Madgigaine Jai Kingsley, was from Senegal, a former purchase herself, who learned to help Zephaniah run his businesses.

I stop briefly on Drayton, visiting with a writer and an artist who live here in a 180-year-old former manor house that was once the center of a sprawling indigo plantation. The directions I follow to reach them are as locked in time as the island itself: they are based not on street numbers but on how many pilings and docks and old boathouses I pass before coming to the correct one. Even then, I have to anchor out, at the edge of the windward sandy bar, and putter in on a small, shallow-draft dinghy.

We seem to care most deeply about rivers when we have invested time and effort actually on them—canoeing, fishing, exploring, observing. We have to put in to get back out. Perhaps, you can invest no more time on a river than to live in a place where that current not just passes you by but surrounds you on all sides. Ashore, I discover there are only eleven families on Drayton, and nearly every need—but friendship—must be acquired back on the mainland. "I like the difficulty of living on this island," the artist,

JUNIPER SPRINGS TO CROAKER HOLE 117

Mary Lee Adler, tells me, clear eyes shining brightly, a choice based not on chain-store expediency but on something more enduring.

Adler, a sculptor who has lived in Miami and England, drives me over the island's lone dirt path in her beat-up white Ford pickup. Here, we pass an ambling gopher tortoise and meet a retired sea captain poking in his garden, his scientist wife, and their young daughter lovingly named for the most predominant natural feature in all their lives, Lake. Finally, with the scientist and Lake in tow, we visit what Draytonites reverently refer to as "the Tree." It is a majestic live oak, surely old enough to be here when Bartram— even Le Moyne—visited.

The leafy canopy is the size of a barn, its lower limbs horizontal and splayed out on the ground, tired perhaps from centuries of holding themselves upright. I walk gingerly up one, picking my way to the heart of the generous trunk. There, I brace myself, standing up inside a natural scaffolding of limbs that extend maternally outward in every direction. I could tell you I felt a lot of things then, and I did. But most of all, high above the ground, inside the cradle of the venerable tree, I felt safe, beyond harm.

Leaving Drayton, I pass a series of fish camps and marinas on the river's easterly shore, a thriving cottage industry to service boaters and sport anglers, modern evidence of the environment continuing to shape culture, just as it did for the Timucua.

In this particular culture, giant largemouth bass are portrayed ferociously. In signs, on souvenirs, and on murals, the predatory fish usually fires itself up from the water like a Triton missile, purple rubber worm lure in the crook of a mouth the size of a small cavern. Within this perspective, this missile fish almost always dwarfs the tiny boat and fishers, far off in the background. Archaeologists of the future, finding icons like this, might come to believe there once lived bass several times the size of boats in the St. Johns.

While coveted, largemouth aren't the only fish of sport. There are also smaller "panfish," usually variations of the stubbed-nosed, disk-shaped little fighters northerners lump together as bluegill and southerners as bream. Taxonomically, there are eleven different kinds of bluegill/bream in the river, and all are linked, if not by genus, then at least at the next step, family. Most are *Lepomis*—including the brilliantly colored redbreast sunfish and the red-ear sunfish. They are all tenacious and daring, if a fish can be such things, every bit as pugnacious as their tough little faces would have you believe. I have flyfished with chartreuse-colored, eraser-sized poppers along the river, and tiny bream one and two inches long have attacked them with fury—even when the popper is too large to fit in their mouths.

The northern mouth of Lake George marks the routine reach of tides, some 110 miles from the sea. And while marine fish, as I have found, roam far upstream beyond here for very good reasons, Lake George northward spells out a more regular territory for them. Although the terrestrial environment still remains decidedly fresh—and will for a while—anything goes underwater. Mangrove snapper and redfish begin to appear, joining the saltwater mullet and striped bass and sea lamprey already here. Of these saltwater visitors, one is federally listed as endangered. It is the shortnose sturgeon, *Acipenses brevirostrum*, and it is found in no other Florida rivers. It may even be endemic. Yet federal protection of such critters can sometimes lag dangerously behind reality: the existence of the shortnose sturgeon hasn't been confirmed since the early 1980s, and its appearance is mostly consigned to lists, on paper and not in the water.

Odd little marine fish also begin to show up here more often, too, critters anglers are seldom likely to encounter. One is the opossum pipefish—a member of the same family as seahorses, looking much like a seahorse would look if someone grasped its snout in one hand and its tail in the other and pulled it until it straightened. Along with the opossum, which is scarce enough to be considered threatened, there are three more of its brethren hereabouts—the chain, gulf, and northern pipefish.

Another oddity is the Lilliputian goby, normally a cylindrical-shaped fish not much longer than my little finger. Found here in twelve different species, the goby is known to rest on the bottom, propped up on its lower front fins. In a surge or current, a suction is often formed between the ventral fins to anchor them in place. As gobies go, one is particularly rare, if also a bit more ambitious when it comes to size: it is the river goby, and it grows to almost a foot, flat head above an olive tan body, crossbars on its pectorals.

If there was a blacktip reported in the run of Salt Springs, there are surely other sharks about as well—although this is not a fact local chambers of commerce are likely to promote. In 1955, Archie Carr wondered about such inland sharks. While admitting that none had been positively identified, Carr said it was "well known" that sharks visited Florida rivers, and shark remora had been seen in the runs. Of the sharks, he figured, the ones most likely to swim upstream would be the massive bull, which can range up to ten feet in length, and the much smaller sharpnosed. A 1995 "Checklist of Fishes Recorded from the Rivers of Florida" cataloged the tiger and scalloped hammerhead as "occasional" visitors to the St. Johns.

All these fishes, however, marine or freshwater, are at least native. Far more bizarre are the exotics, which—by example of the blue tilapia alone—can do very well for themselves here. Most are tropicals released by aquarium keepers and kept under natural check by the colder winter river, which discourages reproduction. But this is not always so. Topping the list of anomalies is the pacu, a sharp-toothed, red-bellied look-alike for the piranha from South America. Even though the fish is said to be vegetarian, well over a dozen have been caught by fishers on bait in the river. A state wildlife biologist predicts the pacu will be the next exotic to become fully established in Florida, with the St. Johns becoming the fish's very own Amazon, a home away from home.

Bulkheaded shores have been appearing and disappearing along the river since Lake Monroe, and I can usually predict their existence by looking closely at the map. If there is any sort of a riverside community present, there is usually a concrete wall built to keep the community from washing away, to make the ever shifting meander behave.

One such place is Fort Gates on the westerly bank. Its name alone implies it was used as a fort or at least an encampment of soldiers during the "Indian Wars," as most all the "forts" of Florida once were. An early schedule from the DeBary-Baya Merchants Line of paddlewheelers lists Fort Gates as a stop, some 106 miles from the main port at Jacksonville. With one exception, there is little remarkable about this old landing. Yet that exception is a grand one indeed, pulled nearly intact from the river's past, as complete as the vision of Bill Dreggors back on Hontoon Island. It is one of the most classical gothic-style mansions I have ever seen—complete with its own gothic boathouse. Gables are piled atop gables, and filagree dances a slow waltz around each window and along the edges of the peaked red roof. At this moment, it is not quite abandoned, but it is not kept up either, and shabbiness is setting in.

An 1880 guidebook to the river describes this home as "one of the finest residences on the St. Johns [belonging to] S.U. Hammond, esq., editor of the Putnam County Journal"—which in that time meant something. Originally, the house was built by a Union officer during the Civil War, and U.S. government soldiers were quartered here to stop Confederate blockade runners carrying supplies up and down the river. What remains of this rich history is a cultural snapshot of an archaic concern for ornate detail, as baroque as a wood duck, as lushly romantic as Billy Bartram's prose. If God is in the details, as the architectural designer Ludwig Mies van der Rohe once wrote, then God is lavish, indeed. Perhaps some romantic will come and care for it all someday.

Awash in such ponderings, I barely notice Mount Royal, which I pass on the right bank, hidden somewhere behind the tree line on a bluff. Like the massive midden back at Blue Spring, it represents one of the major ceremonial centers built by pre-Columbians along the river, back when nomadic bands began to settle, to plant crops and to acquire the markings of a more complex, stratified society. Down deep in the mound are historic snapshots, perhaps thousands of them still waiting to be developed. Another ferry crosses here, this one larger and more serious than the two-car affair back at Drayton. This one is a fifteen-foot-long barge hitched to the side of a tug; the half mile of river it crosses for several dollars is worth the time it saves in land miles. The last upstream road bridge was at Astor, thirty miles south; the next won't appear until Palatka, another thirty river miles north. The ferry splits the difference.

In one form or another, a ferry has been crossing here at least since 1856 when the United States ordered its troops from one bank to another, pursuing Seminoles who refused to do exactly as they were told by a government that made little sense to them. Like the oil barges that tugs still push up and down the St. Johns, the ferry is one of the last working threads of busy commerce the river once commandeered. In this way, the ferry doesn't so much save time as relive it.

The St. Johns, briefly, expands here, and the riverbanks fall back in a hint of what is later to come. In fact, this is not just the channel but a place mapped as "Little Lake George," and it is nearly a mile from one bank of the "lake" to the other. The channel passes to the west, and to the east the river slouches out into two shallow coves. In one called Buzzard Roost Cove, several old sabal palms poke out of a tiny marshy island of grasses, pipe stem–like trunks worn smooth by age. I steer the boat cautiously in the shallow water not far from it and anchor for the night. Cave mapper Hutcheson is still with me, and we throw some chicken on the gas grill on the stern of the boat and wait for the darkness of the cove to settle around us. In the morning, we will explore a powerful artesian spring notable for being located not at the beginning of a run near the river but on the river bottom itself.

For now, I sit on the stern, watching the sporadic lights of sport boats move up and down the river off to the west, until finally there are no lights at all except the blink of a distant green channel marker. It is full moon now, and the pale light of it reflects on the water, as if creating a pathway from the top of the night sky to my place on the river, a path punctuated with the soft, easy calls of a barred owl, the sudden, rumbling grunts of a large gator, both out feeding nocturnally as they have always done here, in the cypress woods and under the water.

Morning comes soon enough, and with it, our drive across the cove to the river-bottom spring. This place, mapped as "Croaker Hole," is not hard to find: by 7 A.M., there are a half dozen small boats of fishers anchored around it, lines dangling down in the water.

Although I am now in the "tidal range" of the river, measuring such events goes far beyond consulting a tide chart to show how much the river rises or falls during flows and ebbs. There are many other considerations beyond moon phases to influence this—including atmospheric pressure, wind, the depth of the bottom and the width of the shores, the discharges of tributaries and of springs, and the wet-dry, seasonal rate of flow from far upstream. Too, water with a high salinity is more dense than water without. That alone affects how a tide moves along the river, with the fresher water sometimes riding up over the incoming tides. At such times, the river may even have two "currents," one flowing north on the top and one headed south on the bottom.

Anchored over Croaker Hole, I now descend into this odd river, after finding an open patch of surface that is clear of the eager lines and hooks and hulls of those who are fishing. The danger of diving in such places is not the potential of alligators or curious sharks or strange, diverging black currents but the spinning boat props of anglers anxious to belly up to the hole or, once satiated, to zoom away—regardless of where one's head might happen to be on the ascent or descent. I have seen alligators underwater before, and I can tell you the primitive madness in their eyes is nothing compared with the obsession of an angler determined to bring home a whopper.

Hutcheson has descended first, long enough to plant our anchor on the fifteen-foot bottom near the opening to the spring cave. Letting the air gradually out of my buoyant dive vest, I flip over and pull myself, hand over hand, down the anchor line, through the murky tea of the river water. I trust Hutcheson has put the anchor near the cave entrance, but the visibility is so poor that I can barely see my hands as I make my way down the rope. During the first ten feet, the bright sun backlights the black-red tannin, making it seem as if I am free-falling through the living veins of the St. Johns itself.

Finally, at the entrance to the spring on the bottom, the water becomes as clear as any swimming pool I've ever been in. But with the dense layer of tannic river to screen the sun overhead, it may as well be midnight down here. I flick my underwater light on, and its beam illuminates Hutcheson, who hovers at the entrance to the boulder-strewn cave. The rounded cavern seems to burrow gradually down into the limestone like a massive natural shaft, large enough to hold a subway train.

As my beam plays over the limestone walls, I watch in awe as reflective shards of light dance inside the cave, much the same way light does back on the surface at night when a flashlight beam bounces from the river to the trees, rippling them with its movement. I settle down beside Hutcheson here on the bottom, as if meeting a fellow traveler at a prearranged rendezvous in the middle of the night.

At his signal, we both rise up and fin across the beachlike white sand, scattering the jubilee of five-pound stripers circling at the portal. We are headed, upstream, as far as we can get into the shaft. As with the other caves we have penetrated along the river, the outflow of water from this hole is spectacular, and simply swimming in with my fins is out of the question. Using my bare hands, I pull my way inside, boulder by boulder, along the cave floor. As I do, I feel the rounded edges of the large rocks, worn smooth by the water's energy. I see the same force has also striated the cave walls around me, making them seem like large carved blocks, quarried and mortared together, nature's own water-filled basement, mineralized black with age. My depth gauge registers the slight incline of the tunnel as we follow it downward, from sand into rock: first, thirty feet, then fifty, sixty, and seventy feet.

The upwelling I am fighting feels every bit as powerful as that of the more famous artesian flow back at Blue Springs. Flow meters once placed in Croaker Hole, in fact, show it pumps out at least 119 cubic feet per second of water—some 52 million gallons per day—which is only 32 percent less than the first magnitude strength of Blue.

Like Blue and Salt and Silver Glen, there is more than one vent inside the cavern, and each seems to function as a separate conduit from the aquifer. I try to pull inside one hole just large enough for me and my tank, but its flow won't let me in more than a few feet. The astounding thing about this single vent is not its power but the way it creates a halocline with its infusion of salts, a visible "layer" distinct from the rest of the fresh, crystal-clear spring waters. I look down at the gauge that shows me how much air I have remaining in my tank and see that the halocline refracts the light. The numbers on my gauge become wavy, out of focus, as if I am looking out through very old window glass. If connate seawater is buried deeper in the aquifer, then this capillary must connect with a reservoir very far away, indeed, in both distance and time.

I release the edge of my rocky holdfast in the side vent, and the current instantly blows me out, effortlessly knocking me over like a rag doll with a hydrological flip of its hand. Finally, I end up flat on my back atop my tank near the tunnel entrance, turned turtle by forces that probably predate the river itself.

Naturalist Archie Carr once wondered why there were croakers in Croaker Hole. Like a good teacher, he also speculated an answer, one in which some springs were already actively flowing when the St. Johns Basin was still a marine lagoon. Perhaps, said Carr, these vents even emerged from *under* the lagoon itself, just as some springs today still bubble up into the sea offshore Florida.

When the sea level last reconfigured itself, some of these upwellings acquired a woody landscape in which they could nestle enchantingly, a site to give man and woman space to settle and grow culturally. Maybe Croaker Hole was among them—like the other springs of the Ocali. If this was so, the meander of the river has surely done its work well since then, fully drowning this particular spring and erasing any trace of its terrestrial existence. In the other possible scenario, Croaker Hole never had a topside presence at all. In this incarnation, it has remained underwater all its life, toiling away here unseen on the river bottom just as it once did on the older lagoon floor, rife with marine critters—a place for the Atlantic croaker, *Micropogonias undulatus*, to visit, or a place that it never left.

Back here in the foyer of Croaker Hole, I look over to see Hutcheson making hasty sketches on a plastic slate, measurements to help define the parameter of this place, mapping the hidden dimensions of Florida's past. Who can say what is deeper inside this vent, beyond what we have seen today? Like earlier cartographers, Hutcheson might well inscribe "Here Be Dragons" at the edge of what we know.

I shine my light around me and see stripers, an American eel, two blue crabs, several bream, a yearling largemouth. Dangling just at the edge of my light beam are the eager lines of the anglers, fifteen feet above and a good eon or so away.

7 Ocklawaha to "Charlottia"

> We turned . . . into the narrow land of the Ocklawaha, the sweetest water-lane
>
> in the world, a lane which runs for more than 150 miles of pure delight . . . as if
>
> God had turned into water and trees the recollection of some meditative ramble
>
> through the lonely seclusions of his own soul—Sidney Lanier, *Florida: Its*
>
> *Scenery, Climate, and History* (1875)

*F*or a river as famous as the Ocklawaha, its confluence with the
St. Johns is unheralded, accomplished through a subtle break in the cypress
woods behind a vast pod of hyacinths and grassy maidencane on the western shore, little more than an aquatic murmur. Except for its presence on my
map, there's no indication that this is even the Ocklawaha at all: there are
no signs, no markers, no classical Florida hype of the sort one might find on
a terrestrial site of this magnitude.

Coming upon the Ocklawaha in this way is like walking into a deserted
movie theater—a show with no ushers or ticket takers, but one where the film
is still playing over and over. Once here, you slip quietly into a solitary seat
in the cool darkness, picking up where the last person left off, a person who
might have been here yesterday or five centuries ago. I point the bow of my
boat toward the river's entrance, following in the wake of the most famous
of all the Florida trips of the late 1800s for tourists—a paddlewheel excursion up the Ocklawaha, all the way into the basin of Silver Springs. Of those
trips, surely the most spellbinding were the night runs, turpentine-soaked
pine knots illuminating the riverbanks in a soft, flickering strobe of bronze
light from an iron box atop the wheel house.

During her own custom-made, two-woman excursion on the St. Johns,
Marjorie Kinnan Rawlings hung a left here, just as I do today, steering her
open boat onto the Ocklawaha, pointed toward home. She was returning to
Cross Creek after a trip that began east of Orlando, following a braided
course that took her upriver to Orange Creek, through Orange Lake and

Lake Lochloosa, back to her little "cracker" farm. The trip away from the creek seemed to refresh her, to renew her affinity for the natural Florida. "I do not understand," wrote Rawlings, flush with the serenity of it all, "how anyone can live without some small place of enchantment to turn to."

This Ocklawaha is singular among tributaries of the St. Johns. Fed by some twenty artesian springs—including the 540-million-gallon-per-day gusher at Silver—it is surely the most steady and dependable. But it is also far more venerable, one of the oldest continuously flowing rivers in Florida. In this way, it moves up and out of the higher and more ancient Central Highlands of the north–south Florida Ridge, winding across a landscape that arose early from the sea, draining almost twenty-eight hundred square miles as it does.

In places, the Ocklawaha Valley is almost a mile wide, and the river itself wanders through it, sometimes creating high bluffs when it knocks up against the steeper contours at the valley edges, such as at the mouth of Eaton Creek. The Ocklawaha also travels along the boundary of another geological territory, one that ranges east and west across the state. It is the physiographic rim, the boundary that segregates the rolling, antiquated dunes of northern Florida from the lower and newer terrain of the central part of the state. South of here, the St. Johns is officially contained in its upper basin; north of here, in its lower.

At forty to sixty feet in height, the terraces that the Ocklawaha flows over are geologically older than the basin of the larger river into which it empties. But how much older is the river itself? Peats, mucks, and freshwater marls have been analyzed from the Ocklawaha floodplain and found to be nearly seventeen thousand years old. From this, we know that the Ocklawaha was behaving like a river long before the St. Johns, most likely sluicing its way from its headwater lakes inside a separate and more ancient marine lagoon basin.

There is history here, surely. It is quantified from the beginning—from the sea-bottom shell fossils found inside the walls of the spring caves to the twenty-four pre-Columbian middens and mounds scattered along its banks and the wrecks of nineteenth-century steamships embedded in its bottom. But there is a biological time line here, too. If the highlands have protected the Ocklawaha from the rise-and-fall fluctuations of more recent Ice Age machinations, they have also created a medium where at least one critter— perhaps more—has adapted especially to the localized environment.

This is the Lake Eustis pupfish (*Cyprindodon variegatus hubbsi*), named for one of the lakes in the original headwaters of the Ocklawaha. It is a small, laterally compressed fish, seldom growing longer than an inch. If the little *Fundulus bartrami* back at Lake Jesup's Clifton Springs is gone, and no other purely local fish are known, the pupfish hold the distinction of being the only endemic freshwater fish confined to the peninsula of Florida. In his earlier evaluation of the St. Johns Basin, ichthyologist McLane described it as a "marine relic," a critter that lived here when this was all a great sprawling saltwater lagoon instead of a freshwater river.

During his survey of the entire basin, McLane also collected a southern tesselated darter (*Etheostoma olmstedi maculaticeps*) on the Ocklawaha at the historic landing of Davenport, seven miles upstream from the St. Johns. Although it is not limited to the river, it wasn't until almost thirty years later that another such darter—a 2½-inch-long fish with chromatic pigments— was found, nearby at Orange Creek. Other rare fish have also been reported here over the years—the bluenose shiner, the snail bullhead, the dusky shiner, and the rainwater killifish, which may be another "ecotype," a marine relic like the pupfish. But are they still here today? And what else unique lives here, still undiscovered, in this ancient river system? If they all—fish and snails and mussels and clams—vanish before they are fully known, I wonder what information they will take with them.

For me, there is also a striking visual illusion at work on the Ocklawaha. When the surface of the water moves, it doesn't so much ripple or splash. Rather, it seems to melt into thick ebony folds, dark mercury taking its time to get where it needs to go, swirling in slow motion around the cypress knees at river's edge. It is moving this way in front of the houseboat now as I navigate the tight turns of the Ocklawaha, crawling upstream.

In no time, I have moored the larger boat, dropped my kayak overboard, and gingerly climbed down into it. Soon, I am slipping back into the creases of this river hidden off the mainstream, sometimes ducking down to avoid low branches or using them to pull my way along, scraping over the top of mossy logs hidden like gators just under the surface. On I go, creeping around islands and oxbows, following inviting meanders through the low shores of this blackwater swamp. Here, uncorseted, the Ocklawaha strays beyond remembrances of itself, bayous and slivers that go nowhere really, except back into time. It is a place of quietude, broken only by the brilliant flash of a painted bunting back in the green foliage, the cry of a red-shouldered hawk somewhere overhead, well above the reach of the flowering trumpet creeper vine.

When I stop paddling, the flora that surrounds me like the walls of a tunnel comes into focus: there are elms and sabal palms, swampbay and dogwood, bald cypress and swamp tupelo. There is the rare needle palm hidden in the understory, among the cinnamon ferns. There are mosses, lichens, liverworts, lilies, and wild orchids. Noise is absorbed back here, creating a moment that is cushioned from anything but the swamp itself. I think of the river's name, saying it out loud to myself. It comes from the original Creek, *ak-lowahe*, for "Crooked River," "swamp," or "muddy"—perhaps all of these.

In one slough, I run out of water, and my shallow keel softly slides to a halt against the bottom, leaving me surrounded by a forest of cypress knees rising like obelisks from the muddy flats. I gently run my fingers over the top of one, right where a knob of new brown-red growth is bursting from the husk, and find it is soft to the touch, like leather upholstered over a sponge. Like the swelling buttresses of the trunk, the knees are another easily recognizable characteristic of the water-loving cypress. The knees are, in fact, extensions of the underground root system, attempts to rise above the oxygen-poor riverbank mud and take a needed gulp of air. Some people also believe that they help anchor the heavy hardwood trunk in the soft ground; I'm not sure if this is true, but I can tell you I've seen huge oaks uprooted after a few weeks in swamp overflow, while the cypress—which endures sogginess every day—never gives way.

Back on the main river, the St. Johns had begun to widen, its banks falling back in imitation of its run to the sea from Palatka, upcoming. And so, I welcomed the shrouded mystery of this tributary, as excited as I am when I enter the mouth of a spring cave in dive gear underwater, always wondering what will be revealed around the next bend.

What is most urgently revealed is how difficult this river—even its deeper channel—must have been for the captains of the steamships to navigate. Poet and musician Sidney Lanier described just such a vessel when he made his own trip up the Ocklawaha to research a guidebook. The writer's steamer was the *Marion*; like other paddlewheelers during these decorous times, its steep decks were jammed with passengers, nattily attired in wool suits with ties and dark hats, or tight-necked, full-length dresses. The *Marion*, reported

Lanier, "is like nothing in the world so much as a Pensacola gopher with a preposterously exaggerated back."

Although Ulysses S. Grant also traveled up the Ocklawaha aboard a similar steamer called the *Osceola*, Lanier is perhaps more closely associated with the river than any other historic figure. His chapter on it was not just a logistical guide of what a passenger could physically expect from a similar trip but a vivid glimpse into how Lanier's own artistic sensibilities were set loose by the river. In this way, Lanier carefully explained how to place a chair near the end of a narrow passageway on the upper deck of the *Marion*, next to where the railing drops by thirty degrees. Thusly situated, a passenger could then straddle one leg on the railing, rest the other on the deck, tilt his or her chair back, and—looking up—then "sail, sail, sail through the cypresses, through the vines, through the May day, through the floating suggestions of the unutterable that come up, that sink down . . . and so shall your heart forever afterwards interpret Ocklawaha to mean repose."

Then again, Lanier was a romantic. And, although Silver Springs seemed to awe nearly everyone at the journey's end, not all agreed that the twisting, convoluted path of the Ocklawaha was a party waiting to happen. As one anxious passenger described it: "The hull of the steamer went bumping against one cypress-butt, then another, suggesting to the tyro in this kind of aquatic adventure that possibly he might be wrecked and subjected, even if he escaped a watery grave, to a miserable death, through the agency of mosquitoes, buzzards and huge alligators."

A few centuries earlier, in 1539, Hernando de Soto, the old trailblazing conquistador, marched overland from the gulf into the heart of Timucuan territory, stumbling on a village either on the banks of the Ocklawaha or close by. Here, in typical conquistador fashion, his soldiers stole all the crops the Native Americans were cultivating, including storehouses of grain as well as the corn still growing in the fields. Although he didn't know it, and probably didn't much care, de Soto was in the territory of a powerful Timucuan tribe. It was ruled by a chief named Olata Ouae Outina, and it nurtured its own special traditions, distinct from those of Saturiwa and his people to the north.

While the Spanish weren't kind to the natives, the more modern American travelers on the river weren't particularly benevolent to the Ocklawaha, despite its value as an early tourism destination. Ironically, it was the narrow, boxy steamships like the *Marion* and the *Osceola* and the *Okeehumkee* that first exposed the valley to the outside world. With that exposure came the opportunity to exploit the land—to create commerce that nearly consumed the river, almost as thoroughly as the Spanish eliminated the Timucua.

First, farming arrived in the upper Ocklawaha Basin, replacing the wet prairie and sawgrass communities around Lake Griffin and then Lake Apopka. These efforts were called "muck farms" because row crops grew in the rich muck of the lake's wetlands. Exposed to the atmosphere, the black soils here oxidized, vanished into air just as the peat soils of the Glades did when corporate sugarcane growers commandeered the natural terrain there. To complete the degradation, nutrient-loaded fertilizers and pesticides soaked the new fields, with the pollutants being drained and pumped into the surrounding lakes, along with poorly treated sewage. Instead of having sandy bottoms and clear water, as in the 1940s, the lakes turned pea green, especially in the warmer summer months. Lake Apopka, once a leading sport fishing destination, became eutrophied. Gizzard shad replaced oxygen-loving bass. By 1966 some one million fish died almost at once in the lake. Fish camps and marinas closed their doors. When a small plane crashed in Lake Apopka in 1989, rescue divers searching for the wreckage were inoculated for tetanus, typhoid, hepatitis, and cholera.

But that wasn't the worst of it. People with even bigger ambitions have squeezed the Ocklawaha and, in places, even girdled it with concrete. The intent was to channelize and dam Lanier's "sweetest waterlane in the world" for its entirety, to turn it into something that would extend from the banks of the St. Johns to the gulf, to make it a busy highway for commerce. It would be the Cross-Florida Barge Canal. Creating a ditch like this wasn't special to modern thinking: as early as 1830, schemers had suggested slicing across rivers of the peninsula to give vessels rounding the dangerous Florida cape a more secure and efficient inland route.

After a fitful start in the mid-1930s, the building of the canal finally took hold in 1964 with the help of the Army Corps of Engineers. Into the blackwater swamp went a fearsome-looking contraption called a crusher-crawler that growled its way down the riverbanks, chewing up and spitting out the sort of enchanting, wild environment I have just paddled through. Wildlife fled like fawns in a Disney cartoon. As it went, the machine chipped its way down into the limestone of the Central Highlands, threatening to lop off the top of the upper aquifer, jeopardizing the drinking water supplies for central and north Florida.

In a few years, the diligent dredge work had created a wide, empty swath where the cypress and tupelo had been. Some sixteen linear miles of river were encased inside two dams, Rodman to the north and Eureka to the south, both named for former landings. The great impoundment that puddled up between Eureka and Rodman covered fourteen square miles of once pristine floodplain wilderness. It was called "Lake Ocklawaha" and was stocked with gamefish to make it somehow more appealing, perhaps to justify its existence.

Ironically, Eureka Landing had figured prominently in Rawlings's first novel, *South Moon Under*, creating a very real sense of place for readers seeking to understand what "cracker" Florida and its people were all about. Art wasn't enough to save it, though, and Eureka drowned under the weight of water and engineering ambition.

Besides costing the public some seventy million dollars, all this ditch digging and land clearing helped demystify the natural poetry of the Ocklawaha, shredding its verse into ribbons. The loss was heartbreaking, enough to make people who cared very mad. This plan for the Cross-Florida Barge Canal galvanized the state's nascent environmental movement, giving it a common enemy, rallying schoolteachers and housewives, hunters and biologists. Science was invoked in the fray; so was poetry: Sidney Lanier's writings about the Ocklawaha were frequently quoted—particularly the part about the "sweetest waterlane in the world." Even the conservative *Reader's Digest* was convinced, reporting of the carnage in a 1970 article, "Rape of the Ocklawaha."

By 1971 the canal was finally deauthorized by a presidential order, marking the first major victory for conservationists in modern Florida, coalescing a unified movement. Simply halting the canal, of course, didn't fix the Ocklawaha. As in the upper basin of the St. Johns, restoring the systems of nature requires patience—as well as a hearty dose of friendly politics.

When it came time to put all the pieces back together again in the mid-1990s, one state environmental official looked at the damage done and pronounced it profound: "Next to the Everglades, the Ocklawaha is Florida's best example of what happens when you don't cooperate with Mother Nature."

It will take years to accomplish, but at last, restoration of a sort has begun: pasture and fields are being bought and reflooded. Already, artificial wetlands—with descriptive names like Emeralda Marsh, all twenty-four square miles of it—have been built to filter lakes eutrophied by the nutrients and lack of oxygen. When funding is approved, holes will be knocked into dams to restore the river's flow.

Still, not everyone agrees with restoration. When the Ocklawaha Basin was first retrofitted, it created its own paradigm, one that existed with little history to guide it. Muck farmers have not given up their land, even for payment, easily. And some sport fishers now covet the vast puddle of "Lake Ocklawaha" for its great lunker fishing. In 1966 the administrator of Putnam County, the home of the reservoir, lamented the dollars anglers will no longer bring to his area when the dam is breached. "It's a major economic benefit to Putnam," he said. "If we lose that we lose a tremendous asset." Although biological studies showed that a revitalized Ocklawaha would actually create a *better* fishery than the artificial lake, legislators right up until the end of the century—grabbing onto the shaky logic of short-term economic loss—refused to destroy Rodman.

Thankfully, there are still untouched stretches of this tributary, and they exist here between the St. Johns and Rodman Dam on the lower Ocklawaha and between Eureka Dam and Moss Bluff on the upper leg of the tributary. Most of the remaining natural shore is protected by public ownership, either in the Ocala National Forest or on land owned by the water management district.

Of this wildness still left, there are surely biological ways to qualify it. But they are just numbers. Here is a better way: in 1978 a local Baptist pastor who was otherwise revered reported spotting a Big Foot–like creature along the shores of this *ak-lowahe*. It was gorilla-sized, odiferous, and wild, and it snapped dry limbs and branches as it lurched through the dense, moss-hung subtropical jungle. I find this fascinating all by itself—not for the melodrama of the report or even the veracity of it but because what remains of the Ocklawaha *seems* like the sort of dark and lonely place where Bigfoot could actually be pictured frolicking about, if he wanted to.

There's still enough room to roam here, enough of what Lanier and Rawlings first saw to sustain an extended family of Bigfoots, if you know where to look. Perhaps someday I can even ride directly on this river from the St. Johns to Silver Springs, floating over the clutch of limestone vents in the ether of the headspring, just like Lanier once did. Or maybe I can go farther west, all the way back to Cross Creek, back to enchantment.

Welaka appears on a high scarp on the easterly shore of the St. Johns, a village named for the original Seminole description of the river itself. Here, I notice a paved street runs smack through the middle of town, under a single blinking traffic light, and then keeps going down the bank into the river itself.

The St. Johns is a theme here, just about the only one around, and it is urgent enough to transmute a main street into a boat ramp in just a matter of yards. Lanier described Welaka as the site of an old pre-Columbian Indian village, a bluff where the Spanish later built their own once flourishing settlement. Like other steamboat landings, it once had ambitious promise, and now it has something else, the endangered taste of Old Florida.

Although pioneer archaeologists C. B. Moore and Jeffries Wyman often found Indian middens nearly this immense when they visited the St. Johns in the late 1800s in separate expeditions, the shoreline scarp that hugs the river northward to Palatka is an ancient ocean dune, a wind-piled marine terrace.

Artesian springs still feed the river north of here. But with the exception of Green Cove, most have a flow of less than 3 cubic feet per second—Welaka, Satsuma, Nashua, Forest, Mud Springs. For instance, nearby Satsuma, named for a small community that in turn was named for a variety of orange, discharges 1.8 cubic feet per second. That's 1.2 million gallons of water per day, about one-sixtieth the outflow of Silver Glen back in the national forest.

Welaka itself is a village of four hundred–odd souls, mostly natives salted with a handful of newcomers fleeing the urbanization washing over other parts of the state. Two of these newcomers are Rand Speas and his wife, Marianne, here more than seven years from Key Largo. Although they may be considered "new" by natives, the lifestyle they have embraced is as antiquated—and as thoughtful—as any I encounter along the river. I meet them after tying up to a bulkhead near the rusting metal and wooden dockhouse of what used to be the St. Johns Crab Company. Nearby, Speas has turned a barn-sized, vaulted storage building into a working boat restoration shop, Welaka Landing.

In one corner of his spacious riverfront shop, Rand is restoring an antique motor yacht; in another, he is crafting a gem of a replica from scratch, an eighteen-foot-long steam-powered launch, just like the ones that sometimes plied local waters around the turn of the century, down the St. Johns and up the Ocklawaha. I bend over the hull of the replica and see it is made of finely tooled white fir. I run my fingers over the ribs inside, and they feel smooth, milled and hand-shaped to perfection. It all makes modern fiberglass and metal boats seem clunky, superfluous. "There's no reason in the world to build an ugly boat," Rand tells me. "I carve all my boats first, as models. Then I build them here in the shop."

When he gets a chance, he also takes them out on the St. Johns and the Ocklawaha, happily chugging along in a virtual nautical time warp with Marianne, out in a historic boat, on a historic river. Sometimes, he fires up an old Cris Craft "speed boat" and pulls Marianne behind it, riding a set of half-century-old wooden skis, autographed by Dick Pope, the water-skiing founder of Cypress Gardens. "Engineers design boats these days on computers without ever seeing the real thing," said Rand, a bit wistfully. "How do they know how a boat is supposed to feel?" The result is boats with angry names like Predator, Terminator, Aggressor, swift plastic vessels designed only to go very fast, from one place to another, rather than to absorb the moment.

I walk outside, near where a small spring is capped to keep it from leaking a path of erosion down to the river. The boughs of the cypress and magnolia frame the river, and in the late afternoon sun, the boathouse and the shop and the riverfront seem tinted sepia. My moment of time travel is briefly shaken when I notice a huge house cat lumbering across the grassy riverbank; it is one of the largest domestic cats I've ever seen.

"Owl-proof," says Marianne, explaining the bulk. "When you live in a place like this, surrounded by nature, it's a small price to pay, having bigger cats."

Northward, a tiny clump of woods mapped as Turkey Island passes, then an easterly creek named Acosta, a bluff called Possum. The bait traps of fishers come and go, full of shiners and menhaden—small frame shanties of wood and net rising in strange geometric formations from the water near the shore, each angled as sharply as the head of a triceratops. Submerged pilings are charted almost continuously at every bend as a series of black dots on the map, remembrances of once busy steamboat landings, busy now only with visiting bass and gar, eel and blue crabs. Somewhere here, I pass over another relic, the long-submerged wreck of the Union riverboat the *Columbine*, sunk during a battle with Confederates in 1864.

To the left, the mouth of the actual Cross-Florida Barge Canal—the ditch that runs as straight as a surveyor's transect through the Buckman Locks to the Rodman Reservoir—lurks, distressingly. To the right, the wild grid of tangled islands known as Seven Sisters is split between the meander of the main channel and that of two smaller creeks, Trout and Barrentine. By my count, at least one of the sisters appears to be missing. Perhaps it is, but cartographers are a conservative lot, tending to stay with place-names long after they lose their accuracy—and sometimes, even when they aren't accurate to begin with. I remember Drigger Island back upstream and chuckle to myself.

A railroad bridge looking like something built from a child's erector set rises ahead. Oddly, it is called Buffalo Bluff. There is plenty of bluff about but, as far as I can tell, no buffalo to be found. Buffalo Bluff Bridge lays low-slung and territorial across the river, and I have to call its handler on a VHF radio to ask him to raise it, even for my modest houseboat. Up it goes in a riff of screeches and groans, and under I go, downstream.

Murphy Island, isolated by the channel and Murphy's Creek, reveals itself. I look at a topographical map that shows the middle of the island rising a good fifteen feet above the river's level. This is no escarpment, rather an Indian midden of heroic proportions. Billy Bartram landed here during one of his river exploits, describing it as "the little remote island" with an "almost impenetrable thicket" of trees and undershrubs. Here, traders from the nearby Spalding's Lower Trading Store had once hidden their merchandise in fear of an Indian uprising.

In homage, I anchor out of the channel near Horseshoe Point on the west shore—what pioneers called the "Indian Shore"—and wait for the sun to dip below the crown of cypress. By dawn, I'll put my kayak in the water and paddle over Murphy's Creek to explore.

The St. Johns in the late evening is Billy's river again. In this incarnation, it becomes a place where the great vast bowl of a sky is filled nearly end to end with stars, where unknown critters rustle about in the underbrush of the shore. To sleep and dream in an environment like this, rocked by the gentle swash of the river, is to rekindle its touch.

Morning comes quickly, and I ease my kayak down into the quiet river from the houseboat, steam rising around me from the warmer river into the crisp new air. There, I paddle around the edge of Murphy, looking for a spot with enough flat, hard sand to land. As I pass the crown of an uprooted tree, I spook a log-sized gator three yards away who belly flops into the water so suddenly that the water roils, violently rocking my little craft from side to side. Kayaks are great for sneaking up on critters, to observe them without chasing them away. But on times like this morning, the surprise factor can work both ways.

I wonder, in fact, how I must look to animals when I am in this banana-shaped craft, with only my upper body protruding, arms moving metronomically, head occasionally swiveling, if not with the rhythm, then with some urgent perception, known only to me. Sitting here, low in the water, with my torso splayed out for almost nine feet, green and tapered, I must seem an oddity of nature—half human, half aquatic something-or-other, a modern take on the merman myth.

Finally, I edge ashore on a flat, golden spit of sand where the gator was resting, carefully stepping out of the kayak. As I look up into the dense woods, I am startled to see how steeply the forested mound rises from the shore, almost like an earthen fortress. I hike up the hill, fighting my way through thick vines and briers, feeling relieved that Murphy still seems a bit like Bartram's "impenetrable thicket."

Atop the little summit, I look under my feet and see that the ground is covered with countless snail shells, each about the size of my thumb nail and bleached by time. It is my old friend *Viviparous*. I put my hand down inside a deep burrow some animal has carved into the earth—an armadillo? a gopher tortoise?—and find that the shell layer extends as far as I can reach, up to my shoulder. I pick up a single shell, turning it over in my hand, trying to imagine some Timucua holding it in his or her palm so long ago, perhaps plucking it from a pot of broth, maybe removing the tiny chunk of meat with a sliver of bone. I hike through the thick woods, impressed with the girth of the live oaks, stately old trees dripping with moss, each main stem splitting off into six or seven or more trunk-sized boughs, all humbled by the gravity of age.

By now, I'm several hundred yards inside the interior of Murphy, thinking I may be the first person in a long time to get this far. That's when I see the deserted camp. The camp is made from a massive gray metal ocean buoy, which has been slice-welded in half. Each half has a doorlike opening cut from it, creating what amounts to two round, rustic metal huts. Inside each are piles of rusty Bud cans, rotting mattresses, and graffiti that seem to stop around 1967, rough-hewn territoriality hiccuping its way into a slow death. But then on the wall of one, I notice a scrawl reading: "Fuck You," next to last month's date. At this point, I stop very still, listening for noises, remembering *Deliverance*—half expecting to hear banjo music twanging from somewhere.

Yet there is nothing but the low coo of a pair of mourning doves above in the oaks. I walk outside, picking my way back to the summit above my kayak. As I do, I stop to munch a few wild blackberries and admire a natural bouquet of pinkish fetterbush wildflowers, each of which is hanging like a thimble-sized Victorian lamp globe from a sturdy stem. A beam of sunshine penetrating the thick canopy falls on the little globes, making them seem actually to glow incandescently.

This river has been a magnet for people for centuries, drawing them all here for varied reasons, signifying their intent by what they leave behind, from the slovenly to the sublime—snail shells, discarded trash, the memory of the way the sun illuminates a wildflower, the taste of a wild berry.

Dunn's Creek has already begun its run southward, on a languorous sprint toward Crescent Lake, an oblong, thirty-square-mile water body that sits, like nearby Lake George, deep inside a bowl of ancient sandy terraces. Geologists figure both lakes were once depressions in a prehistoric sea bottom. Counting lakes formed by the river is tricky business. If you consider just those the channel passes through, there are nine. If you add Blue Cypress at the headwaters—bereft of a navigation channel but hydrologically linked—there are ten. If you factor in those tethered by creeks, like Crescent and Woodruff, there are at least twelve. But once you start roaming toward the edge of the valley, computing distant lakes that can be reached in one way or another from the St. Johns—the Ocklawaha Chain, Ruth and Salt and Loughman Lakes, and others—then the count more than doubles.

For a stream that is narrow and winding, Dunn's Creek is surprisingly deep. Except for a few five-foot shoals, it cuts down eight and twelve feet into the earth, wandering under a bridge, past a series of arrow-straight, artificially made residential canals with mobile homes, back into thick swampy woods, and then—except for a sharp westerly jog at Piney Bluff Landing—shoots southward into Crescent Lake. The last several miles are surely the most natural, meandering past a five-square-mile wildlife management area until finally emptying into the lake beyond an old steamboat landing called Moccasin, spreading out at Willow Cove.

Inside this wilderness preserve, white-tailed deer, turkeys, wild hogs, gray squirrels, and rabbits are hunted during assorted seasons—some of which are sportingly limited to the use of replicas of archaic muzzle-loaded, single-shot guns, some restricted to archery. Then, too, other critters here are legally protected from the slings and arrows of a hunter's good fortune, including bobcats, otters, skunks, and fox squirrels. All these rules must royally confuse the Timucuan spirits of the forest charged with nourishing its bounty—this trying to figure out the proper season, the relevant weapon, the right species to watch over.

Crescent itself is long and narrow—almost crescent shaped—ten and twelve feet deep, until it shoals in a southerly cove called Green Bay. Because of the way the pressure on the surface of the Floridan Aquifer is diminished nearby, hydrologists suspect there are artesian springs somewhere along the southeastern edge of Crescent—springs that together create a "diffuse upward leakage" of somewhere in the neighborhood of 10.3 million gallons a day.

This being the St. Johns Valley, all these circuits connect and flow *northward*, confluxing at the mouth of Dunn's Creek, feeding the great and noble river itself. Yet, for the same peculiar reasons, this flow in the lower creek daily *changes* direction, courtesy of the tides that push water backward, into the main channel of the St. Johns.

Here, back in the river channel, Edgewater emerges on the east, a few canals and docks bunched together at riverside. Oddly enough, there is not a water hyacinth in sight—which is strange only because this is where *Eichhornia crassipes* was first introduced to the river in 1884. I have seen these floating plants almost from the beginning, hunkering down together along the shore, sometimes drifting downstream in entire islands, roving gangs of foliage.

When they bloom, from late spring through late summer, a stocky green spike emerges from the green, unfolding a series of lavender orchidlike blossoms up and down its stem. It is no wonder a Mrs. W. F. Fuller was in a swoon with the hyacinth when she first saw them on display at the New Orleans Cotton Exposition. The delicate flower of the hyacinth so impressed Mrs. Fuller that she brought some home to Edgewater to share with her friends, showing it off in a backyard fishpond. The plants, used to competing for space in the jungle rivers of Venezuela, immediately went to work, sending out bulbous runner shoots like some real life Jack-in-the-beanstalk, doubling itself every twelve days. In no time, the hyacinths overcame Mrs. Fuller's little fish pond.

Why not cast it away in the river, for others to share in the hyacinth's beauty? Within a decade, the pretty little plant covered an estimated seventy-eight thousand square miles up and down the St. Johns and its tributaries, sometimes filling the entire river from bank to bank, perplexing paddlewheel captains, who wondered what had become of the channel. Soon, it began to colonize all the rivers and lakes of Florida.

Although chemical spraying keeps the hyacinths from spreading as fast as they otherwise might, total eradication is out of the question. Nearly everything has been tried—deadly herbicides that blacken whatever they touch, hyacinth-eating weevils, and fungus, even a small fleet of Glockenspiel-like boats built as "Hyacinth Harvesters."

And there is the manatee cure. At various times, riverine locals—noting manatees love to chomp on hyacinths—have proposed transporting a herd or two to particularly troublesome sites. Although the plans never went anywhere, there is some off-center appeal to the notion of the manatee-as-natural-avenger, another peculiar vision special to Florida.

As I move downstream from Edgewater, hyacinths begin to reappear, along the shore of the village of San Mateo. Somewhere near San Mateo, beyond the smattering of waterfront homes, is the site of one of the river's most bizarre dreams, Charlottia (also spelled Charlota). Perched on these high easterly banks, Charlottia once sprawled away from the river in every direction for 125 square miles. There were fields of corn and rice and indigo, pastures of cattle, entire forests of live oak harvested for the lumber of naval stores. Tending this vast empire, for a very brief time, were prostitutes from the slums of London.

Charlottia, named for the wife of King George III, was the work of Denys Rolle, Esq., a member of the English Parliament who launched his grandiose scheme here in 1765, when Britain still owned Florida. Rolle, known as a philanthropist, wanted to re-create the success General James Oglethorpe had in Georgia, where he imported convicts to people the swamp and coast there. But the prostitutes, according to one observer, were "imperfectly reformed." Pulling up palmetto stumps and planting crops was nasty work, and when they protested, Rolle cut off their food supply. In no time, the women fled to St. Augustine.

Not missing a beat, Rolle brought in slaves to do the chores. The plantation prospered for a while with their help, soon becoming Rollestown (Rollston). But when the Spanish reacquired Florida from Britain after the American Revolution, Denys Rolle fled with his charges to the Bahamas.

Today, the place where Charlottia more or less was is marked by a modest riverside pub, the Alligator Bar. It is a narrow mobile home with heavily tinted windows, a forlorn, rectangular metal shoebox of a structure where several neon beer signs burn brightly, even at midday, comforting the few thirsty souls huddling inside. The adjacent wooden dock, with its scattered chairs, is deserted. The only clue to life is an outdoor speaker, which—perhaps in evocation of the grandiose vision of Denys Rolle, Esq.—is blaring an old Patsy Cline classic, loud enough to carry a half mile to the opposite bank of the St. Johns. The song is "Crazy."

As Patsy sings her ineffably wistful lament, mullet leap from the tea-colored river, jumping into the summer air with sheer abandon—the fish-dream dance of a long-dead Englishman and his imperfectly reformed party girls of London.

> The tree crashed, flattening everything in its path, and the roar of the fall went
>
> like a roll of thunder through swamp and hammock and scrub. The boy
>
> thought there was a hush after the last echo, as though the men waited before
>
> they began to trim and saw, watching the tree like a great prone animal that
>
> might not be entirely dead.—Marjorie Kinnan Rawlings, writing of logging
>
> along the St. Johns in her novel *South Moon Under* (1933)

*P*alatka looms ahead now, and its arrival means I have seen the last of the narrow river and its elegant solitude. Between here and Jacksonville, the St. Johns becomes a broad aquatic boulevard, averaging two miles from one shore to the other—sometimes as narrow as a mile, other times splayed out between its high banks for three. It now seems more like a sensible northern river than a charming southern one.

Water managers call this the "main stem" of the river; Lanier called it "broad and garish"—but he did so in contrast to the more mysterious, gloomy Ocklawaha. It is the main stem that dominates now, a true superhighway that replaces the meander of the country road that has brought me this far. But it, too, has its own charms, unfolding in ways singular to this river, this place. As it moves along, it does so through a basin that—except for the urbanization of Jacksonville's Duval County—is two-thirds forest.

In this northern river valley, there are still half-wild, swamplike creeks yet to come. In fact, there are some twelve tributaries charted along the lower river, beginning with Crescent Lake back upstream. Although they don't have the spring-fed consistency of the Ocklawaha, each introduces water, sediments, and nutrients—good and bad—to the St. Johns, drawing from streams and floodplains that stretch away from the river for hundreds of square miles.

You can think of each tributary basin as a shallow culvert, gathering the rainwater that falls around it—on parking lots, rooftops, lawns, marshes, and swamps—and funneling it off to the St. Johns. Some basins, like that which drains the Arlington River in Jacksonville, are a modest 32 square miles; others, like the one surrounding Etonia Creek just north of Palatka, are engorged with landscape, to the tune of 355 square miles.

The appearance of Palatka marks another change as well, a geological boundary as significant as the rise that first launches the St. Johns back near Lake Okeechobee. It is the arrival of the higher "proximal" zone of northern Florida. Older than the central region, and far more ancient than the flat southern tip of the peninsula, this northern range is distinguished by continuous high ground instead of the rolling hills and valleys of the central zone. Geologically, the surface is characterized by "dead zone" karst features, like abandoned springheads and steep-walled sinks, dry beds of streams and lakes, which have become prairies.

At my final approach to Palatka, I find the river configures itself into a classic oxbow, twisting itself like a Hindu contortionist until the compass shows I am headed due south, before I can again point north. The name Palatka derives from a Seminole word meaning ferry, ford, or crossing—*pilotaikita*—and it is clear why: the throat of the river narrows here, affording the last easy crossing at the "Devil's Elbow," a narrow shoal of swampy land jutting out into the water from the southwest shore. Ten miles north of Palatka, the St. Johns will have widened itself by twenty times this distance.

Depending on your sensibilities, you will be either delighted by Palatka or startled by it. There are communications towers and power plant smokestacks and a concrete bridge that sweeps high across the water. There are municipal docks and marinas and boatyards. There is a riverfront Burger King here on the eastern shore, a place where I can—if so inclined—tie up at a dock, climb a wooden stairway up the steep bluff, and dig right into a Whopper. The efficiency of doing so is not lost on everyone: an author to a boating guide of the river selected the Burger King landing as one of his "Top Ten St. Johns Destinations."

A bit farther downstream, on the opposite shore near the bridge, I can check into a Holiday Inn, the first high-rise I have so far encountered. Once inside, I can enjoy a Burger King of an experience, one in which every ingredient is carefully prescribed, no different here—on the site of an ancient pre-Columbian Indian town—than in a midwestern suburb of Chicago. And would you like fries with that irony?

Yet, if you factor in its richly textured history, Palatka seems a bit like Jacksonville in miniature—which is no surprise because Jacksonville is about what Palatka's founders would have had it be. Since this was the last, high river bluff with an easy ford before the upstream river tightened, the Spanish set up outposts early here, building over shell mounds left by the Timucua. By the Revolutionary War, Seminoles were living on the same middens, growing oranges, corn, pumpkins, and melons in surrounding fields.

Created as a town in 1853, Palatka rivaled Jacksonville as a busy shipbuilding and transportation hub. Seven steam lines based their operations here, some of which serviced Savannah and Charleston to the north and, through them, New York City. By 1880 five separate railroads were carrying passengers and freight to and from the city in all directions. Opulent hotels, like the Lafayette—with a fireplace in every room—and the Larking House, were an oasis of luxury in the raw Florida interior. When Lanier arrived to write his 1875 guidebook, he described "Pilatka" as "a considerable resort for consumptives" with luxuries like a telegraph office and a newspaper. The paper, reported Lanier, was noted for "alligator stories to such an extent that its editor is universally known as 'Alligator Pratt.'"

Like Sanford, though, Palatka's ambition was tempered by trauma: an 1884 fire burned down most of the business district, and the "Great Freezes" of 1894 and 1895 destroyed the citrus industry. With oranges gone and the steamship era drawing to an end, Palatka still had the Wilson Cypress Company to drive it. The company did a better job cutting the ancient first-growth cypress trees from the river than practically any other operation. In doing so, its workers removed what one writer of the steamboat era described as "a mighty arbor" of towering 150-foot-high crowns, canopies that met and merged over the tightly wound creeks and spring runs of the river's swamps.

Operating between 1884 and 1944, the company chewed up trees to the tune of forty million board feet of lumber annually, employing up to sixteen hundred people at a time either to cut the cypress, float them over the river, or operate the buzz-saw machinery. "It was," wrote one historian in awe in 1943, "the most magnificent lumber mill on earth." But loggers in Florida didn't harvest selectively or replant trees in those days. Even if they had, the slow-growing *Taxodium* was not much of a candidate for agronomy, taking a single human lifetime even to make a log the size of a mast of a small ship.

As a result, when all the huge, buttressed cypress had been cut, there was nothing to replace them—ecologically or economically. The Wilson Cypress Company, which had constructed its own buildings and warehouses and wharves out of cypress, finally performed the real-life act that spelled its end: with no magnificent trees left to fell and shred, it disassembled all its cypress structures, milled them into shingles and trim, and vanished, having eaten itself off the face of the earth. The great southern writers of tragedy— Welty, O'Connor, Faulkner—couldn't have invented a better metaphor for a demise to such an existence.

There is an odd, final chapter left from the logging days. Not all the massive cypress floated up- or downstream made it to the mill. Some, especially those cut before their sap had been drained, sank to the bottom. And on the bottom they have mostly remained under the protection of mud until recently. Lumber mills, actively searching for large, uncut logs in a state where the giant timber has been long harvested, are resurrecting the sinkers from the river bottom. This "deadhead logging" has actually gone on for years, at a slow, casual pace. But as timber companies have depleted large first-growth forests worldwide, the value of the behemoth sunken logs has soared to hundreds of dollars each. "Now they are worth some money," one lumberyard owner told a reporter in 1996, "and now everybody's going after them. I wish I had a pile of them."

Still, any tree that settled into the bottom a century and more ago has become part of today's benthic ecosystem, creating habitat for fish and snails and plants. Raising it not only eviscerates that chunk of the system but also stirs up sediments best left unstirred, the same pollutants that deep dredging tends to revive—setting old and sad spirits loose in the present.

Topside, Palatka has been saved from urbanization by the dashing of its dreams, and it is probably a good thing. After all, how many times do we need to see the ambition-driven model of Orlando repeated before a skyline full of boxy, glass towers becomes monotonous? In Palatka, the charms are still real and southern, revealed in its remnant architecture, in which I can still read the details of its history. Quality of life still carries some value here, despite the patina of commercialization.

I have visited Palatka before by car and know it as a place with a healthy share of Victorian homes and brick store fronts, clues to a heritage ungentrified and country enough to be authentic. In town, there is a hidden garden of a ravine carved by the water flowing beneath the sandy flanks of ancestral hillocks, a place Works Progress Administration workers turned into a park during the Great Depression. On the streets, people still seem to have time to stand and chat, instead of marching purposely on to their next appointment. Scattered about this reality are still unpretentious little diners where apples are sliced large and served inside a light flaky crust—not as a torte or crepe or anorexic sliver of nouveau American cuisine but as a hardy wedge of homemade pie.

Five years before his death, Confederate general Robert E. Lee took the steamer *Nick King* from Jacksonville to a landing just north of Palatka, where he overnighted at the orange grove home of one of his former colonels, Robert G. Cole. In the morning, they picked fruit from the grove and ate it. Today, along the water's edge at Wilson Cove, a riverfront street hugs the shore, lined with live oaks and historic wooden frame houses left over from Palatka's glory days. Here, if the light falls just right and if I squint to narrow my vision, I can make believe the next vehicle to travel the trail will not be a pickup or sedan at all but a horse and carriage, maybe with an old, distinguished Confederate general seated in it.

I look closely on my map and see that there are submerged pilings and "ruins" around the entire rim of Wilson cove. This is a virtual graveyard for some twenty steamboats run by the Hart Line and other companies headquartered here, their hulls now hidden under sediment and memory. Scores of the paddlewheelers operated from the docks over the years—so many that the demise of one more wasn't considered much of a loss.

A local historian tells of the unheralded end of the *Astatula*, one of the narrow ships built especially for the "jungle cruise" up the Ocklawaha: not long after the turn of the century, "she was committed to the riverbank not far from Hart's Point, and gradually stripped of her tophamper. . . . For a while, she was a low box on a raft—with a door like aperture in the stern and a tall, tottering stovepipe. Then she was a nest of water-soaked timbers, and finally, thirty years later, two rotting stern-wheel supports slanting above a carpet of water hyacinth." By the time folks begin to understand the uniqueness of the paddlewheelers, they had vanished, saved only in photographs that remain.

The river has been sounded here for depth since 1852, with crewmen dropping lead-weighted lines over the sides of the gunnels to measure the bottom—three to five feet in the coves, sixteen to twenty feet in the channel.

Today, boaters use hand-held global positioning systems, bouncing signals off a satellite to confirm depth locations plotted by fathometers. The distance between the boat gunnel and the lead weight on the bottom and between the river and an orbiting satellite is a fine parable, equal to the distance between the Palatka of two hundred years ago and now, between the gamey meat in a snail shell and that in a Whopper.

Northward, the St. Johns hasn't lost its serpentine character; its turns and twists are just much larger, gulflike in proportion, fat lazy pythons instead of skinny garter snakes. It is here that maps—even the most cursory thumb-nail sketch—mark the change of the St. Johns from a thin pencil-like scribble to a thick bluish tentacle, headed now with some authority toward the sea. To be traveling smack in the middle of this channel—with each bank stretch-ing away on both sides for a mile—surely provides its own water-bound solitude. Like the large lakes on the middle river, this stretch of the St. Johns can be defined by expanse, by superlatives of size.

From the channel, the bronze afternoon light makes the distant shores shimmer, as if I am passing mirages instead of points named Moritani and Hog Eye, Forrester and Warner. I am as locked in isolation as I have been on the river, insulated by distance over water, rather than the foliage shroud of the swamp. Alone here, with the metronomic hum of my engines to put me into a daze, I have time to consider more of the essence of the water beneath my hull.

Although tides have played a role in the flow and the depth of the river for some miles now, the science of figuring the tidal range along the St. Johns seems to have an alchemy all its own. For instance, the difference between high and low tides at Palatka has been measured at 1.09 feet. Yet at Julington Creek, forty miles north of here and much closer to the river mouth, the tidal range is only 0.71. This is a puzzle until I realize the river is wider still at Julington, creating a basin that absorbs the energy of the tides there. As a result, the incoming "wave" from the ocean spreads out in such places, in-stead of ebbing or flowing up and down as it would inside a more narrow constriction.

But there are other natural variables at work here as well. The force of the tide changes routinely with the rain, winds, temperature—even with the lunar pull, when the stronger new and full moons rise during the more intense spring equinox. The Timucua, decorated in natural dyes and incised with tattoos to transmute the powers of nature, revered the equinox in prayer and ceremony along the St. Johns. Now geohydrologists keep detailed graphs and charts, spreadsheets configured on computer software. Both are attempts to reckon with the unknown, to control or protect us from natural forces. I wonder if—cloaked in crisp, clear numbers—our shamanism is ultimately any more profound than theirs.

Of all these nature-driven elements, it is perhaps the wind that seems to lay the heaviest hand on the tides of the main stem. If the wind blows in from the ocean at the river mouth at a sustained velocity of seven miles an hour or more, it can push nearly as much water as the tides upstream—raising the river's level from one to three feet above normal tides.

But what is it inside these tides that matters? For us humans, it is the first taste of chloride, just as it is for those critters who schedule their entire life cycles around the slightest presence of salt. The matrix of fresh and marine spells estuarine for them, a reality that has its own officious designation: the entire lower river is included in the National Estuary Program. At 2,777 square miles, the lower St. Johns is Florida's largest estuary—and for the average person, surely the most unacknowledged.

Long before any such description was officially made, saltwater fish and shellfish knew of this haven, using it as a nursery for their larvae, a place to feed and hide while growing strong. For instance, blue crabs (*Callinectes sapidus*) mate during the warmer months throughout the entire river but descend to the lowest part of the estuary—the last twenty-five miles or so nearest the ocean—to spawn in the cooler months. When the eggs hatch, the newborns endure seven free-swimming larvae stages before settling down to resemble what looks for all the world like a miniature blue crab.

Like other critters with exoskeletons, the blues must leave their shells behind to grow. They do so a number of times in their lives along the river, becoming soft as a mushroom—delectable to predators, including people— for a few brief hours. Females only mate during this time of molting. As they do, the larger, hard-shelled male hovers protectively over his mate, cradling her gently under his own shell with his swimmerets until he is sure her eggs have been fertilized. Sometimes, inexplicably, he lingers long after he is sexually required to, for reasons known only to other blue crabs. Since they must travel downstream to spawn, female blues are more often found in traps at the river mouth than the larger, meaty males. Freed of the siren's call to migrate, the males remain upstream, living out their lives in a calmer, less salty environment where food is plentiful and larger ocean predators are scarce.

And then there are the shrimp. All three major Penaeid shrimp of the St. Johns—white, brown, and pink—spawn offshore, where their eggs and larvae develop before returning to the protection of the estuary river nursery to mature. Although shrimp flit rather well through the water with a flip of the tail, they are energy-conscious little arthropods: when they want to migrate in one direction or another in the river, they rise—or fall—to catch an outgoing or incoming tide, letting that current carry them to where they want to go.

It is hard to place a fixed value of the river to the shrimp, or to people who eat them. Commercial landings, which vary widely, amounted to 1.4 million pounds just in Duval County in 1989. But sport shrimpers—limited to 99 pounds per day—get their share as well. One survey revealed 150 sport boats shrimping between Palatka and Jacksonville in a single day. According to a scientist who has studied the migration of all three species, the lower river is "probably the most important single geographic feature affecting the shrimp population of northeast Florida."

As for salinities, south of Palatka—where the river is augmented by the connate salts of the westerly springs of Lake George—they are higher than they are in this portion north to Jacksonville. After Jacksonville, salinity will spike again, but this time its source won't be the ocean of millions of years ago but the Atlantic of today.

Meanwhile, I will encounter ancient streams, like Rice Creek, Yellow Water Creek, and Black Creek, all of which meander over the relic dunes of the west for miles before reaching the river. Shadows of the Ocklawaha, these creeks are geologically ancient, winding toward the ocean long before there was a St. Johns to urge them on, trickling through protoswamps that were among the first to be exposed when Florida arose from the sea. Because of this, scientists suppose that ancestral animals and plants likely remain in or around their waters, somewhere.

Of these three, Rice is the lost treasure, brimming with pollutants at a rate hardly sustainable to modern life, let alone that of a millennium ago. Its mouth appears to me now, in the broad westerly bend of the river just north of Palatka. The dilemma of Rice is not a simple one but a byzantine puzzle that affects both quality and flow of the water. The Georgia-Pacific Corporation, which turns wood pulp into paper some two miles upstream, continues its practice of discharging the postpulp effluent into the creek—just as it has for the last half century. Chemically, this is not good news at all. But Rice has it own hydrological dilemma, one linked to the very aquifer cave mapper Hutcheson and I had been examining for the last several days.

As sometimes occurs in swamps, there appears to be "upward leakage" from the aquifer into lakes around Keystone Heights, at the westerly edge of the Etonia drainage basin, which feeds Rice Creek. In other words, the aquifer and not direct rainfall sustains the lakes. But when the water pressure of the Floridan Aquifer declines—because of scant rainfall and increased water use—the water level in the lakes there also declines. As this happens, the flow of Etonia and Rice Creeks diminishes, feeding the St. Johns with less water, making the entire river system less noble than it once was. Indeed, a water management district study here showed an average drop of four feet in the level of the upper Floridan Aquifer between 1978 and 1990.

The natural flow of Rice has declined so drastically that during the dry season the effluent from Georgia-Pacific now makes up 97 percent of the its flow; throughout the rest of the year, it contributes 57 percent of the creek's water.

At the bottom of Rice Creek, there is no longer sand but muck, created by erosion and runoff from the poor soil conservation practices over the last century. It is this muck that is particularly good at absorbing carcinogens—the PCBs (polychlorinated biphenyls) and chlorinated pesticides that require six, seven, even eight syllables to describe them. Here, too, are traces of metal contaminants, easier to pronounce but no less deadly—lead, mercury, zinc, copper.

Although the food chain may begin in this bottom, it doesn't end there. Metals and poisons easily pass from worm to crustacean, to small and then larger fish, all the way up the ladder, right to the very top. And for the last several thousand years, the largemouth—even the alligator—is no longer at the very top. Humans are now in that position, with our reserves of spongelike fatty tissue waiting to absorb newly introduced metals, like the muck on the stream bottom.

Today, fish taken from Rice Creek in random samples show high levels of dioxin, a well-known by-product of the pulp industry. In 1997 largemouth bass—Bartram's "great trout"—caught in Rice were among those with the highest mercury content of the entire river. (Even one such fish, afflicted with mercury at a rate above 1.5 millionth of its filet weight, is not safe to eat.) But in 1998 it got worst: female gambusia were discovered with male-like organs. "We're not even sure what aspect of paper mill effluent affects it," biologist Steve Bortone told the *Florida Times-Union*.

Perhaps not surprisingly, Rice Creek has the lowest diversity of species of all the tributaries, a primary indicator of health or the lack thereof. With the outfall of Rice from the west, domestic storm water from the streets of Palatka, and runoff from the agricultural fields that lay neatly gridded back in the woods east of town, the water quality in this segment of the river is no longer good or even fair but is now rated by the state as "poor."

We've done this all by ourselves, piece by piece, over the decades—not because of malicious intent or gratuitous meanness but in the name of economics and jobs. Certainly Georgia-Pacific's payroll alone—seventy-seven million dollars to 1,866 people in 1998—seems to create logic that almost transcends biology. Almost. It's as if we've forgotten that the river is organic, just as we are, and like us is immune neither to abuse nor to the memory of it. It is this memory that still nags us with its presence, even when we try to stuff it down into our unconscious, deep in the mud.

I had thought of fishing here for dinner, but perhaps the idea of a dockside Whopper isn't out of the question after all.

The St. Johns has a language all its own, a dialect separate from that of other rivers. It has spoken to me before in this dialect, spitting and cursing between the whitecaps of Lake George. Now it speaks to me again this morning, turning its surface into a patchwork of prisms, one giant honeycomb of movement and light, a soothing drawl of a speech.

In this way, it almost seems as if the river is cradling the hull of my boat with its optics, keeping me aloof and safe from the rest of the world for a few brief moments—not unlike how the male blue cradles his mate in his swimmerets. Except for a lone tug that grumbled by an hour ago with its oil barge, there is no boat traffic on this river yet today. As I sit on the stern with a cup of coffee, the shoreline nearly hidden by a rising mist, the river does its time-stop illusion trick again. And I think it could be yesterday, or five hundred years ago.

It is on this wet, tannic horizon north of me that I notice a white speck, approaching. As it nears, the speck turns into a churning wake, and in front of the wake is a small Whaler with a large man aboard. This man is Clay Henderson, and—using a combination of cellular telephone and marine radio—we had earlier planned to meet somewhere here along the river today. Henderson is an attorney who heads up the Florida Audubon Society, and he has driven his little kicker-powered skiff more than twenty miles on this fine morning from a downstream ramp. Henderson wants to talk with me a bit about the river and what it has meant to him.

Henderson tosses me a line from his Whaler, I tie him astern, and he joins me here in the middle of the St. Johns. A sixth-generation Florida native, Henderson could be pulling in good money practicing law. But he's seen enough of his home state change in his lifetime to want to direct the state's largest environmental mission to save the best of what's left.

Henderson, a big, affable bear of a man, is also a lifelong aficionado of Billy Bartram's: his young son's middle name is Bartram. Indeed, when Henderson helped direct a statewide program to purchase sensitive lands in fast-growing Florida, he referenced Bartram's *Travels,* letting the record of what the botanist-artist saw 220 years ago help define what we should protect today. "We used *Travels* as a virtual guidebook to acquisition," Henderson explains, "as a way to find out what places ought to be important to us, historically and naturally. . . . If we ever forget, all we have to do is go ask Billy Bartram."

Here on the stern deck, we put our feet up and talk about fishing, about how the old naturalist used a brightly colored "bob" of hair and feathers to catch the great trout up and down the river. In other trips to the St. Johns, Henderson has performed a version of that quest, using a fly rod with deer hair popping bugs, working at the edges of the maidencane and spatter dock for the fish.

The sun rises higher in the new sky, and I drive us toward shore, visible now that the mist has lifted. Here, back in shallow water near a clutch of cypress knees, a bull gator grunts loudly. A great blue heron stands frozen in its hunting mode and then, in a flash of an eye, spears a small bream with its sharp beak. It is this river and its swamps that remain as a natural corridor, providing a refuge to besieged wildlife on the run inside a state that routinely slices and dices its environmental legacy. Despite dramatic comebacks by bald eagles and ospreys in Florida over the last decade, most other birds and animals aren't doing very well at all—especially those who must live outside such corridors.

Henderson tells me that volunteer Auduboners, who began doing Annual Christmas Bird Counts in 1906, have discovered that wild bird populations throughout Florida have decreased by 90 percent since then. There is less woodland, less wetland, less avian life to count inside it all. But Henderson will be the last to throw in the towel. He is more than an environmentalist who fights on theoretical battlegrounds; he is also a sport fisherman, an outdoorsman who sustains a gut link to the river. For him, the St. Johns is a place to retreat, to reestablish a connection with those who came before, even when those who came before were unsure about the worth of the place itself.

"This is the 'Audubon' part of the river you're on now," says Henderson, referring to the namesake of his organization. "Audubon came up here in 1832 and didn't get a whole lot farther than where we are today before he turned back. He didn't think much of it, either. Said Bartram got it all wrong, said the St. Johns was a wild and dreary and desolate place." Henderson laughs heartily at that idea. But it was true.

In fact, in his second attempt to ascend the river, John James Audubon climbed aboard the U.S. schooner *Spark* with the intention of traveling all the way to its headwaters—"as far as navigation will permit"—in search of birds to add to his portfolio. Before he boarded the *Spark*, Audubon had killed five "white headed eagles" in one day at St. Augustine and had seen a caracara fly overhead, a bird not even known to exist in the United States until then. Stoked with Bartram's own written promises of what was to come, Audubon was at first elated about the trip.

But once out on the St. Johns, things did not go well for the high-strung artist. "The fog was so thick that neither of the shores could be seen," he wrote, "and yet the river was not a mile in breadth." Then, blind mosquitoes descended on the boat. "So wonderfully abundant were these tormentors, that they more than once fairly extinguished the candles whilst I was writing in my journal, which I closed in desperation, crushing between the leaves more than a hundred of the little wretches."

At his side was his faithful Lab, Plato, whose job it was to retrieve the birds the artist had shot so they could be sketched in detail. But Plato seemed to not fare well, either, routinely being pecked in the nose by the half-dead birds as he went to fetch them. And then there were the gators, who lurked in wait for the big dog. "Alligators were extremely abundant," wrote Audubon, growing increasingly uncertain about his journey, "and the heads of the fishes which they had snapped off lay floating around on the dark waters." Disgusted, Audubon finally left the *Spark* somewhere just south of present-day Palatka, hiring a boat and two locals to help get him back to St. Augustine. "The stink of river water has caused half of our crew to be sick," Audubon wrote on February 17, 1833. "I look forward to the leaving of it as a happy event!"

"The Garden of America," wrote Audubon finally, mocking Bartram's descriptions. "Where all that is not mud, mud, mud, is sand, sand, sand . . . where in the place of singing birds and golden fishes, you have a species of ibis you cannot get when you have shot it, and alligators, snakes and scorpions."

Several years ago, an environmental organization in Florida assembled an annual "Calamity Calendar," which carefully recorded the sounds of nature backfiring—the sinkholes, the algae blooms, the red tides—in the half-humorous, half-desperate hope of scaring off new residents who flock to the state, thus curbing development. Both Henderson and I agree that John James Audubon's historic observations about the St. Johns would have made a fine entry.

Henderson overnights on the houseboat and by morning climbs back into his little Whaler, getting ready to return to the serious business of saving what is left of natural Florida. Unlike the namesake of his organization, Henderson's affection for the peninsula and the historic river that flows through it is both deep and true. As he disappears in a frothy wake, I hope in my heart that he travels safely. The place wouldn't be the same without him.

Ashore, there is a tiny point here charted as Palmetto, and to the east, back beyond the margin of the river, there are the furrows of Hastings, self-described as the "Potato Capital of Florida," complete with its own suburb, a map dot called Spuds, all a scattered ménage of wood frame farmhouses, tin roofs, and thousands of acres of open space.

Once I met a third-generation potato farmer from Hastings, a congenial man who told me how the warmth of the nearby river helped farmers get their seed potatoes in the ground just a few weeks earlier than anyone else. The early crop at first brought better prices for the farmers of Hastings and made them prosperous, a true potato capital. But by the late 1980s, mechanization and a gradually changing outside world left Hastings and its little downtown and its single blinking traffic light behind again. My new acquaintance lamented this—not so much for the loss of money but because it was a close-knit traditional farm community with children who no longer want to be farmers.

I remember this encounter well, for it let me see the human side of noncorporate farming in the river basin, to understand that there is no well-defined good and evil world populated by caricatures who either pollute or don't—but lots of gray where most of us simply want to do the right thing. Still, doing the right thing by the land and river today is harder than it's ever been, with or without the comfort of old paradigms.

Creeping north through Hastings is a runnel of a stream called Cracker Branch, and it intersects with and is consumed by Deep Creek, which itself winds for some ten miles west to the St. Johns. It is, as its name implies, deep—eighteen and twenty feet and more—and a creek like this carries energy with it. It carries so much energy, in fact, that it occasionally overflows its banks after prolonged rains. Some floods are worse than others: after a nonstop four-day deluge that dropped twenty inches of rainfall onto the basin in the late summer of 1951, Deep Creek imagined itself a lake, sloshing over the fields and into the streets of the Potato Capital itself.

To help remedy this—as well as to protect the wetlands that clean the agricultural runoff—the water management district bought nearly six square miles of floodplain, from the creek's confluence with the St. Johns just above Federal Point, upstream toward Hastings. This conservation area is bottomland hardwood and cypress swamp, habitat for bald eagle and black bear, a place that balances flood control with biology. To leave the broad river at this point and kayak up Deep Creek is a pleasant segue back to the canopied streams of the middle river—an experience made even more so by where it is situated, east of the giant aquatic boulevard and west of Spuds.

Back in the gullet of the main stem, I go with the flow, north, past Deadman Point and Cedar Creek on the west shore, McCullough and Tocoi Creeks on the east. This main stem is fast becoming—how can I say—*monotonous*.

I feel as if I'm in an old Andy Warhol flick, one the filmmaker himself once described as a juxtaposition between the endlessly banal and the haphazardly corrupt. Even the corruption is scant—here a go-fast boat or a tug-barge tandem, there a jet ski. But then, I am the sort of person much happier to be metaphorically cane poling along the darker cusp of the river—at the edges of coves and peninsulas and streams—than trolling in bright, cheery open water.

Tocoi Creek is forthcoming, a welcome gash back in the cypress to the east. Taking its name from an Indian word meaning "water lily," Tocoi is undaunting by tributary standards; in fact, it is not even one of the top twelve systems that flow into the lower St. Johns. That's because it stretches for only 3.6 miles—and during the dry season, it is hardly navigable for most of that distance, tapering quickly to a soft, muddy depression in the swamp. Yet Tocoi has some dandy history to it, mainly having to do with being one of the closest landings on the river to St. Augustine.

As a landing, Tocoi historically rivaled Picolata just to the north, competing for incoming passengers and freight to be carried over a dirt path by cart to the lively resort of St. Augustine. But after the Civil War, Florida went on a railway-building binge. Rail spurs replaced mule-driven carts, and Tocoi was linked directly to the coastal city by a rail spur, making the dusty, teeth-rattling journey a bit more bearable. In this way, Tocoi was the official river "terminus" for the bustling "St. Johns Railway, " a local line with a steam engine and cars that huffed and puffed overland some fifteen miles or so to St. Augustine. Picolata, with no such rail, could no longer compete and went into decline.

Southbound steamship passengers on their way upriver from Jacksonville or Savannah or Charleston could land here, where the rail extended all the way out to the end of the wharf. Or they could land at West Tocoi on the opposite river bank and then ride the ferry across the river to catch the train at the east shore station. When Lanier stopped at Tocoi, there was also a busy "Spanish moss factory" at work, drying and debugging the moss for commercial use. Workers at the moss gin used rakes and hooks to pull the epiphyte from the branches of trees, then piled it in haystacklike heaps or buried it in long shallow pits. When the moss was stored in this way, its gray outer skin quickly rotted, leaving a black, tougher core fiber.

After preparation, the moss was shipped off to be used as stuffing inside mattresses or as upholstery inside chairs, sofas, and railroad car seats. Sometimes the moss found its way north inside boxes of citrus or other delicate items, playing the role Styrofoam and cardboard and little bubbles of plastic serve today.

The little railway that linked Tocoi with St. Augustine, however, soon took on a life all its own, one that went well beyond the spurs of the river landings. Tracks were being laid outside the valley to connect the length of the peninsula. They would eventually make the wharves and the steamships of the St. Johns obsolete. As early as 1880, railroad-run development companies were busy draining the "overflow districts" around their tracks, offering land at $1.25 an acre.

At the creek mouth, there is surely plenty of overflow district to be had, and my kayak takes me there, beyond a generous field of *tocoi*, inside a cathedral of cypress and sweet gum, foliage arches underpinned with wild hibiscus and the purple caterpillar-like flower of the pickerelweed. There are no train whistles, no passengers, just a green clear-wing dragonfly perched atop a red-brown cypress knee, above a glistening set of apple snail eggs. All the tickets for Tocoi have been punched, except perhaps for those silently marking time.

Florida Suite is the music of the river, an orchestral work in four parts. When I first heard it, I was struck with the exotic tranquillity of it all, the laconic, flowing appeal to the natural senses. There seemed to be undertones, a theme, that picked up on the same folk rhythms evoked by Gershwin's *Porgy and Bess*. I liked it a lot, but it wasn't until much later that I found that the inspiration for *Florida Suite* came from the St. Johns—from the year the young composer Frederick Delius spent living on its banks.

He did so here at Solano Point, just north of Tocoi, arriving from Liverpool in the spring of 1884 to manage an orange grove for his father. Orange growing was promoted as easy back then, and the twenty-two-year-old Frederick simply wanted to find some livelihood that gave him plenty of leisure time to study music. But he got more than he bargained for.

At "Solano Grove," he lived in a four-room cypress cottage under the protective canopy of a gargantuan live oak and a magnolia tree. By night, the aroma of orange blossoms commingled with the fresh, wild scent of the woods and the ever flowing river. In a neighboring grove, black workers sang improvised harmony to their folk tunes.

Sometimes, his own servant took Delius out alligator hunting on the river, by torchlight. At other times, he would row the budding composer in a small wooden boat under the moonlight, singing to him. The songs recalled not just plantation life but something long before that, strains of barely remembered African rhythms. They were distant, like the headwaters of the river, but they were also immutable and sure. It was all to change Delius's life, forever.

"His lasting impressions of the wild life about him gave rise to a growing, firm conviction of the supremacy of instinct and the wonder of it all," biographer Eric Fenby later wrote. "The play of light through the dense woods and the gray veil of Spanish moss touched the scene with a mystery he was later to evoke in music." But artists, as the lives of other river travelers have shown, make poor businesspeople. While Delius's sensibilities prospered, the citrus trees didn't, and the young man left the following summer, moving first to Jacksonville, then north, and later back overseas.

There was no escaping the captivating experience on the St. Johns, though. Although Delius earned his share of fame in his lifetime, today he is barely remembered except by classical music buffs. Yet in *Florida Suite* he achieved something he never achieved before—or since. Despite his relative obscurity today, *Florida Suite* is considered by many critics as a world-class work.

As for me, I cannot listen to its four movements without imaging Delius and his servant-friend still here, alive somewhere, exuberant with the wonder of it all: "Daybreak-Dance," "By the River," "Sunset—near the Plantation," "At Night." It's the sound of the river stirring up quiet passion, over a century ago.

Today, the house at Solano Grove is missing as I pass downstream. But unlike other historic wooden structures along the river, it has not been destroyed. Rather, it has been moved to the campus of Jacksonville University, where it is furnished with period furniture and accessories dating from Delius's time, its cypress frame as enduring as the composer's own river vision. "In Florida," Delius once wrote, "through sitting and gazing at nature, I gradually learnt the way in which I should eventually find myself."

There are water moccasins in the creek today. I see them swimming, heads out of the black water as I wade ashore at Picolata, pulling my kayak behind me. It is not exactly the welcome I would have preferred. But they are little snakes, just curious is all, and they quickly swim in the other direction when they see me move.

I am fifty-five miles above where the river empties into the Atlantic. Tidal waters rise and fall here to the whims of the moon, flavoring the woods and swamp with the sea: palm-sized blue crabs scuttle under clear, shallow water across a sandy bottom, barnacles encrust cypress knees, sandpipers flitter next to red-bellied woodpeckers. Saltwater spartina marsh grass spikes out from the bottom, just as I saw it do far upriver, in a tiny and insular connate sea.

There may be no more compelling invitation to a mythical boy riding a raft than the chance to visit an abandoned Spanish fort—in fact, it's pretty damn compelling to a real adult riding a houseboat. There was once such a fort at Picolata, right above Magnolia Landing. Built during the days of the Spanish occupation of the river valley, "Fort Picolata" was cobbled from coquina blocks, compressed seashells like that used to construct the larger, more grandiose Castillo de San Marcos in St. Augustine in 1672.

The blocks were cut from the same quarry at Anastasia Island back on the coast and then shipped upriver and cemented together with lime. Here, the fort guarded a relatively narrow passage in the otherwise broad river, from a cape of land on the easterly bank, a strategic presence in the jungle wilderness of the New World. *Picolata*, it was called, "high bluff." Fort Picolata was modest but formidable: two-foot-thick, pale reddish coquina block walls, a thirty-foot-high square tower topped with a cupola, and at least eight four-pound swivel cannons, two on each side. All of it was surrounded by a moat, a vision of medieval Spain grafted onto a subtropical landscape of sabal palms and cypress and moss.

By the time Billy Bartram and his father, John, arrived here on their first exploratory trip up the St. Johns in 1765, the fort had been abandoned by the Spanish, but it was still in active use: during the Bartrams' brief stay here, it was the site for the "Picolata Congress," in which British colonial governor James Grant persuaded Creek leaders to give him all of East Florida—that chunk of the peninsula between the river and the ocean.

The treaty paved the way for the British Land Grants along the St. Johns. The Creek chiefs, dressed in buckskins and smoking eagle-plumed pipes, accepted a shipload of presents in return for their land concessions. Soon, the western edge of the river became known as the "Indian Shore," a designation that lasted long after the Creeks became Seminoles and were hunted down, chased south, or forced to resettle in the West by the more draconian American army.

On Billy's second, solitary visit upriver ten years later, the fort was still standing but deserted and overgrown. When Sidney Lanier arrived to write his 1875 guidebook, he described Picolata as "a place formerly of importance as a landing for passengers, but now . . . only of historic interest." Along the shore, said Lanier, there are "remains of an old defensive work . . . still to be found."

Ashore today, there is a bucolic, tree-lined river road with an eclectic smattering of structures—ranch style and metal-roofed, log and fancy, gabled stucco—on either side of the road. Nearly each seems to have its own narrow wooden dock stretching out into the river, individual "landings" imitating the steamship wharves of the last century. There is also a Bartram historic marker commemorating Billy's visit to Fort Picolata. But there is no fort, not a trace.

I have made plans to meet an archaeologist here to talk about the vanishing of such things. I park myself in a wooden swing on one of the docks, and soon a compact pickup pulls off the side of the country road. Emerging in shorts and bright pink T-shirt and a pair of Ray Ban sunglasses is Dr. Robin Denson, who did her doctoral work on the study of rivers, of how people who live around them are shaped as the channel constantly reworks itself through the floodplain.

Of such waterways, the St. Johns—in making its way through a low, moist terrain—is far more likely to change course than a river bound by mountains or even low hillocks. In work she has done back on the Ocklawaha, Denson found that banks where Native Americans once lived have been repeatedly undercut and slashed by current until the heart of the midden is more likely underwater than not. Fort Picolata, says Denson, is probably a victim of just such a shifting shore. She taps her finger on my nautical map, a place corresponding to a shallow bar extending out from the capelike shore, not far from where we are now sitting. "It's probably buried out there somewhere," says Denson, now pointing lazily with her hand to the bar, "somewhere between here and the channel." Under the sand and mud, perhaps the walls of Fort Picolata are still intact, holding who knows what stories left to be told, swamped by the rising waters of its own moat.

"We tend to think of the river being where it is today," says Denson. "But it's always moving, even in our lifetimes." A river follows the path of least resistance, altering course when it becomes naturally easier to do so, wandering through its floodplain at will, just as it has for centuries. It is only the conceit of staking a claim on "riverfront real estate" that makes us think it is permanent.

"The shoreline we see right now will change by the flow of the channel, by storms—even by erosion from the wake of boats." Bulkheads, revetments, stone forts only delay that change, not subjugate it. "This is just a single snapshot in time," says Denson, "that's all."

The wild untouched banks are beautiful; but the new settlements

generally succeed in destroying all Nature's beauty, and give you

only leafless, girdled trees, blackened stumps and naked white sand,

in return.—Harriet Beecher Stowe, *Palmetto Leaves* (1873)

*T*he massive Shands Bridge rises up from the water to the north, right beyond the easterly peninsula of Pacetti Point and Palmo Cove. After being lulled into a buzzlike complacency by the broad, repetitive nature of traveling through the middle of this lower river, the appearance of the bridge startles me, looming on the horizon like King Kong over the skyline of Tokyo, one long, low span engorged by a behemoth hump. The hump is the only way for any boat larger than a skiff to get under the bridge, and I aim for it.

I think of this bridge as the gateway to suburban Jacksonville, the tangible arch through which the river passes for another transformation. There are only fifty river miles left before the ocean jetties at Mayport, and they will soon be busy, eclectic miles, indeed. To the right, the confluences of both Six Mile and Trout Creeks slosh in slow motion out into the shallow Palmo Cove, the last bastion of eastern shore wilderness. Upstream, each creek is spanned in turn by SR 13—the "William Bartram Scenic Highway"—in a set of low-slung concrete bridges, of the sort first made popular in Florida back in the twenties and thirties. The country road winds pleasantly along the river for miles, past general stores, under mossy boughs of cypress and oak, and past a little honor-system bait stand with a hand-lettered sign that reads: "Fishing Worms. Self Serve. $1.50 Cup."

Any blackwater stream represents Frost's "road less traveled" for me— tea-colored, wooded passageways that skim through the countryside, door- ways to a lesser-known time. The mouths of both creeks appear as strong, flowing rivers—wider than the Wekiva back in the middle basin—before trailing off into canopied brooks that seem barely known, even unpredictable.

On a warm summer day in 1996, Six Mile Creek became especially unpredictable when a local minister pointed the bow of his sixteen-foot Gheenoe (a stern-backed canoe) up the creek for some solitary bream fishing and found something he wished he hadn't. It was the carcass of a headless dog lying alongside the bank. More than just a dead dog, though, it was the dinner-to-be of one of the largest and most aggressive gators he'd ever encountered. "Suddenly, the front end of the boat just came out of the water," the minister told a local reporter. "The boat spun around so fast it sent a sheet of water into it."

The culprit was an alligator, one that was especially protective about guarding its shoreside meal. "His head was humongous," sputtered the minister. "He was a monster, as long as my boat." Gator trappers later figured that the reptile with an attitude was one they had nicknamed Old Tail Light, because his eyes are so huge they shine like tail lights when a beam hits them at night. It was territorial, wary, and in the fifteen-foot-plus range. Once, a trapper tried to catch it by leaving a baited, outsized steel hook in the water—only to find later his hook straightened by the force of the gator's jaws. Another time, Old Tail Light was spotted swimming with a smaller, eight-foot gator in its mouth.

Certainly, aggressive gators are rare in Florida. But that is little consolation to the angler with alligator teeth marks in his tippy little Gheenoe. Had he not fired up his motor for a swift escape, who knows what might have happened? "I'd have been fishing with Jesus," said the minister.

Huddled on the opposite shore from Palmo Cove is Bayard Point, a 10.5-square-mile conservation area that sprawls southward from the foot of the bridge. It is another one of the low-profile, unsung water management tracts bought to keep riverine wetlands intact—storing floodwaters as it preserves natural lands. Bayard Point is the last truly wild stretch of river I will find before Jacksonville; if I wanted to linger, I could wander through a forest of bottomland hardwoods, pine flatwoods, and communities of sandhills, perhaps encountering warblers and woodpeckers, deer and wild turkey, bald eagles, even the massive but harmless eastern indigo snake.

But there is another mystery to be considered here. And the process of unraveling it is far more sublime than the melodrama of thrashing gators or black snakes as round as my forearm. It has to do with naturalist Bartram, who not only traveled upriver in two separate explorations but actually lived and farmed alongside the St. Johns for almost two years. Over the top with artistic sensibilities, Bartram—naturally enough—became a dismal failure as a farmer. His abandoned five-hundred-acre indigo plantation fell so completely into obscurity that later historians, including his astute biographer Francis Harper, couldn't find it when they looked earlier in this century.

Frustrating as it surely has been for these seekers, the notion of anything this large remaining lost in modern, go-fast Florida is a fascinating one for me—a sign of secrets still to be unlocked along the St. Johns. This particular secret remained sealed until 1995, when history professor Daniel L. Schafer from the University of North Florida did a bit of clever sleuthing. He began by reviewing the only firsthand description of the plantation, recorded by a wealthy Charles Town, South Carolina, merchant, Henry Laurens. The merchant visited Billy there in August 1776 and came away disturbed by the condition of both the writer-naturalist and the farm.

The plantation, wrote Laurens in a letter to Billy's father, John, back in Philadelphia, is "the least agreeable of all the places I have seen, on a low sheet of sandy pine barren verging on the swamp . . . so shoal and covered with umbrelloes that . . . the water is stagnated." Worse was the condition of "poor Billy Bartram"—described as "a gentle mild Young Man, no Wife, no Friend, no Companion, no Neighbor, no Human inhabitant within nine miles of him the nearest by Water . . . Seated upon a beggarly spot of land." Whew! Billy Bartram, a strong swimmer and a fearless adventurer when traveling, had apparently been overwhelmed by the utility of trying to stay put in one place.

Historian Schafer pondered the description of the land. In London, where the Public Records Office recently completed restoration on documents immersed by floods and sewage decades ago, he discovered deeds and maps of the "East Florida Claims Commission." In three of those files, he found references to the land owned by Bartram. The site of the plantation, says Schafer, is a squat peninsula of land known as "Smith's Point," bordered on one side by the easterly footing of the Shands Bridge and on the other by "Little Florence Cove." The plantation house itself—which Laurens described as a "hovel"—likely stood near where Florence Cove Road ends, a relic still awaiting the "ground truthing" of archaeological examination.

It is this point of land I approach by late afternoon. It has been a long day, and I anchor across the river from the cove near the wilderness of Bayard

Point. The sun sets, tinting the sky crimson in the west, launching a sliver
of a crescent moon into the dusk of the east. It is a remembrance of a moon,
accompanied by a dot of astral light that is Venus. Both moon and planet
hang above the site of Billy's old plantation—lonely, wane, beckoning—a
celestial continuum, plaintive in the river night.

Green Cove Springs first comes before me just beyond the Shands Bridge,
and it does so in the form of eleven one-thousand-foot-long piers once used
to mothball a fleet of World War II ships. It is a taste of the industrial riverside sprawl I will see beyond Jacksonville, a giant aquatic, haphazard assem-
blage of metal that seems to have no beginning and no end—working tugs
and disabled seagoing ships and massive metal hulls without cabins or decks.
The whole scene appears like a cartoon alarm clock wound too tight, springs
bursting and hands askew, clock eyes rolled back up into its head.

A couple of the southernmost piers seem to be given over to a marina. I
maneuver the boat next to one pier, spinning the wheel and tugging at the
throttle until the broad-beamed houseboat clunks up against the rubber
bumpers at the edge of the dock. Here, I climb a ladderlike railing up to the
top of the pier and wander about on shore, where the terrestrial motif is
driven by homemade cabin cruisers propped up on blocks and scrap metal.
I am looking for a dockmaster who might supply some fresh water or fuel.
But the blockhouselike structure identified as an "office" seems lifeless.

Back on the concrete pier next to where I am temporarily berthed, two
pickups are haphazardly parked; the doors of one are thrown open, and the
voice of Hank Williams Jr. blares heroically from a tape player, covering a
range of several hundred yards. The pickup truck owners and their girl-
friends—in short denim cutoffs—are steaming shrimp and crabs over a grill
on the dock, knocking back cold Budweisers, oblivious to all else, the pungent scent of shellfish seasoning and testosterone commanding the moment
here. It all seems happily beyond the realm of adult supervision.

Just downriver, the piers give way to a shallow cove. The workaday town
of Green Cove Springs itself pushes up against the point of land bordered
by the cove and Governors Creek just to the north. I have an old colorized
postcard of Green Cove, from the halcyon days when it was the most prominent landing and resort between Jacksonville and Palatka, back when the
town radiated out from the luxury hotels that housed the steamboat visitors.

Like other riverside resorts, Green Cove sported a winter "season," one that both began and ended with the glitter of tony balls at hotels like the St. Clair and the Clarendon, which adjoined the artesian sulfur springs. And what springs they were! In his guidebook, Lanier reported that they were used for "the cure of rheumatism, gout, Bright's disease of the kidneys, and such afflictions."

For the affluent, the St. Johns surely was both their oyster and their antidote, one to be consumed in high-profile, velvet-trimmed luxury. Wealthier snowbirds who nested in resorts like this seldom realized that—just beyond the boundary of their fantasy—hardscrabble crackers were living back in the woods in shacks, eating gopher tortoises and the root of the coontie palm, scrapping out a living by draining pine sap for turpentine and cutting live oak for timber.

But there is a hint of something else afoot in this place. In a letter dated 1870, a steamboat visitor named D. R. Mitchell wrote of Green Cove Springs as a "charming place [with] two large hotels, fine trees, walks, etc. Its principal attraction is a mineral spring which throws 3,000 gallons of water per minute [4.3 million per day]. The water is strongly sulphurous with a temperature of 75 degrees, and of course, not agreeable to the taste, but is said to be nice for bathing."

Today, a hydrological report shows the springs still active, pumping out three cubic feet per second—barely two million gallons per day. If the first report was correct, the outflow has decreased by well over half since 1870, representing a trend I am seeing up and down the entire river. The volume of potable water under our ground has a budget, just like a checking account, and if we continue to write checks while deposits dwindle, mother nature may someday close out the account altogether. The impact on the flow of the river can only be imagined, with the notion of *diminishing* becoming the only sure effect of this cause.

On the opposite riverbank, letter writer Mitchell told of a "similar spring at a place called Remington Park, and a hotel is talked of." But on the spit of land where Remington Park is mapped, there is a clue to a reality far more tangible than the promotional promise of an artesian spring and another resort hotel. At the peninsular tip is a cape with the unlikely name of Popo Point. It is the site of Fort San Francisco de Pupo, a small Spanish fortress contemporary with Fort Picolata—and one every bit as lost in time, so lost that mapmakers have discarded all but one word of its name and converted the *u* to an *o* in what remains. First built of wood by the Spanish in 1737, Fort Pupo was destroyed by the British forces of General Oglethorpe in 1740—and then rebuilt from coquina, like its miniature sister fort of Picolata. Now, it has vanished.

The cannons no longer thunder from Fort Pupo; indeed, there is no longer much acknowledgment of the role the bastion played along the river itself. It is another enigma, another piece of the riverine puzzle waiting to be solved.

I have turned in my houseboat and will travel from here to the ocean in a twenty-five-foot custom-built aluminum-hulled research vessel operated by the St. Johns River Water Management District. Used to monitor water quality along the lower river, the boat and its crew routinely travel the St. Johns in pursuit of science, even on the most grim of days. It is midwinter now, and the skies are swirling with wispy streaks of cirrus up high and gray down low, spitting a cold drizzle. The lower river, which is inviting, if formidable, on a pleasant, sunny day, looks serious and steely and decidedly unfriendly. "Even the fishermen have to respect us when they see us out on days like this," jokes biologist John Burns, a specialist in sea grasses along this stretch of the river.

Off we go from a ramp near Green Cove Springs, headed into a steady chop and a chilled wind made even colder by our speed. Like everyone else, I am in jeans, heavy shirt, and rain parka; although I pull the hood of the jacket tight around my head, I begin to shiver the moment I move from the protection of the open cabin to the stern of the boat. To be in a small john-boat or a canoe on a day like this would be a fatal notion. The lower St. Johns can be cold and windy and even dangerous—in the winter, on the wrong day. It is another part of the complex gestalt of riverine weather and ecology that exists outside the world of sanitized tourist brochures.

Aboard, hunkered down in the lee of the skimpy cabin with us, is environmental specialist Dean Campbell. Campbell grew up in Palatka upstream from here and as a boy remembers seeing the remains of the outdated and abandoned steamship *Hiawatha* gradually slough itself off into detritus, until it became part of the flow of the river itself. Like Burns, Campbell is a scientist with a connection, a feeling for the spirit of this mighty resource. The water temperature of the St. Johns today hovers at sixty degrees. He explains how a lingering swatch of frigid air will eventually chill the water beneath us. "After we get a cold snap and the air gets in the twenties for a few hours, the river temperature will dip down to the low fifties," explains Campbell. "But that's about as cold as it's going to get." For folks like us used to Florida's cozy subtropical allure, that seems nearly brutally frigid by comparison.

Campbell has brought me a stack of very official-looking studies, all done on the lower river—reports on hydrodynamics and salinity, hydrology and biological resources. The studies are careful, precise, full of charts and graphs with peaks as sharp as mountain ridges. Science must have a name for each thing it examines—and so, there are scads of tables, with titles like "Estimated autocorrelations of normalized data of creek flow" and "Correlation matrix of monthly normal rainfall."

This lower river seems to have been analyzed and prodded in ways I wasn't sure were even possible. Yet, because of its sheer size and momentum—and since it largely exists with the natural clout of all that flows from the south into it—there is little tangible "retrofitting" available to the lower river basin. Unlike the upper basin, there are no canals and pastureland to purchase and convert into wetlands, no canals to plug or unplug, no dikes to remove.

There are, however, lots of people and industry huddled next to the shore, upcoming in Duval County. The momentum of all of this is not unlike a steam engine roaring down the tracks, with dozens of engineers each vying to control the throttle to make it go a little bit faster. Scientific reports, even those that warn of a decline in water quality from the impact of this speeding train, more often than not get butted clear of the tracks. The economy means jobs, and even though jobs would still remain if the pollution abated, the paradigm of growth and development is an effective cowcatcher, sweeping clear contrary facts. Even the best, ecologically sensitive management plans get knocked aside, as well, if there is no way to fund them. The little research boat I am in today feels small and alone on this cold winter river, and it is not a bad metaphor for how any conservationist must feel here in this lower basin.

Yet, there is more to all this. The earliest residents of the St. Johns, the Timucua, believed, like many pre-Columbian peoples, in the duality of all things, and so it is for this lower river. Despite my intellectual knowledge of its dilemmas, I find myself in awe at the size and power of this final stretch of the St. Johns—and as fascinated as ever by the shards of cultural history that remain. It is a bittersweet affection, one that must be compounded for each person who lives anywhere here in this lower basin.

Upcoming off our easterly gunnels is Black Creek, a major tributary on the lower river. Steamboats once traveled all the way upstream to Middleburg, and live oak cutters floated their lumber in rafts downstream to the sawmills at Jacksonville. Ship captains routinely stopped to "water" here, believing the creek's waters were both "sweeter" and hardier, less likely to become stagnant on long voyages, even ones that sailed outside the river and down the coast of Florida. With its very own drainage basin of five hundred square miles, Black is in turn fed by no fewer than fourteen other creeks, which trail off in all directions for a combined total of 143 extraordinary miles. The basin itself is still largely undeveloped, just far enough outside the suburban sprawl of Jacksonville to remain safe for now.

It is a good thing, too, because the creek the Spanish first called Rio Blanco has more than its share of uniqueness. The most obvious to any connoisseur of the paddle-driven craft is that—along with the Ocklawaha and the Wekiva—Black Creek is usually the only other St. Johns tributary to be included in most guides to canoeing and kayaking in Florida. As I have already seen, scads of other tributaries do qualify as eminently paddleable. But this trilogy still remains unbroken—at least perceptually—to the general public. I will return to Black Creek by myself later on a bright and cheery winter day, putting my kayak in far upstream and navigating beyond its heavily wooded, ravinelike banks. I will paddle Black Creek until I reach a place in the shallows where the rim of the tea-colored water barely covers the gnarled back of a platter-sized snapping turtle. Here, I will reach down and, as gently as I can, stroke his armored tail, just inches under water. He will twitch it slowly, as if I awoke him from a deep sleep, and then move somnambulantly away, a reptile in rapture with its own primitive memories. I will think, then, of the classic observation writer Margaret DeLand once made in 1889 in *Florida Days*, every bit the timeless riparian truth today as it was then: "The creek is full of quiet life. A sensitive person might be conscious he was an intruder."

Like the Ocklawaha, Black Creek is an ancient stream, one that arises from a steep, prehistoric dune ridge of pine and scrub oak that extends from Putnam County into southeastern Georgia. The result is a river that cuts down into limestone bedrock for part of its journey upstream from Middleburg, creating eddies and riffles swirling over rocky bottoms, and in places, scooping out holes that plunge to ninety feet.

Biologically, there is potential for something special here as well: because it was flowing back in the mid-Pleistocene, long before most of the St. Johns configured itself into its contemporary form, Black Creek had time to speciate critters living in the isolation of its waters. Found here and nowhere else on earth is the Black Creek crayfish (*Procambarus pictus*), along with three species of endemic midges. Many scientists believe *pictus* itself to be the earliest surface-dwelling crayfish to colonize the newly formed peninsula of Florida, truly a living fossil.

Researchers who returned to Black Creek fifty years after *pictus* was first discovered in 1940 confirmed that it still existed here—except at those collection sites with heavier shoreside development. In these places of "anthropogenic activity," siltation and enriched nutrients clogged the water, and channelization reduced the stream flow. *Pictus* vanished from those sites—along with whatever still undiscovered aquatic life form that might have lived in symbiosis with it.

North we go, slicing through the steady winter chop, past Fleming Island and its Hibernia Point to the west and Switzerland to the east, two places named by original settlers with ineffable longings for their European homelands. Both sites seem sparsely settled, far less ambitious today than when they were first pioneered as prosperous plantations along the wilderness of the riverfront.

The Fleming family from Ireland carved out a thriving cotton plantation here in 1790 under a Spanish grant, constructing a grandiose manor house with seven chimneys. Hibernia, they called this place, naming it for the poetic description of their own island across the sea. Author Eugenia Price later fictionalized characters from Hibernia in her historic novel *Margaret's Story*. When the fine manor home was finally demolished in the mid-1950s, there were enough chimney bricks left to build another house on the site.

Switzerland was so named by Francis Philip Fatio, a Swiss from Bern who settled here during the British ownership of Florida in 1772. As a good, neutral Swiss, Fatio endured, even after the territory was returned to the Spanish and his British neighbors fled. Fatio's title to sprawling tracts of land up and down the river endured as well, long after the swampy peninsula of La Florida was later acquired by the new country of America. Today, the Fatio name still appears on real estate deed searches on thousands of acres of land in the basin, weathering more than 230 years of change, from indigo and cotton field to upscale waterfront homesite.

Although we are in the middle of the channel now, the river bottom is only ten to fourteen feet under us. The horizon stretches out from an opaque, steely surface of riffling gray that seems every bit as consuming as that of some of the lakes I have been across on the upper river. The gradient remains slight and the current nigh here, with the dynamics of the water flow diffused and absorbed by wetland edges. But at Jacksonville, the river will narrow as it did at Palatka; when it does, the current will surge, scouring out a much deeper river bottom.

While the notion of keeping a wetland intact seems almost frivolous to those with only short-term designs on the urban riverfront, there are some dramatic lessons to be learned when natural rules like that are violated. Wetlands do absorb and store water—and in doing so, they don't just filter and clean it, but they help abate floods. "You see a lot of creeks here in the lower river," says Campbell, flatly. And then: "The ones with development have fairly significant flooding events."

Indeed, it is flooding most folks seem to understand because it affects them in a very direct, NIMBY—Not In My Back Yard—sort of way. One does not even have to care about ecological ethics to want a yard dry enough so the family pet doesn't have to tread water. District strategies to abate creek flooding by rerouting or storing storm water almost always improve the health of the river, if just a little bit. "We can use issues of flooding to leverage storm water and water quality," says Campbell.

These "overflowed districts," as they were historically called by land speculators aching to drain the state in the late 1800s, have perfectly good natural reasons for being so. A flooding event, particularly a significant one, can raise the water four to five feet above what is normal, swamping docks and boathouses and lawns when heavy rains wash down from the higher upland ridges—if there is no spongelike overflowed district to soak it up.

The mouth of Julington Creek passes to the east, so large that it seems like it may contain the channel itself. Stretching a half mile from shore to shore, Julington easily dwarfs portions of the upper river I have seen below Palatka, and it sports its own arched bridge, which I notice is busy with toy-sized vehicles streaming to and fro over it like slot cars. On the north shore of Julington is the muscular peninsula that holds Mandarin, with its own treasure trove of riverine secrets.

"We're right over the site of the *Maple Leaf*," says Campbell suddenly, referring to the Civil War–era Union steamer sunk in mid-river by a torpedo in 1864. I move away from the security of the cabin and look over the side of the gunnels, but the only thing I see is more water, sleek now and laid down flat by the cold wind.

Under twenty feet of this water and four to seven feet of river-bottom mud are the remains of the *Maple Leaf*, a former luxury paddlewheeler pressed into service as a supply ship. Loaded with four hundred tons of camp gear, food, and tools, it was traveling from Palatka to Jacksonville, where it planned to rendezvous with some thirty other Union ships. There, the small armada would try to recapture Jacksonville—for the fourth time—from Confederate diehards. Sympathies in Florida were so mixed about the war that any partisan voyage on the St. Johns could sooner or later bring a volley of shots from the other side if a ship traveled during the day. And so, the 173-foot-long ship steamed downriver under cover of darkness.

But Rebels had other ideas. Not long before the *Maple Leaf* arrived at Mandarin Point, a team of Confederates rowed out in a small boat and set twelve "torpedoes"—wooden barrels with black gunpowder—in place, anchoring them just below the surface. At 4 A.M. on April 1, 1864, the hull of the Union supply ship smashed into one. The explosion killed four black crewmen and sank the steamer within minutes, along with most of its cargo. While the upper decks were blasted and burned away a few years later to keep the wreck from becoming a navigational hazard, the bottom sank into the soft, oxygen-deprived mud. And there it lay, preserved from both wood-boring teredo worms and rot, a time capsule holding detailed memories of one brief moment in the Civil War—until Jacksonville dentist and avid amateur archaeologist Keith Holland decided to open it.

After careful research—and with approval of state and federal officials—Holland's crew of mostly volunteer divers found the site and began the painstaking chore of excavating it in 1987. Work took place in two-knot currents and total darkness, as mud sediment and tannin blocked out surface light. But the diligence paid off: over the next few years, more than six thousand artifacts would be recovered, including hand-made checkers, an officer's sword handle, a powder flask, a bale of tobacco, and a still playable wooden flute. In 1994 the *Maple Leaf* was even recognized as a National Historical Landmark Shipwreck Site.

But there is more here at Mandarin than maritime history, however fiery it may be. Like other high and dry landings, the site was once a Timucua village, one named Thimaqua. Brit settlers built over it, calling their own village St. Anthony; later, the Spanish translated that to San Antonio. By 1821 Thimaqua became Mandarin, for the hybrid orange sometimes grown here. As recently as 1953, a local history guide described Mandarin as a hamlet of two thousand, "of quaint charm and happy people." By 1998 Mandarin was simply one more busy suburb of Jacksonville, with a burgeoning population that had swelled to thirty times its 1953 size.

Ashore on the edge of Mandarin Point is the former site of writer Harriet Beecher Stowe's home and her thirty-acre citrus grove. Wintering here from 1868 to 1883, the prim New Englander and her husband, Calvin Stowe—the dignified, white-bearded "Professor"—are still pictured in sepia-tinted photos sitting on the front porch, next to where a giant oak grows through the porch roof, under cornices of gingerbread and wooden arbors woven with vine. From her home, the author and abolitionist shipped crates of fruit northward, each stenciled with the label "Oranges From Harriet Beecher Stowe, Mandarin, Florida." Stowe was as messianic about her love for Florida as she was about equality for former slaves, and it was revealed to the rest of the world in her collection of essays, *Palmetto Leaves*, published in 1873. In it, she raved about life on the wild, broad St. Johns, where "our life is so still and lonely . . . that even so small an event as our crossing the river for a visit is all absorbing."

For entertainment, Stowe and friends would travel up into the "wide bayou" of Doctor's Lake on the opposite shore, amid all its islands, swamps, and gator nests. There, they would gather the buds of palms to weave palmetto hats and "all manner of palm work." From her tree-studded porch, she would look through a "spy glass" for steamers coming up the broad river, and when necessary, she would get them to land by hanging out a flag on her wharf. "The great blue sheet of water shimmers and glitters like so much liquid lapis," she wrote one day of her view from the porch, the words of a woman in love with a place. Stowe was also famous in her own time on the river and eventually became a tourist attraction herself: the steamer *Mary Draper* would charge tourists seventy-five cents for a round trip from Jacksonville to Mandarin, promising a glimpse of the writer at work on her porch.

Today, the Stowe house is gone, but a local Episcopal church still has a Tiffany window commissioned by her in memory of the Professor. In it, stained glass forever captures the river she once saw from her front porch, a holy vision of cypress and moss and a sheet of liquid lapis, backlit by the theater of the golden light.

Julington Creek was dotted with sailboats in the days Stowe boated upstream there to picnic. At its edges, "the bottom of the river is of hard, sparkling white sand, into which spikes are easily driven," she reported. Along with Arlington River in downtown Jacksonville, Julington marks the boundary of the zone where the incoming wedge of salt water from the ocean first meets fresh water and mixes with it.

It is also the tributary of the St. Johns with the heaviest residential and industrial development. It is activity with a price: the hard, sparkling white sand is now mud—the same mud that preserved the *Maple Leaf* back on the river bottom. But this mud contains what the water management district chemists call the "greatest metal enrichment" of all the St. Johns—a bottom rife with mercury, copper, cadmium, lead, and zinc—all the result of metal release from fossil fuels, metal stripping, and the use of pesticides on lawns and gardens. There are also organic contaminants aplenty, including cancer-causing PCBs and chlorinated pesticides—even those outlawed for decades.

According to a 1993 water management report titled "Sediment Characteristics and Quality," DDT and chlordane—once widely used to control mosquitoes and termites—were found in "very high levels"; another study in 1988, by the National Oceanic and Atmospheric Administration, showed that portions of the lower St. Johns ranked 17th in the nation (among 212 coastal sites tested) in the level of PCB contamination. Much of this remains hidden from view, secreted down in the mud, as do other pollutants up and down the river.

To the west as we go is the suburb of Orange Park and the former site of Laurel Grove, a once grand slave plantation of Zephaniah Kingsley. It was one of a chain that stretched up and down the river from Drayton Island back in Lake George. The height-challenged Kingsley, who used to wear a tall hat and ride a large white horse in public to make himself seem more formidable than he really was, might appreciate the upcoming Buckman Bridge, a six-lane span of metal and concrete that carries autos for more than three miles across the river at the southernmost loop of Interstate 295, beginning not far from his historic Laurel Grove. Surely, it is a superlative antidote to all things low and short, a place he might like to have ridden his tall white horse, at a gallop.

Plummer's Point appears on the right, at the easterly ramp of this Buckman Bridge. It is here that the nutrients from the wastewater plant at Mandarin surge out into the river. In 1997 the plant dumped ninety-five tons of nitrogen a year into the river—about a 40 percent increase over what it discharged six years earlier. Other "point sources" like this will continue through urban Jacksonville for a simple reason: people use water, and the residue of that use must go somewhere. In 1997 ninety million gallons of wastewater a day was drained into the river in Jacksonville-dominated Duval County. Technology is available to scrub out the remaining nutrients from the flush of toilets and the sump of drains. But, like the treatment of storm water—which contributes half of the nutrient load to the lower river—it is highly expensive.

Oddly, it is considered safe nowadays for a politician to be environmentally responsible—right up to the point where that rhetoric translates into higher taxes or a hike in sewer and water rates. Public spending is bad karma to any elected official these days, especially in an era in which candidates routinely ride the coattails of antitax bandwagons into office. And so the result of that contradiction—between rhetoric and reality—is what we pass today in our little boat, alone here in the river: nitrogen by the ton means fertilizing the river, like one fertilizes a lawn or field. Plants grow out of control, like a lawn with no one to tend it, and the whole system goes into overload.

Compounding all this human-made morass is the reality that the lower river is an extremely complicated estuary to begin with, John Burns tells me. Just nature alone has made it so. "A river is not a lake," says Burns. "There's much more involved than just water flow, however slow it is."

Burns, who specializes in the study of submerged aquatic plants, says light is an extremely vital issue in this part of the river. "It's an estuarine system here," says Burns, "but it's also highly colored because of the tannin in the water." And what is tannin but particulates, minerals and sediments from organic decay? As I graphically saw during my scuba dive back at Croaker Hole in Little Lake George, these tannins effectively block sunlight, keeping the bottom locked in perpetual twilight. Add human-made runoff and effluent to the natural tannins, and the water gets darker still. Encourage surface algae to grow with an effusion of nutrients, and you create an additional blanket that shrouds nearly everything from the light. "It becomes very complicated then to understand what the dynamics of the system are," explains Burns.

Submerged grasses, those that live on the bottom, are particularly important as nurseries for small fish and habitat for others, places to live, feed, and hide. Tapegrass, also known as eelgrass—*Vallisneria americana*—is the predominant freshwater grass in the river for good reason: it only needs 1 percent of surface light to charge the photosynthesis that keeps it alive. But sometimes it doesn't even get that. In the spring of 1997, a Blob-like sheet of stringy green algae stretched from Julington Creek some eight miles north to Christopher Creek, fed by nutrients. Under the algae, *Vallisneria* died a sickly death. Other algae blooms have swarmed over the river before, but none this vast and sudden.

Scientists like to find indicator species to gauge the health of the larger environment. For Burns, that species is bottom grass. The passing of it means more than loss of nursery and habitat for aquatic critters, though. It's a signal that other things are amiss in the food chain. Now, the fish have been sick, turning up with open sores and tumorlike wounds. Largemouth bass, catfish, croaker, and yellowmouth trout have all been found disfigured, flesh eaten away, like something out of a bad sci-fi flick.

At first, it seemed like an affliction called ulcerative disease syndrome (UDS), an illness that did the same sort of damage to fish back in the early 1980s—and one for which there was no readily available answer. A biological report on UDS in 1988 suggested a "pollution-related origin, mostly likely from heavy metals." The pathogens causing the infections were fairly common ones present in many estuarine systems. But it was the pollution that *weakened* the immunization systems of the fish, making them more vulnerable to the bacteria. Not surprisingly, the worst outbreaks were around the industrial Talleyrand docks area farther downtown.

Water in these stretches can be cleaned, even flushed by the tides; but it is the mud that holds the accumulated toxins, releasing them back into the water on a timetable that humans have little success in understanding. Mud is hidden, then, only aesthetically.

By 1997 scientists thought they had the culprit pinned down. It was *Crypto-peridiniopsis*—a microbe from a family of dinoflagellates, one closely related to the more famous fish disease *Pfiesteria piscicida*. Not found outside a laboratory until 1991, *Pfiesteria* has been linked to other fish kills in North Carolina and the Chesapeake Bay, especially in those rivers clogged with the overwash of people and industry. It is similar to the driving force of the red tides that periodically sweep up and down coastal Florida. "Crypto," also found disfiguring fish in Florida on the St. Lucie River, seems to act in the same way as *Pfiesteria*, dissolving the protective mucous coating of fish. Lab studies of the better scrutinized *Pfiesteria* already show disturbing links between the disease and people—in which humans develop skin lesions as well as memory loss and cognitive disfunction.

But even before Crypto was identified, Burns himself had made startling discoveries that did not bode well. The biologist set up two aquarium tanks back in his lab. One was filled with minnows and clean water, and the other with minnows and river water and sediment from sites where diseased fish were harvested. In less than three months, 75 percent of the river tank fish became ill or died, while the clean-water fish lived.

The *Florida Times-Union*, once an ultraconservative, railroad and development-driven daily that reflected the mood of another century, took the lead in exposing problems such as these during the 1990s in lengthy, front-page specials, as well as on its Internet Web site. Although the paper also editorialized for a clean river, it drew the line at directly criticizing those industries that caused the pollution. After all, industry was thoroughly woven into Jacksonville. If industrial sources dumped some 247,906 pounds of toxic chemicals into the urban river there over a four-year period—according to a 1996 study by the national Environmental Working Group—then, well, that was the imagined price of commerce. It seemed a bit like a sailor bailing furiously to keep his leaking dingy from sinking—while at the same time failing to plug the holes that caused the leaks.

Nonetheless, the mood toward the river has shifted drastically since the early 1970s, an era when virtually untreated waste was emptied directly into the St. Johns and environmental issues had an editorial priority a few notches behind stories with useful hints to the housewife. It seemed to reflect the gradual rise in awareness by the community at large: in the summer of 1998, a nine-month undercover investigation by the local state attorney's office into pollution of the river actually resulted in a number of arrests. Dubbed "Operation River Rat," the investigation cited twenty-nine people and eight corporations in the Jacksonville metro area. Many, who faced up to five years in prison and thousands in fines, were secretly videotaped dumping toxins in the river—like oil-soaked debris from commercial barges.

Times have changed, and certainly for the better. To call attention to the sewage dilemma in the mid-seventies, former Jacksonville mayor Hans Tanzler took matters into his own hands. This being Florida, Tanzler selected the publicity option that then seemed most available: he water-skied up and down the river, being extra careful, one would assume, not to fall in.

Freshwater grasses, even the ones still surviving, disappear just south of Jacksonville as the incoming saltwater wedge washes over the river bottom. But unlike other estuarine nurseries, no widespread pastures of sea grasses arise to take their place.

To the west, we churn past Piney Point, upon which the Jacksonville Naval Air Station and its contingent of madly zooming military helicopters are mounted. Just on the other side, the Ortega River joins the main stem, running in the same direction like an acceleration ramp on an interstate highway. The confluence of the Ortega marks the last bit of wide river I will see before the St. Johns reaches the ocean. Here, the broad St. Johns begins to funnel itself up agilely into the "Narrows" of Jacksonville, before dog legging due east, north, and east again, at rather astoundingly unnatural angles of nearly forty-five degrees. The channel here will become especially tight, the current swift, and the bottom deep—up to seventy feet and more in spots. Tides moving in from the ocean shift directions about every six hours, with only a short slack in between.

But we are nearing the influence of the oceanic winds. This force all by itself has the power to raise the river by two feet at Jacksonville, sometimes even pushing the surface water in the opposite direction of the outflowing ebb—disrupting the careful planning of tide tables.

For serious sport boaters with the need for provisions, the densely settled Ortega is widely known for its one-stop shopping: not only are there food markets and marinas up and down the creek, but there are restaurants and yacht clubs, in fact, nearly anything one might expect from a shopping plaza—an anthropogenic matrix of the good, bad, and ugly. There is even a topless bar, wild life of another sort beyond that of the gators and otters and deer I have encountered on natural tributaries of the middle and upper river.

Hydrologically, the Ortega is another spiderwebbing waterway, winding through a ninety-nine-square-mile drainage basin, confluxing with its own set of tributaries, including the Cedar River, and creeks named Butcher Pen, Wills Branch, Fishing, and—the most distant—McGirts. There are sabal palms (*Sabal palmetto*) here, as elsewhere along the river, and they often sport the characteristic "bootjacks" that distinguish the younger trees from the older. Long ago, when I was first beginning to understand the Florida landscape and what lived in it, the smooth, pipe-stemmed-like trunk of the older, taller sabals contrasted so sharply with the heavily gridded younger trees that they seemed like separate species altogether.

But the tough, elastic Y-like husks that cover the trunks of the latter are simply the remaining stem from which earlier leaves once grew. If you rip one away, it does look a bit like an organic bootjack or a horn for a very large shoe. Plastered atop each other on a trunk, the bootjacks catch pieces of decaying leaves and berries, creating minigardens that invite most anything to come and grow, courtesy of wind-driven spores or bird-dropped seeds: I have seen, sprouting from bootjacks, golden polypody ferns, the rare hand fern, and the thin, grassylike shoestring fern, saplings of water oaks and magnolias, even the thin, winding cereus cactus. Tiny reptiles flit about, anoles and sand lizards, and tree frogs sit quietly back inside a dark, handy cleft, waiting for the cool night to be reborn. Even here on the Ortega, there are still links left to the natural river, if you look closely enough for them.

Oddly, all of the Ortega was once called McGirts Creek. It was so named for Dan McGirt, who once set up an outlaw camp on the bank of the stream—civic altruism never being a requirement for memorialization in Florida. McGirt was a turncoat Revolutionary War soldier who fled his regiment, joined up with the Rangers of British East Florida, and, with them, led raids through northern Florida and southern Georgia, torching the homes, huts, and camps of patriots as he went. When the war ended, McGirt's zeal for plundering continued in a most egalitarian fashion: from his river camp, he robbed and raided British, American, and Spanish settlements indiscriminately.

Downstream, past the territory of Dan McGirt, we go under another bridge—this one the Fuller Warren. With its preponderance of no fewer than six road and railroad bridges, Jacksonville is not only the most bridged segment of the St. Johns but also perhaps the most bridged large river in all of Florida—all within just a few miles of waterway.

Bridges helped define this city. Until the Acosta Bridge was in place in 1921, only the Florida East Coast Railroad and ferries carried people and their supplies from one side of the river to the other. Most of Jacksonville's growth was limited to the north side of the St. Johns, where the city was originally settled. By the 1950s and 1960s, other bridges followed, opening up dredged spoil and saltwater wetlands to development on the south side, forever changing the face of this most northern of Florida cities.

We wait for one of these bridges to be raised now, a bascule span that is so low slung that even our small boat can't get under unless it is raised. It is a drawbridge carrying the railroad, a dark vision that seems pulled intact from the Rust Belt, an archaic grid of black steel. Its rise is counterbalanced by a heavy weight, a device that seems for all the world like a medieval catapult, ready to toss boiling oil on the swarming masses. Across it now goes a freight train, sputtering and clacking, the vehicle that replaced the riverboats and that now has been nearly displaced itself by the highways and airports. Urban Jacksonville sprawls out around me, and it is a place of tall, shiny buildings, all mighty testaments to human enterprise on the river, a virtual canyon of ambition.

Yet there is a special aesthetic to all this, especially by evening, when the lights of the riverside city sparkle and the arching spans across the water are electrified, all of it reflected in the mirror of the black river, creating a dynamic skyline as uniquely Floridian as any I've seen. If you are a naturalist at heart, you simply have to suspend disbelief during your trip through this riverine city, accepting the human-made gestalt for what it has to offer, not for what you want it to be.

Through the canyon walls our boat goes now, a skyscraping tribute to insurance and banking headquarters, hotels, and commercial towers, logos and names claiming territory like Dan McGirt once claimed his—CSX and Times-Union and Omni. Chamber of commerce guides brag that the state's largest building—the ten-story Bisbee Building—was first built here at the turn of the century. The city subsequently eclipsed itself in that "highest" claim with the twenty-two-story Prudential in 1955 and the twenty-seven-story Gulf Life structure in 1967. They are all edifices in glass—rectangular and glass, pyramidal and glass, stacked like a stairway and glass, glary even in the winter gray. It is all a testament to Zephaniah Kingsley's belief that taller surely is better.

On the north shore is the pastel ménage of muted oranges and greens that is the Jacksonville Landing, a marketplacelike retrofitting where fountains gush water and banners wave festively and men in suits and ties march brusquely about. We dock here, tie up to a set of pilings, and head inside, past the Victoria's Secret store and its designs on cantilevered womanhood every bit as structurally engineered as the bridges of Jacksonville. When Lanier wrote of the city in 1875, he described the riverfront street of Bay, which the Landing has replaced, as a market alive with the colorful vitality of shopkeepers hawking their wares—including "sea-beans, alligator teeth, plumes of heron and curlew's feathers, crane's wings, angel fish, mangrove and orange walking canes."

We belly up to a fast-food counter inside the landing and order hot black coffee and drink it, hunched over in our winter river clothes, a rough-edged slough of calm, safe from the riptide of crisp efficiency swirling about us. Campbell gives me three maps of the river mouth, showing me how the St. Johns has changed course over time. One is Spanish, one early American, and one is contemporary.

They are more pieces of the puzzle, evidence of a riverine lineage that goes past today, even yesterday, back to a time even before chain stores starting selling *café lattes* and lingerie, evidence of an era that modern skyscraping Floridians can barely fathom.

More than a half century of intensive work and the expenditure of some $18 million in dredging the river's channel and basin have made Jacksonville one of the great inland ports of North America . . . not unlike the waterfront of Cairo on the Nile—Branch Cabell and A. J. Hanna, *The St. Johns: A Parade of Diversities* (1943)

A palimpsest is an ancient manuscript that has been written upon and erased, over and over again, through the centuries. It uses a medium, like parchment, that is too rare, too valuable to discard. The St. Johns itself is surely one long and meandering palimpsest. And perhaps its most worked-over site is Jacksonville. There have been more people here, for longer times, erasing the past and re-creating the present, than anywhere else on the river—perhaps anywhere else in this entire palimpsest of Florida.

But like reinscribed parchment, the eras of the river will reveal themselves if held up to the light—if they are examined closely. There is a theme to this particular palimpsest that emerges repeatedly here in Jacksonville, and that theme is industry. Industry, overlain with a patina of riverside strollways and whimsical retail shops and water taxis zipping about like dragonfly larvae chasing gambusia, has come honestly to Jacksonville.

When entrepreneurs first went inland in Florida to exploit the resources, they came to this place, setting up a water-powered sawmill upstream on Six Mile Creek in 1819 and the first steam-driven sawmill on nearby Trout Creek in 1829. By the mid–nineteenth century, there were around a dozen mills in what is today the greater Jacksonville area, buzzing and slicing the newly valuable live oak and first-growth pine into ship's timbers and hulls. The availability of these "naval stores" combined with an ocean port spawned a frenetic shipbuilding trade. The Industrial Revolution, not due to begin for another quarter century in the rest of the world, got a jump start in Florida right here on the river. Later, in the twentieth century, when industrialists began turning wood into bleached paper on these same shores—and the acrid, telltale scent wafted out for miles around—another layer of the theme was being grafted here, atop the others.

Biologists Campbell and Burns, boat captain Jim Messer, and I leave our warm coffee shop in Jacksonville Landing and walk back out to our docked research vessel at the edge of the river. Huddled against the north Florida winter, we must look like refugees from a Charles Dickens novel, a pack of river urchins sulking in the shadow of the white-collared prosperity of the Landing. On the opposite bank from our dock is the Riverwalk, a boardwalk link to chichi sidewalk cafés and bistros and offices, more yin than a separate yang to the Landing.

It takes a fierce imagination to remember that this is a mere cortex to a deeper body of time, that a Timucua village called Wacca Pilatka—the place where the cows cross—was once here. San Nicolas, for the later Spanish fort of that name, seems just as distant, as does the subsequent British description of this place as Cow Ford. More narrow than the rest of the lower river, this was a natural place to herd livestock—to ford cows—and to ferry supplies and people from one side of the river to the other.

The name Jacksonville seems modernistic in comparison—even though it dates from 1822, when the newly surveyed city needed a serious American name and a soldier who had served under Andrew Jackson came up with one. It was the beginning of an era when the naming of places in Florida no longer had to have any real meaning; a village was known not so much by what it was but by what it aspired to be. Jacksonville imagined itself as bold, tenacious, soldierly—the antidote to low and muddy and full of cows. Even then, though, the ghosts of the Timucua surely outnumbered the settlers by the multitudes: in 1830 the population was only one hundred. Steamboats began to appear a year later with the docking of the *George Washington*, and change has arrived in quantum portions ever since.

Like all of Florida, though, a more authentic heart lurked just outside the civic veneer of commerce. When John Muir wandered through the rural river valley near Jacksonville in 1867, what he found wasn't exactly a chamber of commerce Welcome Wagon. "I came to a shanty where a party of loggers were getting out long pines for ship spars. They were the wildest of all the white savages I have met. The long-haired, ex-guerrillas of the mountains of Tennessee and North Carolina are uncivilized fellows; but for downright barbarism, these Florida loggers exceed."

Out to the middle of the channel we go today, headed for the sea itself. Pelagic creatures—bottlenose dolphins, tiger and hammerhead sharks— wander in and out from the Atlantic, sometimes turning back at downtown Jacksonville, sometimes not. Shorebirds like royal terns have become more common than herons or egrets, which have accompanied me over most of the river. Although the St. Johns has been estuarine for a while, it now seems more fully connected to the sea than it does to an upland dynamic as distant and remote as rainfall and freshwater swamp, almost three hundred miles away, back in another lifetime.

As we bounce along the light corduroy surface of the water, I watch the festive colors of both the Landing and the Riverwalk become more faint in the distance. I think how this designer architecture has again brought people to the river—just as the steamboat landings first did. But this time, they come not for the utility but because the cosmetics have coaxed them here, promising a sanitized experience with no steamship soot or noise or danger, just a pleasant and engaging postcard view of the river, colorized and safe. The railroad-building, hotel-orchestrating magnet Henry Flagler, who wanted the east coast of Florida to be his American Riviera, would surely delight in the virtual reality of all this.

Still, this riverside prosperity hasn't come in one uninterrupted historic continuum, nor has it been painless. The Civil War devastated the town, including most houses and all the sawmills except one. By the time writer Stephen Crane arrived here and met Cora, his temporary wife to be, things were looking pretty ragged. Or, as Crane put it: "The town looks like soiled pasteboard that some lunatic babies have been playing with." Then again, Crane just didn't seem very impressed with Florida's illusionary appeal to consumptives, despite what the guidebooks said. "The same old ladies are sitting on hotel porches," wrote Crane, "saying how well this climate agrees with them."

At any rate, Cora, who ran a brothel at the Hotel de Dream, kept the writer occupied, at least until he could board a supply ship named the *Commodore* and steam off to cover the Spanish-American War in Cuba on New Year's Eve in 1887. The voyage was a defining moment for Crane and his life: in the dead of night, the *Commodore* ricocheted off hidden river-bottom shoals on its way to the Atlantic. By the time it was ten miles offshore Daytona Beach, its damaged hull had taken on enough water to sink it beneath the choppy winter waves.

The subsequent real-life experience of riding the wild seas in a small life-boat gave Crane the material for his classic short story "The Open Boat." It was to become an opening salvo in the new literary genre of naturalism, its man against uncaring nature theme first inspired—or at least aggrieved—by a nasty, uncaring St. Johns River shoal.

Although news accounts often have this river "ending" in Jacksonville, it needs another twenty to twenty-five miles to wind its way from here to the sea. It is headed east now, for the first time in its life. Its shores, which have variously guided the destiny of Florida by acting as boundaries—between the Europeans and the Seminoles, the British and the Spanish, the Union and the Confederates—now draw the line between the compass points of north and south, rather than east and west.

The maps Campbell has given me are fascinating glimpses into the evolution of this grand maritime finale. As we brace ourselves on the bouncing deck of the research boat, Campbell offers a Cliff Notes version of the historic transformation: "The massive sand bar at the mouth of the river used to restrict flow and depth of the current. After the jetties were put into place to keep the channel open, and the government began dredging 'cuts' along the channel, the course of the river was changed forever. Islands disappeared, or turned into part of the mainland."

What this means, says Campbell, is that—unlike the upper river—this lower river can never be fundamentally reconstructed, for to do so would require the jetties to be removed, the channel to become shallow again, the bars to reappear. And the city, built upon spoil banks that once were wetlands, now asserts itself for nearly seven hundred square miles worth of annexed land here in the immediate basin. But there is more. "The biota [the entire inventory of plants and animals] is changed forever. There is more salt in the river now than before because there is more volume of seawater," explains Campbell. "It affects the river far upstream from here."

I look closely at the two earliest maps. The oldest is from December 24, 1791, and it is in Spanish, entitled "Plano numerod de la Barra y Rio de San Juan" (Numbered Plan of the Bar and River of St. John). It shows the "Entrance to the Bar," a fortified "Battery for the Defense" on the southern bank near the mouth of the river, a nearby "Pilot Cone" or buoylike channel marker, a shoreside "Launch Ramp," a house, and, back at the site of the twentieth-century Landing, the fort of "San Nicolas." The cartographer has sketched in creeks, islands, trees, and salt marsh nearly everywhere along the route.

The second map was drawn in 1856, some thirty-five years after the United States acquired Florida from Spain. Engineered by the U.S. Coast Survey Office, it was prosaically entitled "Preliminary Chart of St. Johns River Florida (From Brown's Creek to Jacksonville)." On the American map, there are detailed warnings about approaching the channel from the sea, with advice to use both "the Furnace Chimney of Mayport Mill" and the nearby lighthouse there as reference points. The dozen or so islands in the river now have proper English names: Long, Newcastle, Marian, Crab, Radcliffe, Big Marsh. Otherwise, the St. Johns seems to have held its essential course, wavering here and there as all rivers do as they rediscover easier ways to seep through their floodplain.

In fact, the government didn't begin to unleash its logarithms on the river mouth until the 1890s, when it first began to "improve" the treacherous St. Johns bar. In doing so, it built a permanent rock jetty and, in the earliest years of the new century, began to insist that the channel there be at least twenty-four feet. With a safer and more accessible entrance, Jacksonville began to grow into an international port. Today, as I will soon discover, the improved rock jetties stretch nearly a mile offshore on either side of the river mouth.

As a result of manipulation, the river—which kept its course for centuries—has changed, and that change is apparent when I compare the two historic maps with a modern navigational chart. Entire islands have now disappeared or shrunk to a fraction of their size, and new chunks of terrain, both dredged and naturally shoaled, have arisen—like the triangular "Blount Island"—to take their place. The modern river is sleeker, more focused, less full of whimsical bars and islets that slowed the water, as well as the mariners who sailed and steamed on it. There are now "government cuts," bulkheads and stationary markers scattered along the stretch. There is an "Intracoastal Waterway" that sluices through the middle of Sisters Creek on the north shore, into Pablo Creek on the southern one. Tributaries that have been mapped from the very first, like the Trout and Broward and Arlington Rivers, still wander off from the channel. But they do so with less certainty now, robbed of most of their wetlands, severed from the sheet flow of the marsh—more waterfront real estate than mysterious wooded creek.

A forgiving naturalist, I suppose, could live with some of this. After all, people most often live on the water because they love it there, love the feel of the place, the way the water looks in the morning and evening light. Less forgiving, though, is the industrial sprawl that consumes miles of riverfront, a tableau that begins almost as soon as the gentrified riverfront shops and offices end in Jacksonville. It is a sprawl that Napoleon Bonaparte Broward, who apprenticed his future gubernatorial vision as a steamship owner and county sheriff here at the turn of the century, may have cherished. After all, much of Broward's later policy fixated on the need to drain all the "over-flow districts" of Florida—from the St. Johns to the Everglades—and to populate this once useless marsh and swamp with industrious people and their industrious things.

There are plenty of industrious things here shoreside as we continue our voyage downriver, and they are serious, metallic, byzantine-looking things, indeed. After all, this is the Port of Jacksonville, and it is a sprawl of public docks and private terminals that stretches along the river for nearly fifteen miles to Blount Island. Here, industry takes on nearly any form imaginable, the mechanized counterpart to the biodiversity of the river—maritime commerce, split, reformed, and speciated, encouraged by a city that just hasn't been able to say no to its development.

There are warehouses and berthed oceangoing supply ships loaded with giant shoeboxlike containers—this one the *Cape Domingo* from Norfolk, that one the *Sea Trader* from Moravia. Some of the ships are fitted with huge blue cranes, others with drop-down sterns so the automotive cargo can drive itself in and out. There are smokestacks, concrete wharves, and towers with ten stories' worth of scaffolding. There are massive, floating dry docks and oil terminals and places to unload steel and timber, coffee and Toyotas. There is a gypsum plant with gray vats and tanks, chimneys smoking angrily and pipes hissing, metal detritus scattered everywhere. It is, all of it, breathtaking, looking less like a port and more like a melodramatic movie set for an Arnold Schwartzenegger film, one in which machines with very bad attitudes rule the earth.

Somewhere along this route is the Dames Point Bridge, a giant harplike affair that became the newest major span to be built across the river in the late 1980s. The northernmost link of beltway I-295, it became the access needed to open the last bit of undeveloped salt marsh along the north leg of the river to development. As University of North Florida scientist Carole L. DeMort reported in an analysis of Florida rivers in 1991: "With the opening of the Dames Point Bridge . . . [conservation of natural lands] is on a collision course with economic growth of the area and population surges due to the sudden ease of access."

Nonetheless, this is Florida, and there are always strange, natural touches to be found, even in an environment like this. Here, somewhere along the busiest bulkhead is a power plant, nestled inside a U-shaped pier. River water, pumped into the plant to cool turbines, is returned to the river inside this U, considerably warmer than before it left. Manatees, those gentle, plant-eating mammals who travel to the protection of warmer springs on the middle river during winter cold snaps, also flock here, dodging container ships and shrimp trawlers and speed boats, in order to reach the comforting thermal blanket of the heated effluent. As warm-blooded mammals, the hulking manatees get just as chilled as we do when the temperature drops.

It is one more odd but pragmatic example of the hybrid relationship between ancient Florida and modern humans, and it makes me ponder just how far we can stretch the conventional limits of coexistence here on this river.

A long, slender island off our starboard gunnel hides most of the massive Mill Cove from the main river, trailing next to the channel for some four miles. The cove was once a generous oxbow turn, the place where the river swept south in its meander before resuming its eastward course. The island itself is covered with low-slung foliage—scrub oak and myrtle, yucca, prickly pear cactus, and sabal palm—and its sliver of beach is littered with maritime debris, glass and plastic and scrap wood.

I wonder how this island, so close to the rest of the urban sprawl, has so far escaped settlement. "It's a spoil island," says Burns. "It was created when the channel was dredged and recut." Still, Miami Beach in southern Florida was mostly bottom spoil before it was smoothed out and platted and en-slabbed with concrete. This spoil, though, just might resist that attempt, proving that we Floridians have learned something about ecology in a half century after all. I look closely at the map to match its course to reality, and when I do, I notice that some cartographer—surely one with a dark sense

of humor—has charted this dredged river-bottom creation as "Bartram Island." It's an act akin to, say, naming a breed of feral, half-mad, bird-eating
cats for John James Audubon.

Next to Bartram Island, a real island, one mapped as Reed on the 1856
Coast Guard chart, appears, and it is covered with a grove of ancient sabal
palms, spiked at the edges with spartina marsh grass. "This is an old island,"
says Burns, meaning an authentic one. We pull up near shore here, long
enough for the biologist to probe the bottom with a set of long, wooden
tongs, like oystermen use to harvest their bivalve of choice. Burns is looking for invertebrates, anything living in the sand and mud, something to link
to the health of the local biology and its webwork of benthic ecology. He
gives up after a few tries, finding nothing alive, and we move on towards the
ocean.

Woods thankfully reclaim the shoreline, studded with a few homes. And
then, tucked in amid the thickest wall of foliage, a dream of the past emerges.
It is Fort Caroline—or at least an imagined replica of what the French fort
might once have been—and it sits on a low slab of riverbank along a stretch
of river mapped as St. Johns Bluff. It is a stockadelike defense with wood-
trimmed, picket walls, the sort of fort that would have been hastily built in
1564 in an environment with few solid mediums but trees and dirt. This is
the Fort Caroline National Monument, and it has been constructed this time
not by desperate French settlers but by the National Park Service, which
readily admits that "no physical evidence of the colony has been found."
Instead, this is the "probable area where the early story of European colo-
nization of northeast Florida took place." The triangular fort, surrounded
by a small moat, is based on a drawing by Jacques Le Moyne, the resident
French artist who gave us our first and best illustrations of the Timucua.

We slow next to the replica on the low shore, idling here for a few minutes. Campbell points to a higher, more prominent bluff on a point a few
more hundred yards downriver. "That seems like a lot better location," he
offers. "If I were a Frenchman wanting to build a fort, that's where I'd go.
It's high and dry and has a good vantage point on the river." But then, the
original site of the fort itself, which included an earthen battery and a small
settlement on a nearby meadow, has washed away. There may have been a
bluff here, a natural escarpment connected to the one downriver that remains, before erosion consumed it. In fact, there are two subsequent historic

accounts of the fort's demise—one of natural tides and neglect that first took the structures by 1817; the other of the new jetties and deeper channel that later took a bite out of the land.

Regardless of how it left, the idea of having Fort Caroline back is a dandy notion. Forget Jamestown and the "Lost Colony" of North Carolina and even Plymouth Rock—which would not be reached for another seventy-six years by the intrepid Pilgrims. This is the site of the first known European settlement inside the present-day borders of the United States. And it is a testament to the collective amnesia about Florida's role in early American history that it is not more widely recognized as such.

After an initial landing by Admiral Jean Ribault at the mouth of the river in 1562, the fort and surrounding settlement were built two years later, under the command of René Goulaine de Laudonnière. It was not staffed by farmers and craftsmen who could have helped the colony become self-sufficient but by some three hundred soldiers and sailors, among them only four women, said to be wives. Its purpose was to stake a French claim on this exotic new territory. And it was—like other early European ventures—driven not by religious freedom or a search for a fountain of youth but by the desire to profit from a strange, unexplored new world.

After first touching land on today's Fort George Island at the river mouth, Ribault found both a people and a place that seemed lifted out of a mariner's dream. "They be all naked and of a goodly stature, mighty, faire and as well shapen and proportioned of bodye as any people in all the worlde, very gentill, curtious and of a good nature," wrote Ribault. These gentle people wore pearls as large as marbles and carried arrowheads of turquoise, with an abundance of gold and silver, precious stones, and other riches. They paddled great dugouts standing up, canoes large enough to hold fifteen or twenty people. As for the land itself, it was the "fairest, frutefullest and plesantest of all the world, habonding in honney, veneson, wildfoule, forrestes, woodes of all sorts, palme trees, cipers, ceders, bayes. . . . And the sight of the faire medowes is a pleasure not able to be expressed with tonge."

Despite the lush bounty of fish and game that surrounded them, the French nearly starved during their year here, begging and even stealing food from the Timucua, until they were finally reduced to eating acorns. The Spanish, even more driven by the lure of treasure, and not terribly pleased with the Huguenots nesting on the shores of La Florida, captured and then slaughtered most of the French, claiming the fort for their own. (It must have been a grave disappointment to discover later that most of the riches were not local at all but came from trade with other northern tribes or were salvaged from early coastal shipwrecks.) Only a handful of French escaped to the woods, but among them was the artist Le Moyne, who fled finally back to Europe, where he re-created the detailed illustrations of the people he closely observed for more than a year.

And so, in its present incarnation, Fort Caroline opens the door to a gigantic, sprawling historic landscape. It is a landscape that not just honors the French arrival on the river but also acknowledges the once vital presence of the Timucua, who welcomed them as friends. It does so by protecting a seventy-two-square-mile expanse of forest and wild salt marsh and beach, all veined with some twenty tidal creeks, inside the surrounding Timucuan Ecological and Historic Preserve. Middens here—some thirty feet high—are composed of oyster shells rather than the little freshwater snail that dominates mounds on the river south of Jacksonville. It was the oyster that once rose from the river in giant beds, providing sustenance for the Native Americans and all who came after. Reported Jean Ribault in 1562: "Oysters . . . taken every day along the riverside . . . in so marvelous abundance as it is scant credible."

Yet, while the oyster beds still cover more than thirty-two hundred acres along more than ten miles of creeks in Duval County alone, for the first time since humans arrived on the shores of the San Juan River, they cannot be harvested. In 1997 the Florida Department of Environmental Protection—after many seasons of temporary closures—placed a permanent ban on the shellfish. Fecal bacteria, which causes illness, kept showing up. Officials figured it came from leaking septic tanks and storm-water runoff.

Stretching away from the site of the replica fort on both sides of the river, the preserve covers what was once Timucua territory, from the river north across Clapboard and Cedar Point Creeks, and up to the edge of the sea, all the way to Big Talbot Island and the Nassau River on the coast. This is a place of wild tidal marshes, cordgrass and black needle rush dominating this low-slung terrain, interposed with stands of tree islands, beds of exposed oysters gurgling and spitting at low tide. From the air, the flat, grassy landscape is the salt version of the vast freshwater sawgrass and hammock island headwaters I saw long ago, a place of creation on the edge of the sea.

You can think of it all as homage paid to the historic St. Johns, an act the deeply spiritual Timucua might even regard as a redemptive pathway back to their own gentle values, their place and time. It is especially meaningful in an era in which civilization, and not the water, laps right up to the threshold of the preserve.

The water churning up in our wake is no longer tea-colored but an oceanic blue-green; to our port gunnel, a pod of dolphins cruise by, cutting gentle arches into the surface with their gray dorsals. Ashore is an abandoned, rotting steamboat replica, one made of plywood, not so long now for the world. A car ferry grumbles across the river, from one shore to the other, connecting two halves of SR A1A. I look at its stern and see that it is christened, without a touch of irony, the *Jean Ribault*.

To the south is the fishing wharf of Mayport—in honor of the first French inscription for the river. Shrimp trawlers named *Sassy Lady* and *Papa Hobart* are berthed along its seawall; off in the distance, framed by the rock jetties, another trawler returns from the ocean, gulls encircling like mad butterflies, outriggers down to give it balance, or perhaps to fill one last seine with seafood.

And now, finally, here is the full view of the sea, a perspective that consumes half of the far horizon, even at this distance. Off to the right, the human-made Mayport Basin holds a Brobdingnagian aircraft carrier, one that draws thirty-five feet of water. There is a naval station and air base here, and on the tip of the barrier island at St. Johns Point, not far perhaps from where Ribault first placed the stone column with a French coat of arms to claim the *rivere du Mai* and its land for his country, is a U.S. Coast Guard Station.

Perched incongruously in the midst of all of this, its sturdy glass and iron head poking up from behind a filigree of modern ship rigging, is a red nineteenth-century lighthouse. Built in 1854, the tower replaced two others that first marked the harbor in 1830 and 1833—until being decommissioned and replaced, itself, by a lightship in 1929. In 1887 this area was still so heavily wooded that a new iron lantern was proposed to be placed on the top, raising the tower by fifteen more feet. The improvement was abandoned when, by the next year, settlers were reported to be cutting enough trees so the light was no longer blocked. When Audubon first crossed the bar of the St. Johns so many years ago by night, he reported seeing a "star-like glimmer of the light in the great lantern at the entrance," watching in awe as the arrival of his ship spooked "thousands of snowy pelicans."

A black pilot boat crunches its way through the waves, out to sea, headed for a distant oceanic vessel in need of local navigational guidance, continuing a tradition by other pilots, back to when galleons and corsairs required help crossing the bar of the St. Johns.

The water around us is now full of swirling eddies where the outgoing downstream current introduces itself full force to the incoming tides, the last noble molecule of upland St. Johns marsh meeting the indomitable sea. Some months ago, I stood in the headwaters of this river, up to my waist in a matrix of sawgrass and rain-driven water and peat. And now here the rest of it is, churning under me for thirty and forty and fifty feet, as realized as any river could be, dancing a complex and final jig of tides and currents, a last sweet memory dance of consummation. I have gone from where there is no measurable current—except perhaps the longing for one—to a place where hydrologists say 58.4 million gallons of water a minute swirl back and forth, between the river and the ocean.

To our left, I see two surf fishermen, braving the weather, silhouetted on the sliver of Fort George Island beach in a late afternoon mist of spindrift and sea. Ahead, through the bookends of the jetties, is the ocean itself, the medium that brought every European here for centuries, the doorway that first introduced the interior of Florida to discovery and settlement, that chased the Timucua into history.

I reach down over the edge of the gunnel and swipe my hand into the cold winter water, bringing my fingers to my lips. Its salts vaguely hint of other tastes, like the ones I stole from inside Croaker Hole and Salt Springs far upriver from here. Those were prehistoric ocean tastes, the remainder of a distant place encapsulated by geology and time and then fed back to me by artesian pressure. I think how this river, despite the ravages against it, still has the capacity to feed each of us with its own memory, if we let it.

Just beyond is the place where the whales still come to breach, giant mammals that Le Moyne first drew with their heads out of the water, the same animals I once imagined above my own head, in an ancient Florida lagoon, some 310 miles ago. This frothing Atlantic is the beginning of the St. Johns River—as well as its inevitable and timeless end—and I let my heart surge out with it, into the folds of oceanic creation.

Appendix A. Relevant Public and Nonprofit Contact Agencies

COMPILED BY PATRICK HARVEY

Public Agencies

St. Johns River Water Management District
P.O. Box 1429
Palatka, FL 32178-1429
Responsibilities: Managing freshwater and related terrestrial resources, promote conservation and ecological restoration, flood control, and education.

Florida Department of Environmental Protection
3900 Commonwealth Blvd.
Tallahassee, FL 32399-2400
Responsibilities: Acquiring and managing state land and protecting the state's natural resources (including state parks), enforcing state laws regarding environmental regulation.

Florida Fish and Wildlife Conservation Commission
620 South Meridian Street
Tallahassee, FL 32399-1600
Responsibilities: Managing wildlife, including sport fisheries, and regulate hunting, fishing, and nongame wildlife; managing habitat.

U.S. Army Corps of Engineers, Jacksonville District
Public Affairs Officer
400 West Bay Street
Jacksonville, FL 32232-0019
Responsibilities: Navigability of the river, flood control, water resources, recreation.

U.S. Environmental Protection Agency
Region 4 (Southeast)
Atlanta Federal Center
61 Forsyth Street, SW
Atlanta, GA 30303-3104
Responsibilities: Permitting and enforcement of federal laws regarding water and air pollution, pesticides, and solid waste disposal.

U.S. Fish and Wildlife Service
Region 4 (Southeast), Area III
Federal Building, Room 1200
75 Spring Street, SW
Atlanta, GA 30303
Responsibilities: Conserving and protecting fish and wildlife and their habitats, with
special attention to federally protected species.

The administrators of those counties the river borders or through which it passes:

Alachua	Nassau
Baker	Okeechobee
Bradford	Osceola
Clay	Polk
Duval	Putnam
Flagler	Seminole
Indian River	St. Johns
Lake	Volusia
Marion	

Not-for-Profit Agencies

American Rivers
1025 Vermont Avenue, NW
Suite 720
Washington, DC 20005

The Nature Conservancy
Florida Regional Office
222 South Westmonte Drive
Suite 300
Altamonte Springs, FL 32714

Trust for Public Land
Southeast Regional Office
206 North Monroe
Tallahassee, FL 32301

Save the Manatee Club
500 North Maitland Avenue
Maitland, FL 32751

Florida Audubon
1331 Palmetto Avenue, Suite 110
Winter Park, FL 32789

Florida Defenders of the Environment
4424 NW 13th Street, Suite C-8
Gainesville, FL 32609

Florida Wildlife Federation
2545 Blairstone Pines Drive
Tallahassee, FL 32301

Sierra Club, Florida Chapter
c/o Geraldine Swormstedt
1075 22nd Street
Sarasota, FL 34234

Friends of the Wekiva River
P.O. Box 6196
Longwood, FL 32791-6196

Friends of Lake Jesup
P.O. Box 195567
Winter Springs, FL 32719-5567

Florida Canoeing and Kayaking
P.O. Box 837
Tallahassee, FL 32302

Appendix B. Access Points on and near the St. Johns, from South to North

Contact individual agency for more information. About 90 percent of all St. Johns River Water Management Conservation areas are open to the public, although some may require permits.

Public Agency Initials:

DEP	Florida Department of Environmental Protection
DOF	Florida Division of Forestry
FFWC	Florida Fish and Wildlife Conservation Commission
SJRWMD	St. John's River Water Management District
USACE	U.S. Army Corps of Engineers
USFS	U.S. Forest Service

Upper River

Ft. Drum Marsh Conservation Area
SW Indian River County
[SJRWMD]

Blue Cypress Conservation Area
Fellsmere area
[SJRWMD]

Three Forks Conservation Area
Lake Hell 'n Blazes
[SJRWMD]

Bull Creek Conservation Area
East of Holopaw
[SJRWMD]

River Lakes Conservation Area
Lakes Washington, Winder, and Poinsett
[SJRWMD]

Canaveral Marshes Conservation Area
North of Lake Poinsett
[SJRWMD]

Tosohatchee State Reserve
North of Lake Poinsett
[DEP]

Seminole Ranch Conservation Area
Puzzle Lake
[SJRWMD]

Econlockhatchee River

Little-Big Econ State Forest
North of Chuluota
[DOF; SJRWMD]

Hal Scott Regional Preserve and Park
Upper Econ
[SJRWMD; Orange County Parks]
**

South Lake Harney Conservation Area
Lake Harney
[SJRWMD]

Lake Jesup Conservation Area
Lake Jesup
[SJRWMD]

Lemon Bluff Boat Ramp
Osteen
[Volusia County]

Kratzert Conservation Area
South of Osteen
[SJRWMD]

Wekiva River

Wekiwa Springs State Park
[DEP]

Rock Springs State Park
[DEP]

Wekiva Buffers Conservation Area
[SJRWMD]

Seminole State Forest
[DOF]
**

Gemini Springs Park
DeBary
[Volusia County]

Blue Springs State Park
Orange City
[DEP]

Hontoon Island State Park
Deland
[DEP]

DeLeon Springs State Recreation Area
DeLeon Springs
[DEP]

Middle River

Lake Woodruff National Wildlife Refuge
Northwest of DeLand, entrance near DeLeon Springs
[U.S. Fish and Wildlife Service]

Lake George Conservation Area
East Lake George
[SJRWMD; Volusia County]

Silver Glen Springs Recreation Area
Silver Glen Springs
[USFS]

Ocala National Forest Campground
Salt Springs
[USFS]

Salt Springs Recreation Area
Salt Springs
[USFS]

Alexander Springs Recreation Area
Alexander Springs
[USFS]

Juniper Springs Recreation Area
[USFS]

>   *Ocklawaha River*
>
>   Caravelle Ranch Conservation Area
>   (Near Rodman Dam)
>   [SJRWMD; FFWC]
>
>   Rodman Recreation Area
>   Near Rodman Dam
>   [USACE]
>
>   Ocklawaha River Recreation Area
>   (Near Rodman Dam)
>   [USACE]
>
>   Sunnyhill Restoration Area
>   Upper Ocklawaha River Area
>   [SJRWMD]
>
>   Ocklawaha Prairie Restoration Area
>   Ocklawaha
>   [SJRWMD]
>   **

Haw Creek Conservation Area
South Crescent Lake
[SJRWMD; DOF]

Dunns Creek Conservation Area
North Crescent Lake
[SJRWMD]

Lower River

Watson Island State Forest
East Palatka
[DOF]

Deep Creek Conservation Area
North of Hastings
[SJRWMD]

Riverdale Park
Tocoi
[Clay County]

Baynard Point Conservation Area
Southeast of Green Cove Springs
[SJRWMD]

Old Shands Bridge Public Fishing Pier and Ramp
Green Cove Springs
[Clay County]

Arlington Lions Club Park
Jacksonville
[City of Jacksonville]

Arlington Road Boat Ramp
Jacksonville
[Jacksonville Dept. of Parks, Recreation and Entertainment]

Mayport Public Boat Ramp
Jacksonville
[Jacksonville Dept. of Parks, Recreation and Entertainment]

Fort Caroline National Memorial and Timucuan Preserve
Jacksonville
[USNP]

Huguenot Park
Jacksonville
[City of Jacksonville]

Little Talbot Island State Park
Ft. George
[DEP]

For information on specific canoe and kayak outfitters and guide services on the St. Johns, Econlockhatchee, Wekiva, and Ocklawaha, contact:

Florida Professional Paddlesports Association
P.O. Box 1764
Arcadia, FL 34265

Bibliography

Alice, Mary. 1996. *The Mullet Mystique*. Sanford, Fla.: Published by the author, P.O. Box 1311.

Associated Press. 1996. "Pulp Friction: State Moves to Cut Back Underwater Logging." *Orlando (Fla.) Sentinel*. September 12.

Bartram, William. 1996. *Travels and Other Writings: Travels through North and South Carolina, Georgia, East and West Florida. Travels in Georgia and Florida, 1773–74: A Report to Dr. John Fothergill. Miscellaneous Writings*. Philadelphia, Pa.: Library of America.

Bass, Gray. January 1995. *Checklist of Fishes Recorded from Rivers of Florida*. Holt, Fla.: Florida Game and Fresh Water Fish Commission, Blackwater Fisheries Research and Development Center.

Bell, June D. 1993. "A Treasure Dive Comes Up Literary." *Florida Times-Union* (Jacksonville). May 1.

Bennetts, Robert E., and Wiley M. Kitchens. 1994. *Numbers, Distribution, and Success of Nesting Snail Kites in the Blue Cypress Water Management and Conservation Areas*. Palatka, Fla.: St. Johns River Water Management District. [Final report].

Bergman, Martinus J. 1992. *Surface Water Hydrology*. Vol. 2 of the Lower St. Johns River Basin Reconnaissance. Tech. Pub. SJ92-1. Palatka, Fla.: St. Johns River Water Management District.

Berry, Thomas. 1988. *Dream of the Earth*. San Francisco: Sierra Club Books.

Breedlove, Dennis, and Associates, 1986. *Seminole County, Florida Wetlands Field Guide*. Sanford, Fla.: Board of County Commissioners, Seminole County.

Brody, Robert W. 1994. *Biological Resources*. Vol. 6 of the Lower St. Johns River Basin Reconnaissance. Tech. Pub. SJ94-2. Palatka, Fla.: St. Johns River Water Management District.

Brooks, Mary. 1998. "Jesup Ideas Are Almost Ready." *Orlando (Fla.) Sentinel*. March 8.

Brooks, Mary, and Katherine Bouma. 1998. "Growth Hits Wekiva: Seminole Suburbs Creep Closer." *Orlando (Fla.) Sentinel*. September 20.

Brown, Robin C. 1994. *Florida's First People: Twelve Thousand Years of Human History*. Sarasota, Fla.: Pineapple Press.

Cabell, Branch, and A. J. Hanna. 1943. *The St. Johns: A Parade of Diversities*. New York: Farrar and Rinehart.

Campbell, Joseph, with Bill Moyers. 1988. *The Power of Myth*. New York: Doubleday.

Carr, Archie. 1994. *A Naturalist in Florida*. Edited by Marjorie Harris Carr. New Haven: Yale University Press.

Carter, Elizabeth F., and John L. Pearce. 1985. *A Canoeing and Kayaking Guide to the Streams of Florida*. Vol. 1, *Central Peninsula and Panhandle*. Birmingham, Ala.: Menasha Ridge Press.

Cerulean, Susan, and Ann Morrow. 1993. *Florida Wildlife Viewing Guide*. Helena, Mont.: Falcon Press.

Cooke, C. Wythe. 1939. *Scenery of Florida Interpreted by a Geologist*. Florida Bureau of Geology Bulletin 17 Tallahassee, Fla.: Florida Geological Survey.

————. 1945. *Geology of Florida*. Geological Bulletin No. 29. Tallahassee, Fla.: Florida Geological Survey.

Cooper, Helen A. 1986. *Winslow Homer Watercolors*. New Haven: Yale University Press.

Copelon, Dianne. 1995. "Gone but Not Forgotten: Historian Lives for Old Town." *Orlando (Fla.) Sentinel*. August 3.

Cox, James; Randy Kautz; Maureen MacLaughlin; and Terry Gilbert. 1994. *Closing the Gaps in Florida's Wildlife Habitat Conservation System*. Tallahassee, Fla.: Office of Environmental Services, Florida Game and Fresh Water Fish Commission.

Cruickshank, Helen G., ed. 1986. *William Bartram in Florida*. N.p.: Florida Federation of Garden Clubs.

Deland, Margaret. [1889]. Reprint, 1983. *Florida Days*. Sarasota, Fla.: Pineapple Press.

DeLoach, Ned. 1988. *Diving Guide to Underwater Florida*. 6th ed. Jacksonville, Fla.: New World Publications.

Dennis, Jerry. 1996. *The Bird in the Waterfall: A Natural History of Oceans, Rivers, and Lakes*. New York: HarperCollins.

Denton, Cheryl. 1992. "The Wekiva River Basin: A Resource Revisited: A Technical Report of the Friends of the Wekiva River, Inc." FOWR, P.O. Box 6196, Longwood, Florida 32791.

Derr, Mark. 1989. *Some Kind of Paradise: A Chronicle of Man and the Land in Florida*. New York: William Morrow and Co.

Dreggors, William J., Jr., and John Stephen Hess. 1989. *A Pictorial History of West Volusia County, 1870–1940*. DeLeon Springs, Fla.: E. O. Painter Printing Co.

Duncan, Wilbur H., and Marion B. Duncan. 1988. *Trees of the Southeastern United States*. Athens: University of Georgia Press.

Fenby, Eric. 1971. *Delius*. New York: Thomas Y. Crowell Co.

Fernald, Edward A., and Donald J. Patton, eds. 1985. *Water Resources Atlas of*

Florida. Tallahassee, Fla.: Florida State University, Institute of Science and Public Affairs.

Florida Rivers Assessment: The St. Johns River. 1989. Tallahassee: State of Florida, Florida Department of Natural Resources.

Florida State Parks Guide. 1996–97. Tallahassee: State of Florida, Department of Environmental Protection.

Gannon, Michael, ed. 1996. *The New History of Florida*. Gainesville: University Press of Florida.

Giguere, Bob, and Bill Belleville, coexecutive producers. 1996. "In Search of Xanadu." Television documentary. Tallahassee: BBG Productions; Florida Public Television.

Gilbert, Carter R. 1978. *Rare and Endangered Biota of Florida*. Vol. 4, *Fishes*. Gainesville: University Presses of Florida.

Gilbert, Terry, and John Wooding. 1994. *Chronic Roadkill Problem Areas for Black Bear in Florida*. Tallahassee, Fla: Florida Game & Fresh Water Fish Commission. February 24.

Gleasner, Bill, and Diana Gleasner. 1988. *Florida: Off the Beaten Path*. Chester, Conn.: Globe Pequot Press.

Graff, Mary B. 1978. *Mandarin on the St. Johns*. Gainesville, Fla.: Regent Press and Publishing.

Green, Deborah. 1994. *Wekiwa Springs State Park Habitat Tour*. Longwood, Fla.: Published by the author.

Grogan, Mike. 1995. "Bartram's Plantation Site Located—at Last." *St. Augustine (Fla.) Record*. December 30.

A Guide to Common Aquatic Plants in Urban Lakes. 1987. Brochure. Tallahassee: Florida Game and Fresh Water Fish Commission, Resource Restoration Section.

A Guide to Florida's St. Johns River: A Compendium of Romance, History, and Little Known Facts about this Much-Loved River. 1988. Sanford, Fla.: Rivership Romance.

Harper, Francis, ed. 1958. *Bartram Travels: Naturalist Edition*. New Haven: Yale University Press.

Heritage Management on the Ocala National Forest. Undated brochure. Umatilla, Fla., Seminole Ranger District: U.S. Forest Service, Southern Region.

Hickman, Cleveland P. 1967. *Biology of the Invertebrates*. St. Louis: C. V. Mosby Co.

Hobbs, Horton H., Jr., Zoologist Emeritus, Smithsonian Institution. 1996. Correspondence to Eric Hutcheson on collected troglodytic specimens, June 25, September 16, October 8.

Hoffman, Wayne. 1996. *Survey of Wading Bird Utilization of the Upper St. Johns River*. Tavernier, Fla.: National Audubon Society. August.

Hopwood, Fred A. 1992. *The Rockledge, Florida Steamboat Line*. Published by the author.

Into Tropical Florida, Or a Round Trip upon the St. Johns River. [Ca. 1880]. Jacksonville, Fla.: Passenger Dept. of the DeBary-Baya Merchants Line.

Jennings, Senator Toni. 1994. SB 2120 Lake Jesup Restoration. Bill presented to the Senate Committee on Natural Resources. Tallahassee, Fla. February 25.

Jewell, Susan D. 1995. *Exploring Wild Central Florida: A Guide to Finding the Natural Areas and Wildlife of the Central Peninsula*. Sarasota, Fla.: Pineapple Press.

Johnson, Richard A. 1979. *Geology of the Oklawaha Basin*. Tech. Pub. SJ79-2. Palatka, Fla.: Water Resources Dept., St. Johns River Water Management District.

Julavits, Joe. 1996. "Minister Escapes Huge Gator." *Florida Times-Union* (Jacksonville). June 23.

Kastner, Joseph. 1977. *A Species of Eternity*. New York: E. P. Dutton.

Keller, Anne E., and John D. Schell Jr. 1993. *Lower St. Johns River Basin Reconnaissance: Sediment Characteristics and Quality*. Vol. 5. Technical Publication SJ93-6. Palatka, Fla.: St. Johns River Water Management District.

Kranz, Tom. 1995. *Boating and Cruising Guide to the St. Johns River*. East Aurora, N.Y.: Camp Longacres.

Lane, Ed, and Ronald W. Hoenstine. 1991. *Environmental Geology and Hydrogeology of the Ocala Area, Florida*. Special publication no. 31. Tallahassee: State of Florida, Florida Geological Survey.

Lanier, Sidney. 1875. *Florida: Its Scenery, Climate, and History*. N.p.: Great Atlantic Coastline Railroad Co.

Larson, Ron. 1995. *Swamp Song: A Natural History of Florida's Swamps*. Gainesville: University Press of Florida.

Livingston, Robert J., ed. 1991. *The Rivers of Florida*. New York: Springer-Verlag.

Lytle, Tamara. 1998. "St. Johns River Is Set to Get a Beauty Boost: Honor May Bring Federal Aid, Extra Attention to Waterway." *Orlando (Fla.) Sentinel*. June 29.

McLane, William McNair. 1955. "The Fishes of the St. Johns River System." Ph.D. diss., University of Florida.

Marth, Del, and Martha J. Marth, eds. *Florida Almanac*. Updated. Gretna, La.: Pelican Publishing Co.

————, eds. 1990. *The Rivers of Florida*. Sarasota, Fla.: Pineapple Press.

Milanich, J. T., ed. 1972. *Francisco Paraja's 1613 Confessionario: A Document for Timucuan Ethnography*. Tallahassee, Fla: Department of State, Director of Archives, History and Records Management.

Miller, James Joseph. 1991. "The Fairest, Frutefullest and Pleasantest of All the

World: An Environmental History of the Northeast Part of Florida." Ph.D. diss., University of Pennsylvania.

Mitchell, Robin, executive director of Florida Defenders of the Environment. 1998. "Legislature Passes on Funding for Ocklawaha Restoration." *Monitor* (Gainesville, Fla.; newsletter of Florida Defenders of the Environment). Summer.

Morris, Allen. 1995. *Florida Place Names*. Sarasota, Fla.: Pineapple Press.

Morris, Frederick W. 1995. *Hydrodynamics and Salinity of Surface Water*. Vol. 3 of the Lower St. Johns River Basin Reconnaissance. Tech. Pub. SJ95-9. Palatka, Fla.: St. Johns River Water Management District.

Mueller, Edward A. 1986. *St. Johns River Steamboats*. Jacksonville, Fla.: Published by the author.

———. 1984. *Steamboating on the St. Johns*. Melbourne, Fla.: South Brevard Historical Society.

Nelson, Gil. 1995. *Exploring Wild North Florida: A Guide to Finding the Natural Areas and Wildlife of North Central and Northeast Florida*. Sarasota, Fla.: Pineapple Press.

Nyenhuis, Michael, and Laurie Casady. 1994. "The Maple Leaf." *Florida-Times Union* (Jacksonville). December 18.

Oppel, Frank, and Tony Meisel, eds. 1870–1910. Reprint, 1987. *Tales of Old Florida: Anthology of 19th century articles published variously*. Secaucus, N.J.: Castle.

Our Vital Wetlands. [Undated]. Tavares, Fla.: Lake County Water Authority.

Patterson, Steve. 1997. "Effluent Is Pushing St. Johns into Decline." *Florida Times-Union* (Jacksonville). May 14.

———. 1997. "Once a Bounty, Shellfish Now Wasted." *Florida Times-Union* (Jacksonville). November 6.

———. 1997. "Mercury Levels High: St. Johns Fish Study Troubling." *Florida Times-Union* (Jacksonville). May 23.

Pritchard, Peter C. H., and Herbert W. Kale. 1994. *Saving What's Left*. Winter Park, Fla.: Florida Audubon Society.

Proby, Kathryn Hall. 1974. *Audubon in Florida*. Miami: University of Miami Press.

Purdy, Barbara A. 1981. *A Study of the Flintworking Techniques of Early Florida Stone Implement Makers*. Gainesville: University Presses of Florida.

Ramsdell, Marcia, and Linda A. Lord. 1993. *Guide to Florida Environmental Issues and Information*. Winter Park: Florida Conservation Foundation.

Randazzo, Anthony F., and Douglas S. Jones, eds. 1997. *The Geology of Florida*. Gainesville: University Press of Florida.

Rawlings, Marjorie Kinnan. [1933]. 1977. *South Moon Under*. Dunwoody, Ga.: Norman S. Berg.

————. [1931]. 1988. *Marjorie Kinnan Rawlings Reader.* Jacksonville, Fla.: San Marco Bookstore.

Recreation Guide to District Lands. 1997. Palatka, Fla: St. Johns River Water Management District's Office of Public Information and the Division of Land Management. Fall

"Restore Ocklawaha Flow." Editorial. 1998. *Orlando (Fla.) Sentinel.* March 18.

Restoring the Ocklawaha River Ecosystem. August 1989. Gainesville, Fla.: Florida Defenders of the Environment.

Robbins, Chandler S.; Bertel Bruun; and Herbert S. Zim. 1966. *Birds of North America: A Guide to Field Identification.* New York: Golden Press.

Robison, Jim. 1990. "Fisherman's Paradise of Wekiva Keeps Soldiers' Mess Well Stocked." *Orlando (Fla.) Sentinel.* March 22.

Roman, Dave. 1998. "Local Political Right Builds Opposition to River Initiative." *Florida Times-Union* (Jacksonville). March 8.

Schafer, Daniel L. 1995. "'The Forlorn State of Poor Billy Bartram': Locating the St. Johns River Plantation of William Bartram. St. Augustine, Fla: El Escribano." *St. Augustine Journal of History,* 1–11.

Shafland, Paul L. 1991. *Management of Introduced Freshwater Fishes in Florida.* Boca Raton, Fla.: Florida Game and Fresh Water Fish Commission, Non-Native Fish Research Laboratory.

Sincock, John L. 1958. *Waterfowl Ecology in the St. Johns River Valley as Related to the Proposed Conservation Areas and Changes in the Hydrology from Lake Harney to Ft. Pierce, Florida.* Report of P-R Project. W-19-R. Tallahassee: Florida Game and Fresh Water Fish Commission.

Stobbe, Mike. 1997. "River Toxin Revealed: Studies Back Claim of Mental Effects." *Florida Times-Union* (Jacksonville). December 20.

Stokes, Donald, and Lillian Stokes. 1996. *Stokes Field Guide to Birds* [Eastern Region]. New York: Little, Brown & Co.

Stowe, Harriet Beecher. [1873]. Reprint, 1968. *Palmetto-Leaves.* Gainesville: University of Florida Press.

Tibbals, C. H. 1990. *Hydrology of the Floridan Aquifer System in East Central Florida.* Paper No. 1403-E. Washington, D.C.: U.S. Geological Survey, U.S. Government Printing Office.

Toth, David J. 1993. *Lower St. Johns River Basin Reconnaissance: Hydrology.* Vol. 1. Palatka, Fla.: St. Johns River Water Management District.

Turner, Richard L. 1994. *The Effects of Hydrology on the Population Dynamics of the Florida Applesnail (Pomacea paludosa).* Special Publication SJ94-SPC. Palatka, Fla.: St. Johns River Water Management District.

Upper St. Johns River Marsh, Type II Wildlife Management Area Recreation Guide.

1996–97. Map and Regulations. Palatka, Fla.: St. Johns Water Management District.

Varnum, John P. 1885. *Florida! Its Climate, Productions and Characteristics. A Hand Book of Important and Reliable Information for the Use of the Tourist, Settler and Investor.* Passenger Dept. of Jacksonville, Tampa and Key West Railway. 1982 facsimile. DeLand, Fla.: St. Johns–Oklawaha Rivers Trading Company.

Wagman, Jules. 1988. *Jacksonville: Florida's First Coast.* Northridge, Calif.: Windsor Publications.

Wakefield, Vivian. 1998. "Arrests Continue in Operation River Rat." *Florida Times-Union* (Jacksonville). July 10.

Weisman, Brent Richards. 1989. *Like Beads on a String: A Culture History of the Seminole Indians in North Peninsula Florida.* Tuscaloosa: University of Alabama Press.

Wekiva River Writers. 1988. *The Wekiva River: Scenic and Wild.* Apopka, Fla.: Wekiva River Writers.

White, O. E. 1957. "Magmatic, Connate, and Metamorphic Waters." *Bulletin of the Geological Society of America* 68:1659–82.

White, William A. 1970. *The Geomorphology of the Florida Peninsula.* Geological Bulletin No. 51. Tallahassee: State of Florida, Bureau of Geology.

Wilson, Don. 1990. "Anglers Finding Toothy Pacus." *Orlando (Fla.) Sentinel.* December 2.

———. 1997. "St. Johns Heats Up on a Cold Night." *Orlando (Fla.) Sentinel.* January 26.

Wilson, Edward O. 1992. *The Diversity of Life.* Cambridge: Harvard University Press, Belknap Press.

Wilson, Edward O., and Stephen R. Kellert, eds. 1993. *The Biophilia Hypothesis.* Washington, D.C.: Island Press.

Wisenbaker, Michael. 1997. *The American Eel: A Well-Traveled Fish.* Florida Wildlife. Tallahassee, Fla.: Florida Game and Fresh Water Fish Commission. March–April.

Woolson, Constance Fenimore. 1876. "The Oklawaha." *Harper's New Monthly Magazine* 52 (January): 161–79.

The WPA Guide to Florida: The Federal Writers' Project Guide to 1930's Florida. [1939]. 1984. New York: Pantheon Books.

Yates, Susan A. 1974. "An Autecological Study of Sawgrass, Cladium Jamaicense, in Southern Florida." Master of Science thesis, University of Miami.

Zellmer, L. R. 1979. "Development and Application of a Pleistocene Sea Level Curve to the Coastal Plain of Southeastern Virginia." Master's thesis, School of Marine Science, College of William and Mary, Williamsburg, Va.

Charts and Maps

The Map Guide of Florida's St. Johns River: Racy Point to Lake Dexter. Includes Crescent Lake and Lake George. Crescent City: Florida Cartographic Services.

National Oceanic and Atmospheric Administration (NOAA) Charts 11941, 11492, 11495.

Plano Numerod, de la Barra y Rio de San Juan desde su Entrada hasta dos millas [etc.]. December 24, 1791. St. Augustine, Fla.

Preliminary Chart of St. Johns River Florida. From Entrance to Brown's Creek. U.S. Coast Survey. 1856. U.S. Navy.

St. Johns River Central: From Palatka through Lake George to Lake Dexter. Lake Oklawaha, from Eureka Dam to the St. Johns River. Contour Map for Boating and Fishing. Florida. Map No. 314. Clemson, S.C.: Kingfisher Maps.

St. Johns River North: From Palatka to Jacksonville. Contour Map for Fishing, Boating and Recreation. Florida. Map No. 332. Clemson, S.C.: Kingfisher Maps.

St. Johns River South: From Lake Dexter to Puzzle Lake through Lakes: Woodruff, Beresford, Monroe, Jessup, and Harney. Contour Map for Boating and Fishing. Florida. Map No. 331. Clemson, S.C.: Kingfisher Maps.

Index

Acosta Bridge, 179

Acosta Creek, 134

Adler, Mary Lee, 117

airboats, 5–6, 16–17, 27, 50

Alexander Springs, 96

algae blooms, 50–51, 175

Allapattah Flats, 12

alligators (*Alligator mississippienis*):
aggressive, 162; in Lake Jesup, 52; at
Lake Sawgrass, 19; reputation of, 24,
58–59

Altamonte Springs, 26–27

American eels (*Anguilla rostrata*), 93–94,
114

American shad (*Alosa sapidissima*), 42–43

anhinga, 57

apple snails (*Pomacea paludosa*), 10, 31

Aquifer, Floridan, 149

aquifers, 55, 67, 68, 131, 149

archaeological survey of Salt Springs, 109

Army Corps of Engineers, 4, 5, 49, 66, 75,
130

artesian springs, 37, 45, 49, 54, 67, 111

artifacts, 7, 12, 31, 99

Asian grass carp, 18

"Assum Pit" underwater cave, 114

Astatula (steamship), 145

astor, climbing, 9

Astor landing, 101

Atlantic Coastal Ridge, 17

Atlantic Croaker (*Micropogonias
undulatus*), 124

Atlantic Ocean, in formation of St. Johns, 2

Audubon, John James, 24, 30, 95–96,
152–53

Australian pine, 20

Axle Creek, 104

Aztec artifacts, 7

bald cypress, 11, 18

bald eagles, 40, 106, 151

Banana River, 76

Bartram, John, 45, 60

Bartram, William (Billy): Baxter Mound
discovery by, 38; at Blue Springs, 82; on
Drayton Island, 116; at Idlewilde Point,
97; at Lake Beresford, 86; at Lake
George, 104; at Lake Harney, 45; at
Lake Monroe, 60; limpkin observations
of, 24, 70; on Murphy Island, 135; at
Picolata, 158; plantation of, 163; at Salt
Springs, 109; with Seminoles, 46

Bartram's Travels, 46, 104, 151

Bartram Trail, 101

basin, St. Johns: development's effect on,
5; geological formation of, 2;
management of, 11

bass: fingering, 40; largemouth, 6–7, 38,
117, 150; striped (*Morone saxatilis*), 113

Battle Lagoon, 97

Baxter Mound, 38

Bayard Point, 162

bear, Florida black (*Ursus americanus
floridanus*), 71

belted kingfisher, 57

Berry, Father Thomas, 26

Big Scrub (Ocala National Forest), 109

biodiversity: in Blue Cypress Lake, 14; fire
and, 10–11; in Ocala National Forest,
109; of Wekiva River, 70–71

biological transition area, 70

Bird Island, 51

birds: extinct, 8; decreased population of,
152; wading, 19, 24, 29, 33, 51. *See also
entries for specific birds*

Black Creek, 148, 168–69

Black Creek crayfish (*Procambarus pictus*),
169

Black Hammock, 50

bladderwort, 8

Bill Belleville is an award-winning
environmental journalist and filmmaker who lives
in Sanford, Florida. His work has appeared in
Sierra Magazine, Audubon, Islands, Sports Afield,
and other publications.